→» BOOKS BY BRUNO WALTER «←

GUSTAV MAHLER (1958)

THEME AND VARIATIONS (1946)

These are Borzoi Books

Published in New York by ALFRED·A·KNOPF

Gustav Mahler

Meinem lieben Freunde
Bruno Walter
Wien, Dezember 1907.
Gustav Mahler

Bruno Walter

-》》-》》-》》-《《-《《-《《-

Gustav Mahler

Translation from the German supervised

by Lotte Walter Lindt

NEW YORK

Alfred·A·Knopf

1968

64126

L. C. catalog card number: 57-7551

© Alfred A. Knopf, Inc., 1957

⟶⟩⟩⟩-⟩⟩⟩-⟩⟩⟩-⟩⟩⟩-⟩⟩⟩-⟩⟩⟩•⟨⟨⟨-⟨⟨⟨-⟨⟨⟨-⟨⟨⟨-⟨⟨⟨-⟨⟨⟨⟵

THIS IS A BORZOI BOOK,
PUBLISHED BY ALFRED A. KNOPF, INC.

⟶⟩⟩⟩-⟩⟩⟩-⟩⟩⟩-⟩⟩⟩-⟩⟩⟩-⟩⟩⟩•⟨⟨⟨-⟨⟨⟨-⟨⟨⟨-⟨⟨⟨-⟨⟨⟨-⟨⟨⟨⟵

Published January 13, 1958
Third Printing, October 1968
Published in German by S. Fischer Verlag

➸➸➸➸➸➸ • ⧏⧏⧏⧏⧏⧏

Preface
to the 1958 Edition

REPUBLICATION of this study of Gustav Mahler, written twenty years ago, makes me ask myself whether I still share its point of view and endorse its content. The answer is Yes, I do.

True, I wish I had gone more fully into many matters, notably the marked change in his work from his Fifth Symphony onward. An extensive literature has, however, gone thoroughly into this development of his inner sound-image and the resultant enhancement of his polyphony as well as his technique, and even his whole sym-

phonic style. On these matters my tentative indications have been sufficiently complemented.
I do, however, believe that the passage of time
has perhaps given me a clearer understanding of
a highly individual man and musician, which I
would like to put on record.

I have, nevertheless, decided to leave the text
as it stands. This is because I am struck, on
taking it up again, by the unity of its tone. I do
not want to make alterations or additions that
might break the continuity of what I wrote under the strong emotion of the twenty-fifth an-
niversary of Mahler's death—he died on May
18, 1911—still less because this continuity was
itself the product of my intense absorption in
his work and character at the time I was writing.
Therefore, I have made up my mind to leave the
tone, the tempo, and the total impression as
they stand, confining any alterations to this
preface. Here, I must be retrospective, and look
back over a longer period than the two decades
since the book was published. In so doing, I

must take into account the fateful influence of world events on the culture of our century.

Gustav Mahler died three years before the outbreak of the First World War. There was peace in the world in which and for which he wrote and performed his symphonies. The passionate, easily aroused Viennese temperament was therefore forced to find its outlet on the battlefield of music and the arts—a battlefield on which the Viennese citizen felt very much at home. A fighting pose and passionate partisanship characterized the Vienna of that time: Mahler's tempestuous nature was highly conducive to loosing storms about his head. The first performance of his Fourth Symphony led, as I recall, to fisticuffs within the precincts of the Musikvereinsaal. Passionate audience reaction to his daring music, however, was the rule rather than the exception at performances everywhere; their fascination grew out of the opposition as well as the enthusiasm that his works evoked. The impression made by his

Preface

Third Symphony was overwhelming—and for the first time unquestioned—at the performance under Mahler's baton at the Krefeld Festival of the Allgemeiner Deutscher Musikverein in 1902. It established him definitely in the world of contemporary music. In the years that followed, however, performance of his symphonies often led to angry demonstrations and counter-demonstrations. Among his friends, Mahler met all this "for" and "against" with the reiterated conviction: "My time will come."

My own experience in conducting his works, and, so far as I can judge, that of my colleagues, goes to justify his confidence. Of course, we have not silenced hostility; his musical and emotional excess still rouses the critics. But each year sees the impact of his symphonies grow. They triumphed even in Vienna, often so recalcitrant. The strident subjectivity and shrill eccentricity that once roused such opposition came to be recognized as marks of originality. Profound seriousness and lofty ecstasy spoke to the heart.

Simple, often "folksy" themes appealed to the Austrian, while sheer power of symphonic form and masterly instrumentation overwhelmed the more deeply musical. For many years now, a Mahler program has filled the hall. My colleagues and I had the same experience in Germany. Nobody who heard Mahler conduct the first performance of his Eighth Symphony in Munich in July 1910, a year before his death, will ever forget it. It was a high point in his life as composer.

Up to his death in May 1911, he invariably conducted the first performances of his symphonies, though portions of his Second and Third were given by Strauss and Weingartner before the works were heard in their entirety. Two works, however, he did not conduct: *Das Lied von der Erde* and his Ninth Symphony.

Alma Mahler handed the scores to me for final revision before printing. In November 1911, six months after his death, I conducted the first performance of *Das Lied*, in Munich;

and, early in 1912, of the Ninth, in Vienna. It
was a heavy responsibility to take my great
friend's place and introduce his work to the
world. Here was the fulfillment of the sense of
dedication which, when I first had been shaken
by his First Symphony in Hamburg, had made
me see my future as one of service to his work.

The rise of the Nazi regime for a time put an
end to performances of Mahler, first in Germany, later in Austria. During the Second
World War, my own conducting was confined
to America. Acclaim for his work, as conducted
by me and by my colleagues, rose steadily,
despite the obstinate hostility of some influential critics; today, a wide section of American concertgoers has taken him to their hearts.

The War once over, his symphonies gradually
made their way into the European repertoire.
I ought, incidentally, to mention that in England
they were occasionally performed even during
the War. I have conducted them in London,
Paris, Amsterdam, Edinburgh, Vienna, Salz-

burg, Munich, and elsewhere. It is not easy, looking back over these impressions, to say where Mahler stands in the musical world of today. Audiences are no less enthusiastic than in former times, a section of the press still stands aloof. His work appears, if not often enough, on concert programs.

The reaction on thought, feeling, and behavior, and the damage to the spirit and content of culture resulting from two world wars and their long aftermath have been so appalling that it is encouraging to find work, characteristic, despite its originality, of a sane period and developed under the influence of the great classics, holding its place even in our disordered world. Look, for example, at the fatal effects of the crisis after the First World War; art, either "intellectualized" or proliferating into sheer "entertainment," was given over to sensationalism and the worship of mere technical proficiency in music, to atonality, to the twelve-tone system, to experimentation regardless of content, and all this within a general climate of materialism and utilitarianism, and amid the conflict of contending political ideologies. We were, in fact, faced with a chaos making it an act of faith to believe in the continued life of art or in the music native to the heart of the genuine musician, of which Mahler's work was a late, tardy blossom. I am fully aware of the threat to our civilization inherent in contemporary developments. I am, however, convinced that in Mahler the coexistence of highly "modern" harmony and polyphony with profound depth of feeling, ranging from human to divine, ensures the survival of his creative work. What makes me certain of this is that his harmony and polyphony, for all their vivid modernity, remain in the realm of tonality.

The nearest approach to his disturbed and disturbing Ego is, perhaps, *Das Lied von der Erde*. It is his most personal work. His idiom is as daunting and as subjective here, and as hard of approach, as in his late symphonies. But what is always daunting in Mahler is the burning spirit, not the experimenting intellect. That spirit is open to anyone who can feel. Here the approach is made easier by the strange quality of the Chinese poems in which, on the threshold of death, he found inspiration for the fateful color of the songs.

I cannot speak of *Das Lied* without recalling Kathleen Ferrier's unforgettable performance in the three movements for contralto. From the time of the first production, in Munich, I was lucky in my singers. I recall, gratefully, tenors like William Miller, Jacques Urlus, Charles Kullmann, Martin Oehmann, Peter Pears, Julius Patzak, and contraltos like Mme Charles Cahier, Louise Willer, Sigrid Onegin, and Kerstin Thorborg. But one of the most significant encounters of my artistic life was that with Kathleen Ferrier. Her performance in *Das Lied* —as in the *Kindertotenlieder* and other of his songs—remains among the deepest and happiest experiences of my musical life. The lovely timbre of her voice moved me, when I first heard it, as hardly any other sound ever has. And she had a soul as well as a voice. That soul knew and resounded the very soul of Mahler's work. I have often thought how much it would have meant to him to hear the profound understanding in her performance. There was something mysterious about this creature, who appeared so limpid, gay, simple, and direct. This mystery interpenetrated her singing; she sounded every depth, released every treasure in works she had made her own. Her secret was unity. Everything about her was lovely: her appearance, her soul, her voice, her expression. She expressed intense feeling over the gamut from charm to tragedy, and was, throughout, possessed of a loveliness like an aura revealing the mysterious grace of her nature. Perhaps her early death was part of the mystery that brooded over the life of a great artist. Deep gratitude mingles in my grief for her loss. To Mahler she rendered a permanent service; permanent, happily, in that, thanks to technical progress, it lives on in her recordings.

My faith in Mahler's immortality is strengthened by a realization of the enduring character of the reforms he carried through in the Vienna Opera. Contemporary productions, designed to realize the intentions of the composer by stressing the dramatic significance of the work and of what is taking place on the stage, date back to Mahler's time as general director, of which I speak in the following pages. Even in the precarious world in which we live there is ground for hope when the flame of a potent personality lives on, incandescent in creation and in reproduction.

As I mentioned in my opening words, I am, despite—or, perhaps, because of—the distance of time, conscious of closer contact with a man of genius, to whom I owe much in my own life, a man who was, in decisive years, my model, a man whose deep humanity will always remain with me.

Beverly Hills

Contents

RECOLLECTION

1 · First Meeting   3
2 · Hamburg   11
3 · Steinbach   26
4 · Vienna   38
5 · Last Years   63

REFLECTION

1 · The Opera Director   77
2 · The Conductor   89
3 · The Composer   101
4 · The Personality   145

Index   FOLLOWS PAGE 176

Recollection

First Meeting

MEMORY goes back to my first meeting
with Mahler. I was only eighteen. In June 1894
the first performance of his First Symphony,
then called the "Titan," at the Festival of the
Allgemeiner Deutscher Musikverein in Weimar,
called forth a howl of indignation from the musical press; critics poured the vials of their wrath
on a work at once sterile, trivial, and mon-
strously extravagant. In particular, the "Funeral
March in the Manner of Callot" was dismissed
with irate contempt. The excitement with which
I devoured the notices comes back vividly; I

marveled at the singular courage of the unknown composer of the March, and ardently desired to know the man responsible for so extravagant a work.

A few months later, I got an introduction to Pollini, recommending me for the post of co-répétiteur (coach) at the Hamburg Opera, where this same Gustav Mahler, whose work had so excited me, was chief operatic conductor. As I came out from my first interview with Pollini, there he was, in the office of the theater; small in stature, pale and thin: the lofty forehead of his long face framed in blue-black hair, and behind glasses, remarkable eyes; lines of sadness and of humor furrowed a countenance across which an astonishing range of expression passed as he spoke to the various people round him. Here was the incarnation of Kreisler, the arresting, alarming, demoniac conductor envisaged by the youthful reader of E. T. A. Hoffmann's fantastic tales. With friendly kindness he inquired into my musical qualifications and capacity; to his apparent satisfaction I replied with a mixture of modesty and self-confidence. He left me bemused and perturbed.

Having grown up in a middle class environment, I had looked on genius as something that existed in books and scores, in the thrill of the concert hall, the theater, the art gallery, whereas one's fellows were likely to be commonplace, and real life dull. Now higher spheres seemed to open before me. Mahler, in aspect and gesture, seemed at once genius and demon; suddenly life took on a romantic quality. I can cite no stronger evidence of the electric effect of his personality than the swiftness with which its impact transformed my entire feeling about life and my attitude toward it.

My next memory of him is at a rehearsal of *Hänsel und Gretel*, then going into production at the Hamburg Opera. Never had I encountered so intense a human being; never had I dreamed that a brief, cogent word, a single compelling gesture, backed by absolute clarity of mind and intention, could fill other people with anxious terror and compel them to blind obedience. An inadequate piano-accompanist exasperated him; suddenly—oh, joy!—he saw me standing in the wings, and asked whether I could take the risk of accompanying *prima vista* an opera I did not know. My proud "Of course!" produced a smile of amusement; a wave of the hand dismissed my unhappy colleague and set me in his place. In the forest scene, the repeated choral echo was poorly done; he turned to me, saying something like: "I rely on you to know what goes on in a forest; work out the echoes for me!"

This first rehearsal gave me a real impression of his method of working. He led; he commanded; steeped in the spirit of the work, he knew precisely what he wanted to achieve. Brusque and harsh with weakness or inadequacy, he was kind and sympathetic wherever he recognized talent and enthusiasm.

My third recollection is of a meeting as we

were coming off the stage. I was about to take my leave when he stopped me, and said: "Walk a bit of the way with me." Of our talk I recall only that it began with a remark of his about Humperdinck's work, which he said was "masterly in execution, but not really a fairy tale." From the nature of the fairy tale he went on to other topics. It fascinated me to find the same intensity and high intellectual pitch in his talk as in his rehearsing. The violence with which he rebuffed my insufficient remarks—how shyly I made them! His sudden plunge into reflective silence, then the friendly glance with which he picked up a sensible observation; the unexpected twitches of furtive pain across his face; even the curious irregularity of his walk—now he would stamp; now stand stock-still; now rush ahead—all this confirmed and strengthened the impression of someone demoniac. Indeed, I should hardly have been surprised if, after we had taken leave, he had flown off in the form of a vulture as Lindhorst does under the eyes of the student Anselmus in Hoffmann's *Goldner Topf*.

A fourth picture completes my first impressions. Mahler had bidden me to visit him; as I walked into his workroom my eye was caught by a reproduction, on the wall, of Giorgione's "Concerto." Who, I asked myself, was this monk, with his hands on the keys, who seemed to be interrupting his playing to turn and face me? What had he to do with Mahler, whom he so strangely resembled? Then I realized that for a long time I had been unconsciously seeing Mahler in my mind as the reincarnation of the ascetic music-maker in the picture. Actually, there is a family resemblance here, and not to Mahler only. Somehow every genuine musician resembles the monk, if no one else so much as Mahler. Here is a miracle. A genius of the brush, with the prophetic foresight proper to genius, has here created the typical musician; created him, not built him up out of pieces of knowledge. In Giorgione's time, music as we understand it did not exist. Thus the image of a musician was created in advance of music!

The picture gave the point of departure for our talk. Whether we then touched on Giorgione's strange prevision I do not remember, but I do recall our often speaking about it later. I also know that Mahler's likeness to the pious player enhanced my sense of the mystery prefigured in the fifteenth-century portrait. On this or perhaps on my next visit, I at last worked the conversation round to his creative work, and persuaded him to sit down at the piano. Then everything I was capable of feeling and understanding was fused in one single, tremendous impression; then the tyro in music was given a thrilling insight into the soul of a creative artist. Small wonder that when I began to have a share in the re-creative work of a conductor who could penetrate to the very soul of great works and enrich anyone who worked with him by revealing, through example and precept, their universal significance, my spiritual experience literally went to my head! That I did not lose my head entirely was owing to the boundless devotion and reverence I felt for him. I was ready, without reflection or even looking forward or back, simply to follow him, to feel and to work with him. Since such an attitude was as natural and as congenial to me as were Mahler's music and music-making, I luckily never lost myself in my devotion. Years later, at the cost of grave soul-searching, I had to break away from his influence. But I say today, as I felt then in the very depths of my being, that his influence was a blessing on my whole life.

——————➤➤➤➤➤➤➤•⫷⫷⫷⫷⫷⫷

2

Hamburg

I SPENT two years in Hamburg. A few weeks
after I started work there, Mahler arranged for
me to be appointed chorus director. I had thus,
both in that capacity and as co-répétiteur, the
advantage of co-operating in his productions
and becoming directly familiar with his ideas.
Soon I was also conducting opera, and when at
the close of my first season Otto Lohse went to
America, I sloughed off the skins of chorus master and coach to put on the coveted and more
shining costume of a "real" conductor. It was of
course understood that I continued to act as
coach for Mahler's productions. It was of im-

mense advantage to me to share with the singers the effort to satisfy his demands for the utmost rhythmic accuracy and strict obedience to dynamic and other markings; the more so because I was naturally inclined to overstress the element of feeling in music, the dramatic and poetic aspects in presentation, and the full expression of the spiritual content of a work at the expense of absolute precision; in general, to sacrifice accuracy to vitality. He taught me to pay increasing attention to accuracy and precision in my rehearsing. When, for his *Rheingold*, I was rehearsing Loge or Fricka, I would do my utmost to achieve a combination of lively expressiveness with the rigorous exactness Mahler demanded of singers. My wanderings in the woods of sentimental error would have been long had I not learned from his example and precept that the highest degree of rhythmic accuracy is the best means to attain the highest degree of dramatic expression in Wagner; and, in general, that confining the spiritual within strict musical fetters is a help and not a hindrance to concentrated and powerful emotional utterance.

A constant subject of our conversation was rubato—i.e., the subjection of accuracy in tempo and rhythm to a slowing down or speeding up for the sake of increased emotional expression. Mahler, even in Italian music, where he recognized a certain degree of rubato as a legitimate stylistic element, was against the excessive use of it in which German musicians and singers indulged. He gave, in an unforgettable performance of *Traviata*, the perfect example of a controlled use of rubato, the melodic line being dictated entirely by fire and passion, not by the fancy of singers.

We had many talks about Wagner. Mahler's lifelong considered devotion to Wagner clarified and deepened my obsession with the subject. He was a convinced Wagnerian, and remained one to his death. My most vivid impressions from his Hamburg period remain his *Ring* and *Meistersinger;* later, in Vienna, came a *Tristan*

that, both in its total effect and in many details, will live in my ears and heart forever. We
also talked endlessly about Wagner's personality; Mahler never wearied of defending him
against "Philistine" reproaches of being ungrateful and not to be trusted, or of angrily
demonstrating how the absorption of the genius
in his work serves as an explanation of human
frailties. The scope of his analysis was, of
course, by no means limited to Wagner; it ex-
tended to every artistic work on which he was
engaged, although never with any notion of
laying down the law to a man sixteen years
younger than himself. Mahler was, in any case,
no educator: he was far too absorbed in himself, his work, his stormy inner life; he paid
too little attention to other people or to other
things.

Indeed, anything in the nature of that systematic exercise of influence which is the essence
of education was remote from a wholly unregu-
lated nature moved by its own impulses. I soon

learned that nothing in his life was systematic; it was more like the central cataract of the middle Nile than any even-flowing stream. In efforts to describe his personality, therefore, no epithet occurs so constantly as "erratic." Erratic indeed he seemed to me, though there was no sense of any lack of solid ground beneath his feet; he was ready to rush forward again only when the cataract of emotion and thought had subsided into a temporary calm that lasted— until the next impulse foamed up. He hardly ever gave me any conscious teaching, but there is no measure for what I learned in the deeper sense from contact with a man who, in word and in music, overflowed with a sheer abundance of vitality. His abrupt impulsiveness perhaps explains the excitement nearly everybody felt who came near him; especially, of course, singers and members of the orchestra. He diffused an atmosphere of high tension. This was communicated to those with whom he worked, and induced devout admiration in the best of them. It produced performances illuminated by the fiery glow within him which raised the Hamburg Opera to the top rank in Germany. Of course, there were weaker spirits, men of second-rate gifts, who were injured by his absolutism; good will or ill, however, none could resist his sway.

At this stage, an extreme mobility was the outward sign of his intense vitality. I can see him now, at an orchestral rehearsal of *Götterdämmerung*, stepping down from the conductor's desk and hurrying to the trumpets and trombones to examine a particular passage in the funeral music with them, or borrowing the stool of a double-bass player to get up on to the stage in order to deliver instructions that would have taken longer and been more trouble from the desk—for example, about the gradations of tone by off-stage chorus or stage-band. While this went on, the orchestra would wait silently, as though mesmerized by the spell of the powerful man who, himself compelled by his inner

vision of a work of art, had to impose the irresistible demands of this vision on his colleagues.
Not once in the two years I spent with Mahler
in Hamburg, or in the six in Vienna, did I ever
see the spell broken. "The magic worked" from
beginning to end; the tense atmosphere that was
his element prevailed.

Such concentration inevitably and naturally
brings forth its corresponding counterpart: a
considerable absent-mindedness with regard to
everything that lay outside the circle of immediate interest, and numerous comical situations
occurred because of his distraction. One may
serve as a characteristic example. One day, in
the course of an orchestra rehearsal, the stage
director asked him to pause for a few minutes
to allow some important scenic rearrangements.
After a brief period of impatience, Mahler became lost in thought. The director, having finished his business, tried repeatedly and unsuc-
cessfully to call him back, until, suddenly aware
of the silent expectation in the house, he looked

vaguely around, knocked on the stand with his baton, and cried: "Waiter, my bill!" In the laughter that broke out on all sides, he finally joined, heartily. A deep confusion of this kind is the compensation for, and perhaps the condition of, concentration as absolute as his. For such so-called distractions as cards or any other game, he had no use.

As he gradually realized my passionate interest in his creative work, he began to take pleasure in letting me get to know it, on the piano. I can still hear the droll grotesquerie of his singing "*Des Antonius von Padua Fischpredigt,*" its insolence in "*Um schlimme Kinder artig zu machen*" and "*Selbstgefühl,*" its passion and pain in the *Lieder eines fahrenden Gesellen.* Still, too, I can feel the heart-searching excitement of at last getting to know the First Symphony through him. His creative work came more and more to be the substance of our intercourse and our conversations.

As I grew to know him, in these talks, and to

know the books he read, the poets and philoso-
phers he loved, my original impression of a
fantastic, demoniac apparition from the world of
E. T. A. Hoffmann was replaced by one more
just and comprehensive, but also far more difficult to understand. I shall speak later of the
extraordinary spiritual range of a nature full of
contradictions; of the dark forces with which he
struggled; of the spiritual longing that consti-
tuted the central thread in his life and his work.
Here it is enough to say that I understood as
much—and as little—of his complex inner life
as was possible for one so young and inexperienced. What I did understand fed my increasing
reverence for the man, as my growing intimacy
with his work fed my increasing enthusiasm for
the musician.

How could it be otherwise when a man normally incalculable and explosive was invariably
kind, helpful, and sympathetic to me? He never
assumed the teacher's attitude; there was no
question of his regularly listening in when I

conducted opera, or of his supervising my work in detail. But he was interested enough in my conducting to sit in on a performance from time to time, and to give me his opinion on it afterwards. Once, when I was conducting *Aïda*, the chorus behind the scenes came in about ten measures too soon, probably because the chorus master was expecting a cut often made at that point. I quickly speeded up the orchestra; then, all of a sudden, the chorus stopped, and I had another "rescue" on my hands! It appeared that, at the critical moment, Mahler had dashed from his box and appeared behind the scenes to silence the chorus and give them the entry signal himself; he had not counted on my taking in the situation quite so quickly. I tell this story simply as characteristic both of his impetuosity, and of how entirely co-operative he could be.

Particularly precious in my memory are the occasions when we played piano duets, Schubert being our favorite. We had great fun; Mahler, sitting on the right, would play my top notes

with his left hand, and leave his own lower line
to my right; each of us thus had all the time to
read both *primo* and *secondo*, which introduced
amusing complications. He used to invent words
to go with various marches, singing as he played.
He was great at simple nonsense of this kind;
in conversation he loved witty sallies, sometimes comic in their irrelevance. Yet all at once
his carefree laughter would be clouded over; he
would sink into a gloomy silence that one dared
not break.

Quite apart from these sufferings, which had
their source in the depths of his being, circumstances in his life gave grounds enough for deep
depression. In 1895 his younger brother Otto,
of whose musical gifts he had had high hopes,
shot himself. There were two symphonies in the
drawer of his desk, one of which had been performed but once, and only in part, the other
having been received with total lack of understanding—nay, with derision. There were a
number of songs with orchestra; three books of

lieder, which nobody sang; a third symphony was nearly completed.

Moreover, Mahler's relations with Pollini deteriorated, as was but unavoidable in view of their wholly divergent standards and values. This led to an unhappy situation in the theater. It made Mahler eager to get away from Hamburg, back to his familiar Vienna and its incomparable musical climate. When his doorbell rang, he would cry: "Here comes my appointment as the God of the Southern Zones!" But the appointment was long in coming, and he felt a mounting need for some satisfying experience, some major artistic achievement to clear his path for him. He decided to produce his Second Symphony in Berlin, with the Berlin Philharmonic and the Stern Gesangverein. The work was performed in its entirety for the first time on December 13, 1895 (the first three movements had already been given earlier that year). For the composer it was a decisive day. Of the work he once wrote: "You are battered to the ground with

clubs and then lifted to the heights on angels'
wings." The effect, after what I recall as a
superb performance, was overwhelming. I can
still feel the breathless excitement, in the last
movement, upon hearing the mysterious cry of
the bird after the end of the world in the *Grosser Appell* and the profoundly moving entry
of the chorus—"Arise, yea, arise!" Even then,
of course, there were hostility, misunderstanding, belittling, and malice. But the impression
of a great and original work and of the power
of Mahler's personality was so great that his
emergence as a composer dates from this performance.

And yet, everything might have gone wrong.
He suffered intermittently from migraines
which, like everything of his, were violent in
their onset. They paralyzed his energies. When
an attack took place he could only lie completely motionless. In 1900, just before a concert
with the Vienna Philharmonic at the Trocadero
in Paris, he actually lay thus immobile for so

long that the concert had to open half an hour late, and it taxed him to the utmost to carry it through. On this earlier occasion in Berlin, after great sacrifices he was staking his whole future as a composer on this event: but there he lay, that very afternoon, with one of his worst migraines, incapable of moving or partaking of anything. To this day I can see him, later, on the exceedingly high and far-from-steady podium, pale as death, his superhuman will-power conquering his pain as he conquered performers and audience. For me, a young musician, that day and its victory were of profound significance. I had thought I knew the work, which I had transcribed as both a piano duet and a piano solo. But when I now heard as living sound what I had only known in my own mind and in its piano setting before, I felt with complete certainty that here was a mission for my life. The music itself, its acclaim, and my resolve to devote my life to Mahler's work made me happy.

Meanwhile, I realized that I had gone as far

in my work with the Hamburg Theater as a young man like me could go. There was no room for promotion for me there. Moreover, my relations with Pollini had become difficult. Mahler advised me to look for another post. He had Breslau in mind, where a second conductorship seemed to offer a favorable opportunity. On his recommendation, Dr. Löwe appointed me, and I left Hamburg after two years. My experiences during this time had shown me the direction; to follow it was my solemn resolution.

3

Steinbach

ARLY in July 1896 I got a letter from
Mahler, which, although it has already appeared
in his collected letters, seems in place here:

> Steinbach am Attersee
> July 2, 1896

Dear Friend,

I send a brief reply and invite you to come
and see us about the 16th, unless, for reasons I
don't know, you have made other plans for your
holiday. Perhaps my sisters have told you that I
haven't been idle; indeed, I hope that a few
weeks will see the entire Third [Symphony]

happily completed. The first sketches are already quite clear and now I am working on the orchestration. I have no doubt that our friends, the critics, appointed or self-appointed, will once again suffer from dizziness, but those who enjoy the pleasant strolls I offer will find them fun. The whole thing is, of course, tainted with my deplorable sense of humor and "often takes the opportunity to submit to my dreary taste for dreary noise." The players frequently "do not pay the least attention to one another, and my entire gloomy and brutal nature is nakedly exposed." It is well known that I cannot do without trivialities. This time, however, all permissible bounds have been passed. "One often feels one has got into a pub, or a sty!" Do come soon, and in your armor! If your taste has been purified in Berlin, be prepared to have it ruined! Warmest greetings to you and your family, and Au revoir!

As ever,

G. M.

This cheerful letter proved that the completion of the first movement of his Third Symphony and the prospect of early completion of the entire work, whose other movements dated from 1895, had put him in good spirits. I looked forward eagerly to the weeks I was to spend with him at Steinbach.

I arrived by steamer on a glorious July day; Mahler was there on the jetty to meet me, and despite my protests, insisted on carrying my bag until he was relieved by a porter. As on our way to his house I looked up to the Höllengebirge, whose sheer cliffs made a grim background to the charming landscape, he said: "You don't need to look—I have composed all this already!"

He went on to speak of the first movement, entitled, in the preliminary draft "What the Rocks and Mountains Tell Me." But I had to curb my impatience to hear the Third. Nothing would induce him to show me or to play a single note of a work that was not completely finished. This was his invariable rule.

Steinbach

At Steinbach, Mahler was unbuttoned as never before. Close to nature, free of the cares of the opera, wholly occupied with his own work and thoughts, he was relaxed: he could and did let the riches within him play over his surroundings.

On the meadow between the lake and the boarding house where he lodged, he had had four walls and a roof set up to make a room. This little, ivy-covered "composer's hut" was furnished with a piano, a table, an armchair, and a sofa. When the door opened, masses of beetles fell on your head. Here he spent the morning undisturbed by noise from the house or the road. He went there about six a.m. At seven breakfast was silently set before him; the opening of the door at midday recalled him to ordinary life. This ought to have happened punctually at twelve; often, however, it was three before the hungry members of the household and the cook's anxiety about her dishes were relieved. Not that he stayed continuously in his hut; he

29

would wander about the fields, and often took long walks up the hills, returning in order to "bring the harvest into the barn." On such days he would appear at lunch highly animated, and conversation was lively. He took a child-like delight in good food, and had keen relish for a tasty sweet; he declared that the cook, being an imaginative person, had to surprise him in this line every day for four weeks! One of his favorite jokes was to assert that this excellent dish must be enjoyable to anyone but an ass— and then to ask his guests how they liked it. In the afternoon we went for walks or made music; in the evening we talked or read. Sometimes he would break silence by reading aloud something that had struck him in the book on which he was then engaged. I remember that he could not keep his enjoyment of Cervantes's *Don Quixote* to himself, and especially that he laughed so that he had to stop reading when he came to the attack on the windmills. He laughed uncontrollably over the doings of master and servant, but what moved him most was the idealism and purity of the Don. He said that, much as it amused him, he could never lay the book down without having been deeply stirred.

He took great delight in two kittens, whose play he never tired of watching. When out for a short walk he would put them in his pockets and enjoy their gambols while he paused for a rest; the little creatures were so used to him that he would play a sort of hide-and-seek with them. He had a warm feeling for all living things and felt a loving concern for dogs, cats, birds, and all the creatures of the woods. He watched them with sympathy and understanding; he would reply with an involuntary cry of delight to the song of a bird or the jumps of a squirrel. He told me that he could never forget an occasion in the country when, listening in the night to the long, deep bellowing of the cattle, he had felt a sympathetic pang for the animal's dumb soul.

Summer in Steinbach passed with the restful uneventfulness that his creative work required.

Composition had to be done during vacation-time if, as he wanted, he was to return to the city with the score completed in sketch. Definitive instrumentation and final polishing could wait until winter, but his work as musical director was incompatible with musical creation. At last, at the end of the summer, came the day when he could play me the completed Third Symphony. Thanks to our talks, full of the overflow of the creative frenzy of his morning's work, I was familiar with the spiritual atmosphere of the Symphony long before I knew its musical content. Yet it was a musical experience of an undreamed-of and shattering kind to hear him play it on the piano. I was literally dumfounded by the power and novelty of this music, and bowled over by the creative ardor and loftiness of the work as he played it to me. This music made me feel that I recognized him for the first time; his whole being seemed to breathe a mysterious affinity with the forces of nature. I had already guessed at its depths, its elemental quality; now, in the range of his creativity I felt it directly. Had he been an ordinary "nature lover," a devotee of gardens and animals, his music would have been more "civilized." Here however, the Dionysiac possession by nature, which I had learned to recognize, sounded through music that expressed the very root of his being. Now I seemed to see him in the round: I saw him as possessed alike by the stark power of the crags and by the tender flowers, as familiar with the dark secrets of the life of the animals in the woods. Notably in the third movement, he brought everything —aloofness and whimsy, cruelty and untamability—to life. I saw him as Pan. At the same time, however—this in the last three movements—I was in contact with the longing of the human spirit to pass beyond its earthly and temporal bonds. Light streamed from him onto his work and from his work onto him.

The lovely summer came to an end. Mahler's mood was clouded by the approach of the

Hamburg opera season. He sighed, with renewed longing, for the "appointment as the God of the Southern Zones." I parted from him, but I carried the music of the Third with me, and it was a long time before its disturbing presence passed into secure possession.

In the next five years we kept in touch through steady if infrequent correspondence while I was successively at the theaters of Breslau, Pressburg, Riga, and, finally, the Royal Opera in Berlin. The end of my Breslau contract found me with nothing definite in view. I was considering whether the best way of dealing with a possibly useless period was to do my military service, when Mahler, without one moment of deliberation, wrote offering to cover my expenses for the year. Luckily, I did not need to accept his sacrifice—for it would have been one; at the last moment I was offered an engagement in Pressburg. This, to my delight, carried the prospect of frequent visits to Vienna and of seeing him and hearing some of his performances. He, meantime, had achieved his desire; the appointment had come: on May 11, 1897 he appeared for the first time on the conductor's stand at the Vienna Opera. His *Lohengrin* was a "volcanic" event; in the autumn he was made Director of the Opera. It was a thrilling experience to see the man I recalled in a series of vivid pictures of relaxed summer holiday on the Attersee now sovereign over the most brilliant of opera houses. What a change from the limited artistic resources of the small theater in Pressburg—beginners on the stage and a drab public in the auditorium—where I was "first conductor," to the glories of Vienna, with the Philharmonic Orchestra in the pit, and on the stage, established artists and the fresh talent Mahler was discovering; a festive audience filling the grand house, and at the desk, Mahler! I reveled in performances of, among others, *Dalibor*, *Djamileh*, *Eugene Onegin*, and *The Flying Dutchman*, which he conducted; his shining example saved me from getting used to insufficiency in my own work. Thanks to my visits to Vienna I got fresh artistic impressions and renewed intimacy with Mahler. He took me into the circle of his friends there and gave me the spiritual stimulus I had so sadly missed during my time in Breslau.

For me, two years in remote Riga followed my stint in Pressburg, years during which contact with Mahler was confined to letters. At this time we had a misunderstanding, luckily our only one! In October 1898 he offered me the post of Assistant Conductor in Vienna, dating as from 1900, at the expiration of my contract with Riga; he added that it would suit him if I could be available in the autumn of 1899. Here was a problem. I wanted to go to Vienna and to Mahler. He created a horrid moral dilemma for me by saying that it was important to him to have me come before 1900 because if he had to go on working the way he was working, he would be dead by then. But I was twenty-two; I wanted to try out my powers and develop my own responsibility as conductor at a relatively good opera house like that in Riga: I was afraid of falling under his spell again at that stage, and —though I had never thought of this before—of thereby perhaps deflecting the course of my own natural development. I wrote to him in this vein. He refused to appreciate my qualms: I had disappointed him and left him in the lurch. A coolness that hurt me badly sprang up between us. All the same, I felt I had to stick to my guns. When, in 1900, I was called to the Berlin Opera, I accepted, of course letting Mahler know and recapitulating the reasons for my former refusal. He sent a kind and forgiving reply. It made me hope that unhappy episode was buried. I went to Berlin, and after a few months there, received another invitation from him. This time I had no hesitation or doubt: I arranged to be released from my Berlin contract at the end of the year, and in the autumn of 1901, full of hope and happiness, took my place at the Vienna Opera.

4

Vienna

IT IS hard to speak in terms of calm reminiscence of Mahler's period at the Vienna Opera; it seems more natural to recall a ten-year festival to which a great musician invited fellow artists and audiences. It was highly fortunate that, for a decade, a musician of genius and a man of potent will, passionately devoted to the theater, had in his hands the rich resources of a noble institution; fortunate, too, that his activity there came at a time when his own powers were at the full, and in a period of relative political calm which permitted concentration on the arts.

Vienna

Mahler was at his zenith. The flame of his spirit burned, during those ten years, with ever more brilliant clarity. His energy grew with the reckless demands he made on it; there seemed no limit to a conscious artistic achievement which the enthusiasm of the public confirmed. When I took up my appointment he had been with the Opera four years: nevertheless, each time before he appeared in the orchestra pit, the audience seethed with the high tension that precedes a sensational *première* performance. As, with his quick, firm steps, he approached the desk, the house fell silent. If there was a whisper or a latecomer edging in, Mahler would turn; whereupon a deathly stillness would fall. He began; everything was under his spell. Before the third act there was invariably such a storm of applause as made it hard to get the performance going again.

It was thus throughout the entire period of his directorship. He conquered Vienna with his first appearance on the podium. His dominion

over audiences was unbroken to the last. No attacks on Mahler the opera chief or the composer
could dislodge Mahler the conductor. His popularity in this city obsessed by music and the
theater was really extraordinary. As he crossed
the street, hat in hand, gnawing his lip or chew-
ing his cheek, cabmen would turn to look at
him and mutter, in tones of awe: "Mahler himself!"

To be popular is not necessarily to be beloved.
Beloved, a "darling of Vienna," he was not; for
the comfortable he was too uncomfortable. Yet
this strangely unobliging, uncompromising, vehement man certainly exercised an intimidating
fascination both in public and in private, on the
Phæacian city which Vienna was before the
war. He interested the Viennese enormously.
All his doings were eagerly discussed. He did
away with the claque. He canceled the cuts in
Wagner. He shut out anyone who arrived late
for the overture or the first act—a Herculean
achievement at that time! Singers were refused

leave. Long-established singers were brushed off. His gruff remarks were the talk of the *Kaffeehäuser;* his caustic repartee was on every lip. He had a marked gift for neat summings-up. It happened that in his presence I told a Tristan to make a change in his attitude and expression when he swallowed the love-potion, so as to convey total loss of self-control and restraint, and to express this in his voice. Mahler interrupted, saying: "You have got to remember, dear X, that before you drink you are a baritone, afterwards a tenor!" An influential person recommended a new opera, saying that the composer, though of no particular standing, had this time produced something really lovely. Politely, Mahler replied: "Nothing is impossible, but it is improbable for a horse chestnut to produce an orange!" He told me that he was inclined instinctively to state things in this drastic fashion, and experience had taught him that it was the quickest and surest way of making himself understood. With a grin he added that this practical result was more important, for his purpose, than the complete accuracy of expression inevitably sacrificed for a neat *mot*. His sayings took the public fancy; a journalist who did a Sunday gossip column was perpetually bothering me for characteristic comments or actions of his at rehearsal: anything of the sort interested his readers. I am afraid he was much annoyed by my refusal to talk.

During Mahler's first years his great performances were hailed with enthusiasm and steadily supported by artistic Vienna; I found there an atmosphere of high-pitched give and take. Mahler rejoiced in being able to use the great resources of the Opera to give a music-loving public great productions of works he loved; the public responded by coming in festive mood. True, before I joined him, he had had fearful rows with the Philharmonic Orchestra about his changes in the instrumentation of Beethoven's Ninth and about his performance with the entire string section of Beethoven's String Quartet in F minor, but there was hardly a trace of this left when I arrived. Musical Vienna was in a state of wild enthusiasm about his incomparable *Tales of Hoffmann*—a perfect model of imaginative recreation, both scenic and musical. Over this mood of restored amity only one shadow lay—his casting policy. He brought out significant young artists and used them in his magnificent performances. Every time a new star rose at the expense of the old the resultant hard feelings were not confined to the artists concerned. Mahler's attempt to build up a fresh generation of singers disturbed the public also for another, more important reason. By nature an optimist, he had confidence and interest in everything new. Artistic creation and skepticism are opposed to each other—he confidently expected each new voice, each fresh talent to fulfill all his wishes. At auditions he would listen hopefully rather than critically, eagerly on the lookout for the happy surprise of discovery. It irked him to be surrounded by an atmosphere of cool objectivity. His constant hopes for great new singers involved a constant presentation of guest artists; this tended to overload the repertory, and sometimes carried disappointment; hopes raised at rehearsal were let down by public performances of leading roles. Then his impulsive nature would swing to vehement rejection. No such experience, however, succeeded in damping his native optimism. Certainly, when one looks back over the period one sees that he had a golden touch in selection; when one looks at what he found, the eagerness of his search is more than justified. No need to cite the names of his artists; they belong forever to the great days of opera in Vienna.

There was some shaking of heads about his tendency to pay less heed to a singer's purely vocal gifts than to his personality. For instance, to give an outstanding example of a rule followed primarily in the casting of minor parts, he gave the role of Kasper in *Der Freischütz* to a baritone personally admirably qualified to fill the dismal role, because no available bass, however excellent his voice, measured up to his conception of this sinister figure. He never hesitated, when it seemed right to him, to put the dramatic viewpoint before the musical.

His repertory, like his choice of novelties and revivals, was a fine balance among care for established works, for the unjustly neglected, and love of the new. The fresh life he breathed into opera of every genre from Gluck and Mozart to Pfitzner and Charpentier reflected the breadth of his outlook. It was enriched by the inclusion of works that had previously failed to find general acceptance, but showed their worth when presented with imaginative mastery such as his: e.g., Boïeldieu's *La Dame Blanche*, Goetz's *The Taming of the Shrew*, and Halévy's *La Juive*.

As Mahler's repertory left no scope for criticism, attacks had to be directed against his serious handling of new problems. What is now seen and accepted as pioneer work on his part was then in its trial phase; it roused excitement and resistance. I am thinking of his and Alfred

Roller's productions of *Tristan, Fidelio, Walküre, Don Giovanni, Figaro, The Magic Flute, Iphigenia*—productions marking stages on his way toward solving what he clearly saw as the whole problem of operatic presentation. I mention this here in passing. I shall deal later with his work as director and conductor. Here it is enough to say that while, to the end, he commanded the support of the worthwhile members of the musical public, who admired the manner in which his daring spirit was pressing beyond normal bounds into the heart of problems, and saluted the reckless vehemence of his pursuit of this goal, there were others. The duller and weaker among his collaborators detested his fanaticism and the violence of his personal utterances. And the more conservative element of the press and public was antagonized by his artistic daring. Anything new irked them. They grumbled. They did not realize that the experiments of today were setting the pattern for tomorrow.

Vienna

If, in the last analysis, hostility was caused by the challenging stature of his achievement—as is the case with anything new that matters—it must be admitted that he himself was often innocently guilty of giving personal offense. The steel in him reacted against the "softness" of the Vienna of his day; it was really a salute, with standards in reverse. The dynamic man and fascinating conductor over-whelmed resistance from the very beginning. To maintain this position in a world inclined to take things easy demanded unyielding refusal of any sort of concession. But as his pioneering search led him away and up from the level tract of the accustomed, his artistic demands grew even loftier and more complicated.

Moreover, Mahler, with all his kindliness and sensitivity, was in outward behavior dominating by nature. He had the gift of command, unfamiliar in a Royal and Imperial Opera House highly conscious of its glorious past. The *genius loci* of the splendid and magnificently equipped theater resembled, before Mahler's advent, the young man of the world in Giorgione's "Concerto" rather than the earnest, exalted monk. It was the latter spirit that Mahler brought in, and he was determined to place his stamp on an institution previously characterized by the brilliance of its singers, the sensuous charm of its music-making, and the richness of its décor. Something new and exciting was injected into the sensuous culture of the city by the approach and demands inherent in the profound sincerity of his whole personality, in his spiritual attitude toward his art, and in his relation to the operatic masterpieces.

In his first year as director, he had an audience with the Emperor Franz Josef, who declared proudly that "Mahler has succeeded in making himself master of the House." Mahler was determined to maintain this mastery in order to achieve his artistic aims. He succeeded. But his sights were constantly raised, therefore his demands grew more exacting and his methods

more severe. Artists of genuine gifts and sincere
intentions, however, never encountered the
sharpness of his edge; he had patience with their
failings and showed his appreciation both artis-
tically and in personal contacts. For instance, a
highly gifted singer whom he liked used always
to make the same mistake at a certain point in a
Mozart opera. During a performance of this
work smoke appeared on the stage as a result of a
short circuit. The audience showed signs of disturbance. Panic was prevented by Mahler's
presence of mind, the reassuring words he spoke
from the desk, and the self-control of the singer,
who went on singing and did not make his
habitual mistake. At the end Mahler tapped him
on the shoulder, saying with a laugh: "It seems,
my dear X, that we need a fire to make you
sing that phrase correctly!" The kindness of this
reprimand was in sharp contrast to the uncompromising acerbity he could and often did show
when an artistic question was involved. During
a late, possibly the last, rehearsal of a new pro-

duction, the cast for which had already been announced, he was entirely dissatisfied with the performance of the leading singer, a well-known and popular figure. From the conductor's desk he said just what he thought. He replaced the singer, thus exposing him to the public humiliation of having someone else sing his role at the opening performance.

At other times he could be all kindness and consideration. A member of the company was mortally ill; he was at endless pains to help him financially and otherwise, even getting him a new contract in order to relieve his mind and deceive him about the hopelessness of his condition. Here, of course, artistic considerations were not involved; where they were, as in the earlier case, he was completely "amoral" and unable even to see that he should have softened the blow. Once in an endeavor to get him not to be so ruthless, I discussed a case of this kind with him, only to receive the unforgettable, and really naïve reply: "Look here, once the first unpleasantness is over, I am immediately good again!" He simply could not see that the other fellow was entitled to feel badly about it, or that weaker natures could not accept the strict line he drew between the moral and the artistic.

In his beautiful farewell letter to the members of the Opera, he said that "under the pressure of the fight, in the heat of the moment, neither I nor you have escaped hurts and mistakes." Now, when the Mahler period and the contribution of its artists has achieved an almost legendary stature, it can be seen how much was at stake, and what a significant and determinant battle was actually won. And Mahler never treated anyone else as ruthlessly as he treated himself. At every rehearsal he demanded the utmost of himself, and never spared himself, even when he was ill. It is well-nigh inconceivable that he should have written his Fourth, Fifth, Sixth, Seventh, and Eighth symphonies and a series of songs with orchestra during the brief summer vacations of his years as director, and that for ten years he only exchanged the immense burden of directing the Opera for the greater burden of creative work. His life was an artistic cycle: he poured his energy into art and received it back renewed from art. Except in his very last years in Vienna, I never saw him other than vivid, inspired, bursting with vitality.

His working day began early, at home, with a couple of hours at his desk orchestrating his latest work. Then he walked to the Opera and dealt with correspondence and business until rehearsal time. At midday we would often go out together, and I would accompany him, often after a stroll in the Stadtpark, to his home in the Auenbruggerstrasse. Sometimes we would meet in a café in the afternoon; sometimes there were stimulating evenings at his home or with friends. There were unforgettable evenings, too, at restaurants after his glorious first nights; the job done, he would discuss it in detail. I reveled in his talk, it was always suggestive and stimulating, the outcome of a mind forever on the move. Nevertheless, it seems to me that in Vienna, with his intense preoccupations and all the responsibilities a director has to carry, the tone of his talk was in general less aimed at the heights, less transcendental and more worldly. Yet even when speaking of day-to-day matters, he never lost the "above-the-battle" attitude of the artist whose home is not here, but in the realm of art, and who carries his isolation about with him. Metaphysical questions would suddenly, abruptly arise in his mind and in his talk. An inner *basso ostinato* could be overlaid but never silenced. Every contact with his creative work, whether at his own desk in the morning or in its production in Vienna or elsewhere, would remove his gaze from the day's pressing demands and turn it toward his inner life.

His Fourth Symphony, begun in the summer of 1899, was completed in 1900. In December 1901 it was performed in Munich and fiercely attacked. I was not present, and only learned from a friend how badly things had gone. The first Vienna performance, in 1902, I recall vividly; the explosion of contrary opinions was so violent that fisticuffs ensued between opponents and enthusiasts. In Vienna, Mahler won his place as a creative artist very slowly. While the musical public was almost unanimously devoted to his conducting, it was for a number of years largely opposed to his compositions. The year 1902, however, was to bring the victory of his life with the triumphant reception of his Third Symphony at the Krefeld Music Festival—a victory that had lengthy repercussions. From that day on, other conductors became interested, they performed his works, he was an accepted composer. The *première* of his Fifth Symphony in Cologne stands out in my memory for a special reason; it was the first, and, I believe, the only, occasion when the performance of a work of Mahler's under his own baton left me dissatisfied. The orchestration failed to bring out clearly the complicated contrapuntal tissue of the voices. Mahler himself said plaintively to me afterward that it seemed to him he never would be able to master the orchestral treatment. Indeed, he later revised the orchestration more drastically than he ever did before or afterward in any other work. The reception was, I recall, highly enthusiastic, showing how the composer's status was rising in general esteem.

Mahler always presented a stoical front to approval or disapproval; the embattled reception of his Fourth Symphony in Vienna left his withers unwrung, and while the success of the Third Symphony in Krefeld pleased him, he was wholly unaffected by the heady wine of success. This made it really shattering to see him reduced almost to tears by the adverse verdict of a very prominent musician on his Sixth, the so-called "Tragic" Symphony. No similar experience comes to my mind, and I am sure that the gloomy cast of the work itself had a good deal to do with this most unusual sensitiveness on his part. In general, critical praise or blame left him unaffected. On the morning after the performance of one of his works or of an important produc-

tion at the Opera, he would say jokingly:
"Well, what have our superiors to say?" and
receive the report with unruffled calm. One of
my happiest memories is of a concert to which
the Verein der schaffenden Tonkünstler, of
which I was a member, had invited him; he
responded with warmth to the reverence then
shown him by such younger composers as
Schönberg and Zemlinsky.

The evening, devoted entirely to songs with
orchestra, was really a Mahler Festival; it took
place in the Kleiner Musikvereinssaal, and the
executants were excellent singers from the Opera and a chamber combination from his Philharmonic. It was a happy evening; the devotion
of these young musicians meant more to him
than the noisy plaudits of a great audience: their
hearts responded to his own in the message that
his songs conveyed. The impression he made on
such occasions on gifted, eager young artists
like these was wholly sympathetic: he was full
of interest and outflowing kindness.

In personal intercourse the key to his heart

was talent and high endeavor. I do not believe that anyone who was gifted and of a serious turn of mind ever met his harsher side. He was, however, far too much a child of nature ever to feel at home in what is called "Society." Its conventions, conversation, and formalities put him off; to what was authentic, genuine, spiritual, he responded instinctively. In company he was an intimidating element, and he avoided it as far as he could. When he was in good spirits and feeling conversational, he would be the center of a cheerful group; but if he was upset, such a thundercloud brooded over the gathering that only he could dispel it.

While he could be outgiving, sympathetic, and helpful, he was also capable of a quite staggering lack of consideration for others. One day as we were leaving the Opera we were joined by a musician whom, as a rule, he liked, but whom at that moment he did not want to see. In the middle of a sentence from him Mahler, without a word of explanation or farewell, dashed to catch a tram and was gone. He did not mean to be rude: he merely escaped, in-stinctively, from what was for the moment an unwelcome conversation. Again, one hot day in June, a composer came to play his opera for him. I came in toward the end of the last act to find composer and director in shirt-sleeves; the composer was bathed in sweat; Mahler was obviously sunk in an abyss of boredom and dis-taste. He did not utter a single word; the com-poser, incensed by his silence, also said nothing. I saw no way to save the situation. Finally, the composer put on his coat, picked up his score, and after a few more moments of painful silence, ended the uncomfortable scene with an *"Au revoir!"* of chill politeness. A crowded life of every kind of personal contact had not endowed Mahler with that minimum of *savoir-faire* needed to wind up this encounter normally. Yet, when his feelings were touched, he could be both polite and obliging. His bearing and manner were those of a well-bred man of the world. But he was stiff-necked and showed it in his ordinary contacts, in public, and with officials.

Indeed, it says much for these last that they had
enough respect for a great artist and a self-willed
individual to support him through thick and thin.
But it is not surprising if, at the end of ten
years during which his enemies in the press and
the official world had been hard at work, the
ground had been dug from under his feet.

I cannot now recall the final reason for his
resignation; it was, anyhow, only the final
drop that made the bucket overflow. Shortly
before it happened, Mahler, jogging his chair
back and forward as he spoke, said in his caustic
way: "This is my present case. If I want to
stay put, I have only to lean back firmly to hold
my place. But I am making no resistance, so I
shall go down in the end." Soon after this he
called me out of rehearsal one day at noon. We
left the Opera together and I can see him now
as we walked down the Ringstrasse and I heard
him say in a calm and gentle tone of voice that
he had resigned. I recall his admirable words:
"In these ten years at the Opera, I have ful-
filled my cycle." In the deeper sense, he was

59

right. His artistic task at the Opera was completed; it must now give place to his own last great works and to the settlement of his own problems. We spoke, I remember, of his future plans, of the work in America that would provide a comfortable livelihood and a quieter life, and so on. When I got home I was moved to write him a serious letter about what had happened; he acknowledged it in a few very beautiful lines.

Far more serious and disturbing was what he told me in the autumn of this same year, again as we walked along the Ringstrasse. His doctor had suddenly discovered that his heart was seriously affected. As he spoke I recalled an incident during a rehearsal of *Lohengrin* which had troubled me at the time. He found a lack of vigor in the delivery and action of the swan chorus; to show what he wanted at the point where *"Ein Wunder . . ."* begins, he seized two members of the chorus by the hands, and with an expression of enthusiastic excitement, dragged them half across the stage toward King Henry. I had often seen him in this sort of way, stimulating the chorus to incredible feats. This time, however, he suddenly let their hands go and stood, deathly pale and motionless, with his own hand on his heart. I imagine that he then, for the first time, felt his heart deficiency. Now he spoke of the serious consequences of the discovery of his illness and of the revolutionary change in his life and work which would result from the precautions he would have to take from then on. Accustomed to relying on long walks, even on mountain-climbing, for the inspiration of his music, he had now to restrict all bodily movement as much as possible. This discipline entailed not only a heavy sacrifice, but anxiety about his work. Even more important, however, than the serious but inevitable changes in his working habits, seemed to me the marked shift in his whole outlook. The mystery of death had always been in his mind and thoughts; now it was within sight; his world, his life lay under the somber shadow of its proximity. The tone of our talk was unsentimental and "realistic"; behind it I felt the darkness that had overspread his being. "I shall," he said, "soon get used to it." *Das Lied von der Erde* and the Ninth Symphony, both composed after his illness, are eloquent witness to the courage with which he strove, and to his success.

In October 1907 he took leave of the Opera with a performance of *Fidelio;* and, in November, of his Vienna friends with one of his Second Symphony. Their tributes of love, devotion, and sorrow at his departure gladdened and moved him.

A great epoch in the history of opera was closed—the achievements of one man and of the fellow workers whom he had inspired. Every one of us had learned from him; from every one of us he had obtained the best. The manifestations of his artistry created the unforgotten glorious period of the Vienna Opera; the integrity of will that raised it to such heights is a lasting example.

5

Last Years

IN DECEMBER 1907 Mahler went to America for the first time. The hour of his departure was early, but hundreds of people were at the station to bid him farewell as he left Vienna. A strenuous time awaited him, but he felt release as he looked back over ten years' responsibility for the Vienna Opera. At the Metropolitan in New York he would not have to take on new tasks, let alone cope with new problems, but would only be employing resources already available there for the production of works that he knew well. While his concert activities in 1909–10, and again in 1910–11, represented a great responsibility and made great demands on his strength, they were limited in either case to half of the year.

In the last years of his life I saw him but rarely. Instead of the almost constant intercourse of the preceding six years, we had but little time together—a few weeks when he was in Vienna, between the winter's conducting in New York and summer work in Toblach; the days of the first performance, in Prague, of his Seventh Symphony, and of the Eighth in Munich; finally, a few hours in Paris—the last we were to have. Vivid in my mind are the sunny autumn days in Prague. The place recalled experiences of his young days as a young conductor at the Landestheater; the rehearsals and performance of the Seventh Symphony of course provided us with many occasions for lively discussion. He was satisfied with its instrumentation; we knew that every measure told. We made an expedition by car into the pleasant countryside; we talked together or in groups of friends and family; perfect harmony prevailed.

Then in the winter of 1909–10 Emil Gutmann, the concert manager, made arrangements for a performance of the Eighth Symphony which Mahler at first awaited with some apprehension. Gutmann, without consulting him, had advertised a performance of "The Symphony of the Thousand." Mahler described the affair as a "Barnum and Bailey Show" and foresaw all sorts of troubles and difficulties in the organization of its massive effects. At his wish I had chosen and rehearsed the soloists. When he got to Vienna, early in 1910, he sat in on a rehearsal that took place at my home. As we began, a fearful thunderstorm broke out and we had to keep interrupting our work. He patiently accepted this sabotage by the heavens. He murmured approval of the soloists, and I could see the effect on all concerned of this gentleness on the part of the man of wrath. Satisfied next with the choral work, he departed for Toblach, coming to Munich at the beginning of September.

Those were great days for us who shared in the rehearsals of the Eighth. The hand of the master controlled the vast array without apparent effort. All concerned, including the children, who adored him at once, were filled with a solemn elevation of mood. What a moment it was, when at the zenith of his career, and, little as we knew it, soon to be called from us by the hand of fate, he took his place amid the applause of the thousands filling the vast auditorium, in front of the one thousand performers—above all at the point where the *Creator spiritus*, whose fire inspired him, is called on and a thousand voices utter the cry expressing his whole life's longing—*Accende lumen sensibus, infunde amorem cordibus!* As the last note died away and a storm of applause surged toward him, Mahler stepped up to where, at the top of the platform, the chorus of children stood. He went along the line shaking their outstretched hands as they cheered him. This tribute of love from the young filled him with hope for the future of his work and gave him deep joy.

During rehearsals his friends had anxiously noted many signs of physical weakness. But at the performance he seemed at the height of his powers. The lift of his spirit gave his tired heart its old vigor. This was, however, the last time he conducted a composition of his own; he never heard his last two works.

When he first spoke to me of *Das Lied von der Erde*, he called it a "Symphony in Songs." It was planned to be his Ninth. Then he changed his mind. He thought of how, for Beethoven and for Bruckner, a ninth symphony had written *finis*; he hesitated to challenge fate. He gave me the manuscript to study; it was the first time that I learned to know a new work of his otherwise than through himself. When I brought it back, well-nigh incapable of uttering a word, he turned to the "*Abschied*," saying: "What do you think? Is it at all bearable? Will it drive people to make an end of themselves?" Then, indicating the rhythmic difficulties, he said jestingly: "Have you any notion how this should be conducted? I haven't!"

If my memory serves me, he never himself gave me the score of the Ninth, for which, being a symphony, the ominous number was unavoidable. I see from one of his letters that in the fall of 1909 he took it with him to New York "in almost illegible form," in the hope of producing a fair copy there. He must have taken it back to Vienna early in 1910, but I do not recall ever seeing it there; it was only after his death that it came into my hands. It may be that a superstitious shrinking from a Ninth prevented his talking to me about it. Yet in that clear and powerful mind I had never detected any trace of superstition. Nor can there have been anything of the sort here; he knew only too well what the Fates had in store.

Although I actually saw little of him in the last years of his life, I was compensated for this loss by the intensity of his communication by letter and the profundity of our conversations. As in nature, twilight dissolves in the glow of sunset, the gloom thrown on his spirit at the onset of his illness passed into the mild radiance of approaching departure, lending a new loveliness to the "dear Earth" whose chant he had composed, and seeming to cast a secret shimmer over his speech and writing. I shall never forget his expression as he told me that he had never found the world so beautiful as on a recent visit to the Bohemian countryside and as he spoke of the delicious fragrance rising from the soil. Deep emotional turmoil lay behind his talk. Touching on a wide range of intellectual topics, as in the Hamburg days, it reached out constantly to metaphysical issues, and with a higher and more ardent pressure than of old. His mood might have been likened to a sort of travel fever of the soul, interrupted now and then by passages of serene calm: we even talked of plans for the future. We spoke of a house and garden on the Hohe Warte or in Grinzing, and of a *Kaffeehaus* where we might meet of an afternoon. But such idyllic flights of fancy were likely to end in a gesture or glance of disbelief.

A singular grim incident, which happened, I believe, during his last summer, depressed him deeply. He told me that while working in his composition cottage at Toblach he was suddenly startled by an incomprehensible noise. Something "frightfully dark" burst through the window, and proved, when he rose in horror, to be an eagle that filled the small space with its hurtlings to and fro. The dread apparition was brief; the eagle stormed away as swiftly as it had come. Then when Mahler dropped, exhausted on the sofa, a crow flew out from under it. His musical haven had become a battlefield for one of the endless fights of "all against all." His story reflected the horror of this immediate demonstration of nature's awful cruelty, which had always lain at the root of the deep sorrow in his

soul; the incident had brought it all to the surface again.

In the autumn of 1910 he returned to New
York; in February 1911 came the news that he
was gravely ill. When he went to Paris in April
for a serum treatment I determined to go and
see him there. There he lay, the tormented vic-
tim of an unpredictable disease that now affected
his spirit as well as his body. His mood was
bleak and aloof. When, in an effort to turn his
mind to more cheerful subjects, I spoke of his
work, his response was wholly pessimistic for
the first time. I therefore avoided serious topics
and simply tried to distract his mind by talk on
other, unrelated subjects. I was not wholly un-
successful; indeed, I recall that my report of
some remarks on the subject of art, made by a
well-known Philistine, produced a faint smile
in which there was a tinge of the old sense of
humor. Another incident gave a gleam of the
same kind; he wanted to be shaved—a youthful

French barber appeared who seemed to combine the whole elegance of his nation with that of his profession. While he plied his craft with exaggerated delicacy I caught something like a flicker of amusement in the sick man's eye. He may have recalled the fantastic barber of some fairy tale. When the young man had bowed himself out, Mahler looked after him, murmuring softly, but in a lively tone: "Farewell, beard-scraper!" In my efforts to distract him I often failed; his immobile face showed how far away he was. When I tried to describe the future house and garden about which we had often spoken in Vienna, he did not answer immediately and then gave me a sad reply: "That would be nice, but my only desire now is to be allowed enough digitalis to keep my heart going." Then, his mood would change; he listened with interest to everything I could tell him about Vienna and what was going on in the musical world there. While he often showed resentment, the old attachment broke through frequently; at bottom he enjoyed nothing so much as stories of that world he knew so well. I had to leave after a few days. We had no more talk. When I next saw him he was dying.

In May he was carried to Vienna. No bitterness born of the manifold disappointments of his time there could prevail against his desire to "come home" at the last. He found joy in the friendly greetings and signs of devotion that greeted him on all sides. On May 18, 1911, he died. Next evening as we laid the coffin in the cemetery at Grinzing, a storm broke and such torrents of rain fell that it was almost impossible to proceed. An immense crowd, dead silent, followed the hearse. At the moment when the coffin was lowered, the sun broke through the clouds.

Reflection

~>>>->>>->>>•<<<•<<<•<<<~

I

The Opera Director

MAHLER'S dramatic talent equaled his musical gifts; this was the reason for his greatness as an opera director. He was as much at home on the stage as with the score. He could breathe his own fiery glow into the dramatic action as into the musical performance and get his artists to meet the demands, representational or musical, of any given work.

His personality was dramatic; he was a man of intense feeling and imagination. He could enter into Alberich's despair when the Ring is snatched from him, and share the frenzy of the curse he hurls at those who rob him of it;

77

he breathed with Pizarro's prisoners in their
brief spell of release; he knew the jealous
rage that fills Mr. Ford when he believes that
his wife's lover is hidden in the laundry-basket;
he was Wotan as he curbs Brünnhilde's dis-
obedience, and Brünnhilde as she seeks to soften
her father's wrath. Nothing human, nothing
divine, was alien to him: Beckmesser's petty
spite was not too low, nor the St. John's Day
mood of Hans Sachs too lofty for him. He lived
in everything, and everything lived in him.
However remote an action or sentiment, however foreign to his own character, he could enter
into it imaginatively as into the mind of any
man, in any situation. As he sat in the orchestra
pit his heart was on the stage; his conducting, or
rather, his music-making, was governed by the
drama.

When, as a young assistant conductor, I went
from Pressburg to Vienna I heard him conduct
a performance of *Lohengrin* which set me a
permanent standard. In the scene outside the

cathedral, where Elsa and Ortrud are quarreling, I suddenly realized the essential nature of opera. Mahler was not just conducting the orchestral accompaniment to a contralto song: he was with Ortrud in spirit: he *was* Ortrud; he was transporting both orchestra and singer into the heart of a deeply humiliated woman—at the same time his music took in Elsa's terror and her profound belief in Lohengrin. His conducting penetrated to the soul of the music, and directly to its dramatic essence. This scene from *Lohengrin* was a simple case; here music as such has no independent life of its own because Wagner assigns it an almost exclusively dramatic function. The so-called "Mystery Ensemble" is another matter. Even here, however, while the music has more independent significance, the essence is still dramatic, centering as it does on Lohengrin's bewilderment, Elsa's doubts, the varying attitudes taken by others, all overarched by a sense of approaching catastrophe which must find expression in the music. More exacting demands have here to be met: the spirit of the music and of the drama must be expressed simultaneously.

Another profoundly moving experience rounded off the lesson of *Lohengrin*. At the opening of the second act of *Figaro* the first bars of the Countess's aria transported one into the realm of absolute music; the song of the strings and the voice of the singer alike dwelled there; the theater vanished, overwhelmed; the Countess's pain and longing were resolved in the higher sphere of music. One did not feel in any sense removed into the concert hall, but "lost to this world" and to that of the theater. Mahler had conjured the very spirit of music until it held unchallenged sway; and how this spirit overflowed both audience and performers as he evoked it in the shimmering reconciliation passages that precede the presto at the close of the fourth act!

Opera as an art form lives between the two poles I have here tried to indicate. Mahler was its master from pole to pole. He knew when music should unfold its full power and submerge drama; he knew, too, when and in what degree it had to subserve it—when the dramatic aspect should be uppermost.

Understanding as he did how to dramatize music, he also strove to infuse drama with the spirit of music—the most taxing problem in opera. His musical interpretation communicated to his singers the power of dramatic expression. This was not all. Gesture and movement are part of dramatic representation; he used music to infuse and guide that representation. I am not here thinking of mere pantomimic response, as in the string passages accompanying Beckmesser's scrawlings or lending expressive force to the silent play of feeling between Siegmund and Sieglinde. What I have in mind is an interpenetration by music of the mood of any significant scene; an interpenetration providing for the finer shades of expression—a glance, a smile—and allowing no gesture to break the musical texture. He was able to penetrate the heart of the music and realize, within himself, the composer's dramatic vision. Here his own notable histrionic gifts came to his aid; he could show, not merely say, how a given scene should be played in consonance with the music. His will was evoked to a full realization of the author's intentions. But it is only Wagner and works of the post-Wagnerian period that show any "pre-established harmony" between what is in the score and what is taking place on the stage. Mozart also wrote dramatic music, but no scenic directions in his scores, consequently there were no indications for Mahler to go by. Anyone, however, who saw Mahler's *Figaro* will recall how subtly and vividly the comedy of the stage was made to correspond with the spirit of the music. One example may serve—the exquisite way in which the music led the action of the page in Susanna's aria *"Venite inginocchiatevi."*

In rehearsal Mahler was guided by intuition and impulse, not by any fixed method or principle. He knew the work by heart. He had a picture of it. Here was the stage, here were gifted artists. His imagination in a happy glow, he drew inspiration from the dramatic situation, illumination from the score. When he had to deal with artists of talent, his demands rose; when they were inadequate, he would use gentler methods of getting the best out of them. Always he was the imaginative servant of the work of art itself. Never was he tempted by the abundance of his powers to "play his own hand."

Complete unity was the goal he set himself: a mutual interaction of score and stage. He grew to see that such unity was not achieved merely by the fusion of action and music; staging, costume, and lighting had to be brought up to an equal pitch of perfection. At a significant juncture he met Alfred Roller, who had reached the same conclusion from the point of view of the painter. Roller's sets for *Tristan* showed deep visual understanding; thenceforth Mahler and Roller worked together for the realization of his ideal of unity in operatic performance. Up to then it had been assumed that it was enough to have stage décor, costumes, and lighting that satisfied broadly cultivated tastes and were an interesting contribution toward the production; the idea of integrating music and drama and infusing them both with a dominating idiom and mood was in its infancy, in so far as it existed at all. Roller, a painter of imagination steeped in the theater and its possibilities, was, like Mahler, filled with the desire for animation of the opera stage. His decorative use of three-dimensional settings greatly increased the effectiveness of his lighting, which in turn became an element in the suggestive power both of the drama and of the music. The colors and forms he employed were organically related to the mood of the work; even his costumes played their part. An indescribably moving performance of *Tristan* ushered in the great period in Mahler's search for perfection.

His aims were complex and novel. His approach suggested that he was experimenting and gave rise to much public discussion and excitement, more especially because breaking new ground inevitably involved mistakes and imperfections. The most constructive re-creation of this period, his *Don Giovanni*, was obviously experimental, and became the target of lively critical comment. He had the admirable idea of creating a fixed stage frame to facilitate rapid changes of scene; its drawback was that its turrets did not automatically, or even naturally, fit any particular scene. The colors, again, were too strong for the mild glow of Mozart's orchestration; the choice of singer for the leading role proved unfortunate. Nevertheless, the performance as a whole demonstrated clearly the problem Mahler and Roller tried to solve; with all its failings, it can now be seen as showing the way to the most interesting and promising productions of its time. Each subsequent production profited by the ones that had gone before, until that of Gluck's *Iphigenia in Aulis* scaled heights unique in my experience.

Mahler never relaxed his pioneer effort to secure unified performances of opera in which all the elements would be spiritually fused. He knew how to lift his artists to heights of achievement, where personal impact and obedience to the demands of the work, adaptation to the whole, and unfolding of individuality were all linked together. In his own contribution, absolute loyalty to the work—which alone concerned him—was married to the freedom proper to genius. Dramatic interpretation demands a wider imaginative scope than pure music, for the theater has developed no technique of written instructions which could be compared with the accuracy of a musical score. Even Wagner's plastic vision of the dramatic action, expressed as it is in full stage directions, leaves much open to interpretation. This very fact imposes on a stage director's conscience an obligation to select among the possibilities open to his imagination those essential to the work as a whole, underlining them at the expense of what is inessential so as to preserve continuity of style. Mahler's interpretations were a model of this wider view of loyalty to the work.

In his view, changes were permissible only when lack of clarity in the original makes business on the stage hard to interpret, or when the author's intentions might be compromised by an easily remediable imperfection in direction. Mozart and Wagner were, in general, sacrosanct. In *Figaro*, however, he enlarged the court scene in order to clarify the significance of Marcellina's suit against Figaro. Of course he did not alter a note; he merely expanded the *secco* recitative. In the same way, there was an interesting, if belated, justification for his small infringement on Goetz's *Taming of the Shrew*. He struck out the closing scenes, and made the opera end with the beautiful duet between Petruchio and Katharina. Although this proved highly successful with audiences, he was troubled, feeling that a conductor had no right to deal thus with another man's work. It was an immense relief to his sensitive conscience to discover that Goetz, arranging a piano score for

a performance in Mannheim, had made precisely the same change.

It goes without saying that outside the works
of the great masters—Mozart, Beethoven,
Weber, Gluck, Wagner—he felt a freedom, and
indeed an obligation, to put his rich experience
at the service of the composer. Operas such as
*The Tales of Hoffmann, La Dâme Blanche, The
Merry Wives of Windsor, La Juive,* and *The
Taming of the Shrew* profited by this; the more
so as he used such freedom solely in the interest
of securing performances that fully realized
their creators' dreams. About these he knew no
doubt once his intuition had penetrated into
the artist's workshop. It was indeed this intimate
knowledge of the author's intentions which gave
to his interpretations, for all their daring, the
impression of assurance and authenticity. He
had no trace of vanity, no desire for merely
theatrical effect. The work itself was, for him,
the law. His performances, and the Opera under
him, were governed by this sense of dedication.

2

The Conductor

THE WORKS, beyond description glorious, are bright, as on the earliest day." So, in *Faust*, the Archangel sings of God's creations. Mahler's reverence for the great works of music was of this exalted order. "Bright as on the earliest day" he felt them. Thus they sounded under his baton. Thus he made audiences hear them. A sense of something done for the first time, with first intention, spontaneous, was the chief characteristic in his interpretations.

Only penetration into the depth of the great creations of art, as well as those of nature, reveals that element of ultimate immeasurability which is the hallmark of greatness. Only he who enters deeply enough into the work to feel this can always arouse fresh interest and enthusiasm, while the superficial mind, which assumes that it understands all about a given work, knows it through and through, is likely to lose freshness and relapse into routine performance. Intimate knowledge strengthened Mahler's wonder and admiration for works "beyond description glorious," fed and renewed his first intention. He approached them like a lover, constantly wooing; he was always ready to reconsider, improve, plumb new depths. Nothing was routine in his performances; even if he was giving a work for the thirtieth time, he gave it as though for the first. Though his approach seemed free and impetuous, it was invariably governed by the most rigorous exactitude. He observed and demanded from all who worked with him, complete faithfulness to the score, its notation, tempos, agogic marks, and dynamics. Even the

The Conductor

singers had to sing by the book; he was never content until absolute precision had been achieved "above and below"—on the stage and in the orchestra. The transparency of his conducting responded to his demand for absolute musical clarity. The precision of his exemplary beat was never impaired by emotion, however strong. At the innumerable performances I attended, I heard mistakes by singers and instrumentalists, but never any failure in precision or ensemble: the unfailing certainty of his beat always kept singers and orchestra together. But one never had the impression of mechanical precision, nor can I recall an occasion when audience or critics even mentioned his accuracy. With him, precision was a means toward bringing the soul of the work to life. Talents, however high, were, if not controlled by a well-nigh pedantic sense of form, dismissed as mere sound and fury; only when his fiery hold over singers and orchestra had established an absolute clarity of interpretation did he permit himself

the free flight of spirit which gave his performances the effect of improvisation.

His interpretation was never arbitrary. That
he was accused of this was owing to the wide
difference between his inspired renderings and
what audiences were used to. When he made
changes in the classics, they were designed to
make the spirit live rather than reproduce the
dead letter. Hence his much criticized retouch-
ing of the instrumentation of Beethoven's Ninth
and other works in which, knowing as he did
the resources of the modern orchestra, he used
them to clarify and realize Beethoven's intentions. When attacked on this ground in Vienna
he defended his action in a public statement
in which he drew attention to the contrast between the power of Beethoven's conception and
the limited instrumental capacities in Beethoven's day. He cited the example of Wagner and
stressed the obligation on the conductor to let
the voices soar out clearly.

I have noted his fanatical devotion to the

score; it never blinded him to the paramount duty of realizing the composer's intentions. Now most people accept modifications of this kind, though there are still differences as to how they should be effected. In Mahler's case, they derived from his amazing ear for the inner meaning, even when contemporary instrumentation left it obscure. "Your Beethoven is not my Beethoven," he grunted to a well-meaning friend who took him to task for unfamiliar renderings. So in truth it was; he knew Beethoven by direct experience, and his performance of him was an experience. His Beethoven had nothing in common with the smooth classic presented in so many routine performances. His *Fidelio*, his Third *Leonora* Overture, and his indescribable *Coriolanus* Overture are vivid enough in my memory for me to testify to his spiritual kinship with the real Beethoven. He had within him his thunderstorms, his power, his love. Scrupulous as he was for detail, he had also the simplicity, the truthfulness, and the symphonic understanding that respect the primary claim of organic form.

Arbitrary or subjective renderings were incompatible with his penetrating divination of the depths of a work. The picture in his mind's eye was complete; there were no gaps to fill. The real explanation of arbitrary alteration and subjective transformation is sometimes mere pretentiousness and a craving for originality, more often the imperfection of the interpreter's vision, his lack of the seeing eye, of the penetrating divination which can reach the heart of a work. The poor man, eager not to appear shallow, has to compensate for his defects with his own meager resources.

Clarity ruled Mahler's interpretation of masterpieces. But it was not daylight clarity. Music is no daytime art; it does not yield its secret roots or its ultimate depths to the unshadowed soul. It comes out of the dark, and must be understood and felt in the dark; it is akin to the somber heave of the ocean, not to

the clear blue of the Mediterranean. Darkness
surged in Mahler's soul; his eye, native to the
night, was born to realize the depths of music.

"The best in music," he used to say, "is not
set down in the notes." This best, this essential,
soul leaped forth with such passion from his
conducting, with such an effect of personal confession, such elemental force, as to cause occasional doubt as to whether the composer was
speaking or Mahler, whose stormy spirit compelled the voice of another to utter his own
feeling.

Mahler's sole desire was indubitably to reveal the ultimate depths probed by another—
in fact, the work itself. To ask whether interpretation such as his reveals the soul of the interpreter, or of the composer, or a mingling of
the two, is to confront the very mystery of
musical re-creation. In art, as in life, the fully
personal voice, the complete "I," alone carries
conviction and moves us to the depths. The
well-meant but mediocre interpretation fails by

never establishing identity between interpreter and composer. Not so with the genuine interpreter, whose enthusiastic abandon carries him over into a state where he is "beside himself." Then, ecstasy transcends individualism, and the re-creation of another becomes almost creation in its own right. Then, his talent becomes like that of Proteus; heart and imagination, flooded by "the other," generate a kind of fusion; the barriers between creator and re-creator seem to disappear, and the conductor might be conducting a work of his own. Then, he can speak as "I," feel as "I," and this "I-feeling" gives his interpretation immediacy, complete compulsion. So, in perfect re-creation, loyalty and freedom coincide. To understand that Beethoven's Ninth when conducted by Richard Wagner was filled with the spirit of Beethoven, but also alive with Wagner's personality—moreover, that the full expression of Wagner's individuality was necessary to set Beethoven's spirit free—is to know the meaning of musical interpretation.

The Conductor

→≫-→≫-→≫• ≪-≪-≪

Mahler's conducting was of this order. His powerful personality was wholly dedicated to revealing the work of another in all its clarity and strength; it was his joy to unite two spirits in such performances.

There are cases where difficulty of understanding and an alien approach impair entry into the mind of another. Even then, however, neither personal feeling nor a dominating "I" justifies distortion. Even of unsympathetic works, Mahler, often to the amazement of their composers, who knew the gulf between them and him, gave performances that were at once faithful to the composer and true to himself. What matters in such case is a direction of will toward the "other"; this, as interpreter, he never lacked. Where there is such a sense of service, the scholastic dictum quoted by Jean Paul—"Forty thousand angels can sit upon the point of a needle"—applies. The structure of a genuine work of art permits without contraction of its scope, any and every expression of the interpreter's imagination. There can, indeed, be no convincing performance unless this kind of spiritual collaboration exists.

As years went on, the picture Mahler presented on the podium was simplified. Böhler's excellent silhouettes, drawn in his first period in Vienna, show him in fierce, violent movement at the desk. He always sat to conduct, but in his first Vienna years, as in Hamburg, his mobility was astounding. But his movements were not excessive or superfluous—they seemed rather like some kind of fanatical conjuration. Gradually posture and gestures became quieter. The spirit behind his technique developed to a point at which he had no difficulty in securing a combination of force and precision by an apparently simple beat, almost without moving his body. A glance, a rare gesture would keep singers and players under his spell without any of the agitation in which he formerly indulged. In his last period in Vienna, the picture was one of almost uncanny calm, with no loss in intensity

of effect. I remember a performance of Strauss'
Symphonia Domestica in which the contrast
between the wild storms in the orchestra and the
immobility of the conductor who unleashed
them made an almost ghostly impression.

At stage rehearsal with orchestra, despite intense preoccupation with purely musical matters, the dramatist in him was Argus-eyed;
nothing that happened on the stage escaped his
vigilance—action, lighting, and costumes were
under perpetual observation. Through example
and precept, sometimes tranquil, sometimes vehement, he got the result he wanted. Not because he wanted it, but because he had to get it.
His own tremendous "must" exacted obedience
from all who worked with him.

I want, however, to stress once more the
fact that the decisive quality of his conducting
and the source of its power was the warmth
of his heart. That gave his interpretation the
impressiveness of a personal message. That rendered unnoticeable the meticulous study lying

behind the result he achieved: its virtuosity and accomplishment; that made his music-making what it was—a spontaneous greeting from soul to soul. Here, in the borderland between art and humanity, the nobility and potency of his mind were revealed. The secret of his lasting fame as conductor and director is his ideal combination of high artistic gifts with the ardent sensibility of a great heart.

3

The Composer

THE FUNDAMENTAL element in Mahler's work is the simple fact that he was a genuine musician. At first he was a romantic at heart—witness *Das klagende Lied* and the *Lieder eines fahrenden Gesellen*—but his later development shows conflict between, and blending of romantic and classical elements. Classical is the determination to give form to the music that gushed from him, to control and master his virile power, imagination, and sensibility. Romantic, in the wider sense, is the bold and unbounded range of his fantasy: his "nocturnal" quality; a tendency to excess in expression, at times reaching the grotesque; above all, the mixture of poetic and other ideas in his musical imagination. His was a turbulent inner world of music, impassioned humanism, poetic imagination, philosophic thought, and religious feeling. As he had both a feeling heart and the formative power of ardent expression, he was able to subject his individual musical language to the tyranny of symphonic form. This form came to dominate his creative activity; he was to develop into clear symphonic forms a content that had originally been various and rich to the point of chaos.

His First Symphony, although conceived as a personal credo, already showed how completely he was dedicated to the symphonic idea. From the Second Symphony on, his advance along the symphonic path was more and more conscious and determined, and was characterized by the steady development of movements from a thematic core whose musical completeness is deflected by no poetic idea or musical interjection sacrificing the principle of organic coherence. He was to develop symphonic form and expand its scale immensely, above all in his development sections, where he heightened the use of the motif as created and employed by Beethoven —always keeping the idea of the whole structure in mind when forming the single parts. Here he simply follows in Beethoven's tracks. The glorious, singing quality of many of his themes, like the happy-go-lucky Austrian coloration of his melodies, shows traces of the influence of Schubert and of Bruckner. The choral theme in the Second Symphony, the breadth of its layout, and the traces in it of solemnity, also recall Bruckner. There are echoes of Berlioz, too, in the daring use of bizarre and grotesque means for the purpose of reaching the utmost keenness of expression; he perhaps learned more from the great French genius than from anyone else.

However, there was another ancestor in his

family tree: the "unknown musician," who sang the folk song. Many important themes, not only in his songs but also in his symphonies, derive from folk song—nay, are folk song. The feeling, the idea of the poetry of the people gave the original impetus that set his musical imagination going. The folklore of the mercenaries tugged at his heartstrings, and gave birth to many of his songs. As he had destroyed his earlier work before I knew him, I do not know either his "Nordic" Symphony nor the operas and chamber music of that period. I do not even know whether they derived from "folksy" feeling or, as I guess, from Schumann. The youthful works in the first volume of his songs for piano certainly show traces of Schumann's influence, with the single exception of *"Hans und Grethe,"* a song charmingly reminiscent of the dance music of his German-Bohemian home. The first major work to reveal Mahler's original genius derives from folk poetry though it has nothing to do with the mercenaries; he put

The Composer

Grimm's tale *"Der singende Knochen"* (The Singing Bone) into verse to form the basis for *Das klagende Lied*, a composition for chorus, soloists, and orchestra. The music is inspired and thoroughly original, full of dramatic and human feeling. There followed the more subjective *Lieder eines fahrenden Gesellen*, in which a passionate experience finds artistic expression. In either case, his imagination seems to be in full sympathy with the poetic atmosphere of *Des Knaben Wunderhorn*, though he did not, in fact, read the work of Arnim and Brentano till some four years later. A deep insight into a mind plainly akin to the creators of this masterpiece comes if we realize the close correspondence between his verses and those written or collected by Arnim and Brentano; in any collection his and theirs would be indistinguishable. The music to which they are set, like the verses themselves, is tender and simple, folksonglike in feeling. Here are the roots from which his art grew.

When he finally read the *Wunderhorn*, he must have felt as though he was finding his home. Everything that moved him is there—nature, piety, longing, love, parting, night, death, the world of spirits, the tale of the mercenaries, the joy of youth, childhood jokes, quirks of humor, all pour out, as in his songs. Out of the happy marriage of native poetry and a music intimately related to it was born a series of enchanting works. They reveal a personality of virile cast and strong originality.

Mahler's songs—the earlier with piano, the later with orchestral accompaniments—constitute a refreshingly varied, characteristic, and significant part of his work. Each has the mark of creativity, musical invention; none is a mere piece of emotional declamation. I cannot mention them all, but I do want to glance at the various fields to which they belong, for they illustrate the nature of the man. There are soldiers' songs: some spirited: "*Aus! Aus!*" and "*Trost im*

Unglück," some sad: *"Zu Strassburg auf der Schanz"* and *"Der Tambourgesell";* next, three highly expressive of the nocturnal side of his nature, in which there was a region on which the sun never rose. *"Der Schildwache Nacht-lied"* is one of the most impressive vocal compositions of this comparatively early stage. Night itself pervades the talk of boy and girl, the tramp of the evening round, and the foreboding of the ending. *"Wo die schönen Trompeten blasen"* is the most touching of the three—nocturnal, again, in its mood and with a gripping ghostly conclusion. The most impressive of them all is *"Revelge,"* unique in its reflection of Mahler's own consanguinity with night and death, as in its inexorable marching rhythms, its ghostly coloring, and the emotional tension that brings us into terrifying contact with his demoniac being. Next, a group of pious songs; *"Urlicht,"* an expression of simple faith, quite unlike *"Himmlisches Leben,"* in which it is presented as a childhood dream—a mood paralleled in *"Es sangen drei Engel."* The humorous songs are highly characteristic; *"Selbstgefühl," "Ablösung im Sommer,"* and *"Des Antonius von Padua Fischpredigt."* This last, from which Mahler took the thematic material for the inspired scherzo of his Second Symphony, is a masterpiece of originality and humorous expression, as of formal unity. The droll *"Ablösung im Sommer"* produced the central theme of the scherzo of the Third Symphony. Then, there are lovely folk songs like *"Scheiden und Meiden," "Nicht wiedersehen,"* and, in pride of place, the fourth song in the *Lieder eines fahrenden Gesellen, "Die zwei blauen Augen von meinem Schatz,"* which reappears as the moving central section of the Funeral March in the First Symphony. Another significant early vocal work of the folk period is *"Das irdische Leben."* This belongs to no group. It exists in itself, and he rated it high, as was natural, for the story expresses in its simple, yet powerful way, the woe of the world which haunted him all his life, and which he grew to express with the mature force of his expanding personality. Moreover, this song is one of the first in which his own musical idiom is fully evident.

The smile of a man with a tendency toward deep gloom has a peculiarly refreshing and infectious quality. There is a special charm in the little group of songs in a cheerful vein, e.g., "*Verlorene Müh*," "*Rheinlegendchen*," and "*Wer hat dies Liedlein erdacht?*"

After his Fourth Symphony, Mahler moved from folklore to classic poetry. He felt, in a sense, akin to Rückert, whose exquisite mastery of language, combined with the truthfulness and simplicity of his feeling, attracted Mahler strongly. His choice of the five most beautiful of Rückert's more than one hundred poems for the cycle *Kindertotenlieder* showed his rare understanding of poetry; the work as a whole is a stirring piece of lyric art. The poems themselves are in no sense folk songs; the music too is far removed from the folk-song style of many

of his earlier songs. It has a noble melodic substance, as have the five songs, likewise based on
Rückert's poems, which followed. There is in
"*Ich atmet einen linden Duft*" a melodic and
poetic jewel; a firm belief in God speaks from
"*Um Mitternacht*"; while "*Ich bin der Welt
abhanden gekommen*" is deeply moving both
as song and as personal confession. A characteristic idiom marks all these songs, and however
strong their dramatic expression, Mahler never
oversteps the limits of the medium.

His songs with orchestra contain perhaps the
most sublime examples of the lofty height he had
reached in his orchestration. They are perfect
illustrations of an exquisite dynamic relation between voice and orchestra. The symphonist in
him found particular pleasure in exercising his
craft within the limits of the small apparatus of
the lied. Master of orchestration, he would ex-
pend loving care on getting exquisite sounds
out of a reduced orchestra. The variety and even
the contrariety of his compositions in the vocal

field impressively foreshadows what he was to achieve in the wider field of the symphony.

Has this rich personality given us music of equal stature? I put the question fairly and squarely: did Mahler possess a "genuine faculty of musical invention"?

When speaking of his songs I suggested that none of them lacks a musical idea. In a song everything depends on the musical core; in a symphony it is ultimately a question of how the idea is worked out. To put it in a somewhat exaggerated form—in a song the idea is what matters: in a symphony idea is a means to an end. In Mahler's symphonies the thematic material reveals the inspiration of an authentic musician, genuine and sound: one who could not work out a major thematic construction from motifs in themselves paltry or artificial. For the sustained development of his symphonic works he required the continuous stimulus of the inspired idea, of the theme given in blessed moments of insight. In music, in the broad sense of the word, everything depends on invention: both the "material" and its symphonic development. Mahler's inventive faculty carries, in the first place, the stamp of a personality whose originality no one can deny.

I attach importance to recognition of the mingling of classical and romantic in his thematic material, as in his nature. But where he draws on themes from the sphere of folklore, he never merely imitates, let alone adapts; it is the genuine voice of the people with which he speaks, and which comes from deep within his own being.

The counterpart here is the "symphonic" theme, in Beethoven's sense: broad in construction, meaningful in substance, which forms the core of symphonic work. The last movement of Mahler's First shows a dominant symphonic theme of this kind, although the movement as a whole is governed by emotion rather than by symphonic design. With the powerful opening

The Composer

→>>->>>->>>•‹‹‹-‹‹‹-‹‹‹-

measures of the Second, a great symphonic composer begins his work and at the same time continues the great tradition of the classical symphony. The broad layout of the major theme remains characteristic; it was to be further developed and enlarged in the Sixth and Seventh, and,
above all, in the Ninth. Like the old masters,
he generally sets opposite his main, masculine
theme a singing, feminine one. With it folk music
is left behind; here is lyricism on the model of
the classical second theme. The thematic substance of the slow movements is song—a long-
drawn-out, grave singing—as is the case with
Bruckner. The same broad thematic layout appears also in the last movements.

The inventiveness shown in his scherzos deserves a word. A musician with his strange sense
of humor was bound to produce scherzos of
notable, even singular, distinction of invention.
A quite special place must be given to the
scherzo of the Second, both as a piece of composition and as a specimen of musical inventive-

ness; it certainly is a high point in symphonic scherzo literature. That of the Third is both droll and charming; that of the Fourth mysterious and exciting. The scherzo of the Fifth is not humorous, but has immense vitality. In the Sixth the trio of the scherzo has a singular and wholly Mahlerish charm. In the Seventh the scherzo is a spooky night-piece; in the Ninth the Austrian country dance is employed with consummate mastery and delicious grace.

In general, Mahler made happy use of the Austrian musical dialect. It sounds in the trio of the second movement of the First, with echoes of Schubert, and with some of Haydn in the main theme of the first movement of the Fourth; there are Styrian touches in the country dance in the Ninth, to which I have already referred. The traditional opening bar of the Austrian military band, played by drums and cymbals, is wittily reproduced in the March of the Third, and its scherzo "sounds off" in true military fashion. There are echoes of Vienna's folk

The Composer

songs in the secondary theme of the Fourth and even a Viennese waltz in the scherzo of the Fifth; one of the variations in the andante of the Fourth behaves very Austrian indeed. Austrian military music, of which he was very fond, permeates his marches. When he was a two-year-old, his nurse used to leave him in a barracks yard while she enjoyed the company of a soldier friend: he listened to drums and trumpets, and watched soldiers marching; the romantic aspect of the military, often present in his work, may perhaps derive from these infantile barracks impressions. The reveille sounds twice; the *Grosser Appell* in the last movement of the Second symbolizes the call to the dead to rise for the Last Judgment; the first movement of the Fourth completes the picture, with the finely modulated *Kleiner Appell*, as he called it. Military, again, are the repeated trumpets in the introduction to the first movement of the Third, the wild music of the "charge," and the closing march-rhythms on the drums. Military romance also colors songs like "*Der Schildwache Nachtlied*," "*Der Tambourgesell*" and "*Revelge*."

Marches recur in Mahler's work. In his First and Fifth symphonies, the funeral march carries a singular, tragic-ironic meaning; in the finale of his Second, a vigorous quick march plays an important part. A fiery march—"*Der Sommer marschiert ein*"—occupies a large portion of the first movement of his Third. There are march rhythms in the first movement of the Sixth, the second movement of the Seventh, and the last movements of the Fifth and Seventh.

With his Second Symphony, Mahler begins to think in contrapuntal terms. Its polyphonic structure and artful formation and transformation of motifs show the work's classical affiliation. Mahler's absorption in problems of technique grew steadily right up to his Ninth; by the time of the Fifth they had produced a radical change in his style. Far from being a poet setting poetic visions to music, he was, as I said at the

The Composer

opening of this chapter, a musician *pur sang*. As such, he was primarily concerned to achieve his aim by the plastic use of thematic material. This aim governs the shape of every movement, the development of every theme: the use of counterpoint, the molding of rondo, fugue, etc., in the sonata form. His first four symphonies are infiltrated with ideas, images, and emotions. From the Fifth to the Seventh inclusive, purely musical forms dominate. Between these two periods, he was absorbed in Bach; *The Art of the Fugue* had a profound influence on his counterpoint. This is plain in the rondo-fugue of the Fifth, in which a tendency to imaginative deepening of the rondo itself is also evident. The exalted *Veni, Creator Spiritus* of the Eighth, like the contrapuntal mastery of the third movement of the Ninth, dedicated to the "Brothers in Apollo," shows immense advance in his polyphony. He was also particularly interested in the art of variations. He was a passionate admirer of Brahms's *Variations on a Theme of Haydn* and

loved to explain how high a standard Brahms in
this composition had given the whole concept of
variations. Mahler's use of variations is confined
to the andante of his Fourth, but the "variant"—
the transformation and elaboration of a given
theme, lying, as it does, at the basis of variation—
is a significant element in development, and one
by which he was constantly preoccupied. In
each of his later symphonies the art of variation
is progressively used, and enriches both recapitulation and coda.

There was, also, a notable advance in instrumentation, based in his case on an unrivaled
capacity for vivid sound-imagination and on an
intimate knowledge of the orchestra. Yet his
imaginative mastery of sound never seduced
him into attaching too great importance to
coloration. He used his rare aural gifts to achieve
the utmost orchestral lucidity. Where special
color was needed to fulfill his intentions, he
mixed it on his own palette, as only one of his
amazing sensibility could do. The heightening

of his polyphony, with its complex interweaving of orchestral voices, taxed even his instrumental mastery: in his Fifth he himself had difficulty keeping pace with the growing complications of the structure.

Mahler's instrumentation deserves study. A theoretical analysis of his progress in expanding the idea of the symphony, and of the development of his polyphony, his harmony, his thematic style, his technique of variation, could be rewarding. This however, is no place for such a professional study. It is a task a young composer would find well worth his while.

His work forms a musical whole, with no gaps in musically logical continuity or structure. And yet no evaluation in strictly musical terms can be just, for his work was the outcome of his entire inner life. It has to be viewed as the expression in music of a great spirit. Human as well as æsthetic values must enter in, if his creative significance is to be realized. I propo to look at the part played by his experiences, cast of thought, his poetic vision, and his religious feeling in each of his symphonies, for in each it is unique. One word in advance: if "program music" is the musical description of extra-musical processes, he never wrote it.

His First Symphony might be called his *Werther*. There a heart-rending experience finds artistic release. I do not mean that he expresses in tone something he has lived—that would be program music; what happens is that a mood born of recollection and of present feeling produces themes and affects the whole shape of the musical development without breaking the musical context. Thus a self-contained composition becomes a personal message from his heart. I am not going to examine the symphony in detail; no need to dwell on the youthful fire of the first movement or the powerful scherzo, with its enchanting trio. Anything of the kind would detract from their rich musical content. The third movement, however, sounded something

new in music, and its significance justifies ex-
amination. A spiritual reaction to a tragic event
is translated into music in the "Funeral
March in the Manner of Callot" and in the
finale; there, the young composer frees himself
from personal experience. The very vehemence
of Mahler's emotion may well have made him unaware of his own audacity in using the spectral
creeping of the canon, with its tones of brazen
scorn and shrill laughter, as the musical medium for dull, lowering despair; but the imagination, novelty, and relentless veracity of the
work bear the imprint of genius. It is not surprising that the audience was dumfounded at
the first performance. Then, in the fourth movement, all his passionate vehemence breaks out,
and with unrelenting force, wins a victory over
life.

Sometime in December 1909—the last year
but one of his life—Mahler wrote to me from
America after a performance of the First: "I
was pretty well satisfied with this youthful try-

out. I have a queer experience when I conduct any of these works. A burningly painful sensation crystallizes. What a world is mirrored in these sounds and figures! The Funeral March and the storm that follows are a flaming indictment of the Creator!" After years during which he had not heard it, this elementally expressive music could still shake its composer. In its emotional excess, its unconditional and unconscious audacity of new expression, its wealth of invention, the symphony has the unique impact of the youthful work of genius. Proliferating in invention and pulsing with passion, it is music that has been lived.

From then on, the composer turned aside from personal experiences. The natural bent of his mind shifted his gaze to the tragic existence of man. He conceived the elegiac vision of the opening movement of his Second Symphony—the mourning chant of a suffering world. It starts and every hearer feels: thus begins a symphony! With irresistible force and Beethovian majesty it takes hold of us; the sense of controlled tragedy finds concentrated expression. The gloomy theme is wrought into a movement powerful in invention, development, contrast, architecture; a master has found his style. Here is the sonata form—exposition, development, recapitulation, coda. No one regarding this lofty structure, brilliant in light and shade, with drastic contradictions and fateful contractions of musical polyphony, can accept the laconic description—"a funeral service"—which was all that Mahler could indicate when asked what he "had in mind." It seems incredible for anyone to speak of program music, looking from that concept to this music, but there were some who did so at the time.

The music of the First, especially in its third and fourth movements, is still tinged with and influenced by personal experience. In the Second the world of thought and feeling is farther away from the music. That world, in the first three movements, is a mere background of moods without any continuity of thought, without constant influence of emotions on the music, which lives its own life: it has dissolved mood, feeling, thought, into itself and transformed them into music. The second movement, a charming, delightful andante, is even more absolutely musical than the first; Mahler, in conversation, used to call it a happy episode in the life of the hero, whose obsequies occupy the first movement. The third derives from a sinister mood; it is as though suddenly the wild chaos of existence were seen as unreal, ghostly. Perhaps the most original of the scherzos, this one is full of fantastic life; a scurrilous humor and wild flashes of light play over its sinister, dank-flowing surface, to emerge in a lamenting "Call of the Wild," with no definite idea or thought behind it. It has become a masterpiece of symphonic music.

At this point, I want to interrupt the course of my survey to indicate that while a composer can translate moods, ideas, and feelings into music, music, in its turn, calls forth ideas. In his *Birth of Tragedy from the Spirit of Music* Nietzsche says that music scatters pictures like sparks, though its nature is such that its pictures are different in kind from those which may have sponsored them. In the creative process there is often a loosely woven interplay between music and idea. Dreamlike images rise and fade, give stimulus, feeling, and color to the music; they alternate with periods of thought and indistinct moods, while music follows its own path, obeys the law of its own logic. An example of the unconnected dreamlike unreality of the world in which music floats is given by Mahler's story of how, at the bold conclusion of the first movement of the First, he saw Beethoven before him, breaking out into peals of laughter and running off. The laughing Beethoven has really nothing to do with the experiences out of which, by Mahler's own account, the First Symphony arose. It is indeed so unprogrammatic as to constitute in itself a *reductio ad absurdum* more effective than any æsthetic argument of the view that Mahler wrote program music. Again, apropos of the eerie atmosphere of the scherzo in the Second, Mahler said that it was as ghostly as the distant sight of couples dancing to unheard music —a picture that makes it impossible to see the Second as an unfolding of program music.

In the fourth movement—to return to my survey—words are sung: with the *Urlicht*, they light up the impenetrable flood of tone, woven of moods, but shaped in accordance with its own laws. Man sings—in pious words taken from *Des Knaben Wunderhorn*—of his confident trust that God will give him a candle to lead him to the life of eternal bliss. Here we are—nearly —given a program for the next movement: wandering in the shine of the *Urlicht*. Some such vision did determine the general form of the movement; idea and music draw close: Mahler's imagination is dominated by the Last Judgment, and from the opening of the fifth movement on, one can sense a conflict between a succession of mental images and the course of the music. Music has to give way, and that is easy to understand when one recalls the emotions of a man possessed by such ideas. Yet, with the marchlike development of the choral themes, the musician is again in command; he hands over to the poet only with the entry of the *Grosser Appell*. With the sublime music into which Mahler transformed Klopstock's poem on the Resurrection —and to which he added in verse the expression of his hopes and convictions—he answers for the first time the sorrow, the doubt, the questions that wrung his soul. In transfigured sounds, inspired by the lofty message of his heart, he reaches the solemn assurance of the close: "I shall die, to live!" "Rise, yea, my heart, thou shalt rise after brief rest, and what thou hast endured shall carry thee to God!"

Now he can look out hopefully, with an enhanced sense of life. "How fair the meadows seem today," says Parsifal, looking in reverence on the face of nature. Such was Mahler's mood;

as he gazed on nature with love and deep emotion, he felt it within himself, felt its heartbeat in his own heart. In his Third Symphony nature itself seems to be transformed into sound. In it alone the movements follow a determined sequence of idea. The original headings to the movements were *Pan erwacht: der Sommer marschiert ein* (Pan awakes; summer marches in); *Was mir die Blumen auf der Wiese erzählen* (What the flowers in the meadow tell me); *Was mir die tiere im Walde erzählen* (What the animals in the woods tell me); *Was mir die Nacht erzählt* (What the night tells me); *Was mir die Morgenglocken erzählen* (What the morning bells tell me); and *Was mir die Liebe erzählt* (What love tells me). The night now speaks of man, the morning bells speak of angels, and love speaks of God—we can see the basic structural unity of the symphony. For this very reason, he could do without the titles, which were dropped like a scaffolding when the house is ready; he wanted to have the work taken as pure music. He was right; it had become music.

The Composer

But there is one exception: with the trumpet calls, drum rolls, drastic vulgarities, and fiery march-rhythms of the first movement, with its majestic trombone solo and humming trills on the muted strings, an abundance of strange events and thoughts seem to be rather musically described than composed. They are only insufficiently explained by the title—*Pan erwacht: der Sommer marschiert ein*. Some of the subsidiary titles are yet stranger. On one—*Was mir das Felsgebirg erzählt*—I have already touched; others are—*Das Gesindel* (The Mob), where, in the development section, cellos and basses open a grotesque episode; and *Südsturm* (Southern Storm), with wild string passages near its close. Indeed, when one assembles all these headings and ideas one perceives with astonishment that there is, in fact, no internal connection, and that, in many cases, the music has evoked the picture rather than the picture the music. What, one asks, is the real content of the movement? What is it about? Two opposing, panic-filled basic moods—primordial inflexibility and lust-driven wildness—have been transformed into a wealth of musical images. Out of them Mahler builds a movement extraordinary in architecture and not less so in content. In the ecstasy of composition, new images, new thoughts were thrown in from moment to moment; unconnected as they are, they might produce confusion rather than clarity, and are not at all suited to be formed into a "program." In regard to this movement—and to this one alone —I must admit that the effort to take it in musically is frequently thwarted by the intrusion of non-musical matter, of fantastic images, that break the musical texture. And yet, I feel that here, for once, the wild unconcerned genius should compensate us for the problematic style. In this movement Mahler decided to dispense with titles confident that the unique creation of a wide-ranging imagination would be accepted as the voice of nature, all the more as æsthetic lines are likely to be blurred when humor— under the sign of which the work exists—flickers brightly.

The Composer

Beginning with the second movement, it becomes different. Here a delightful theme is developed purely musically; even if tinged by the
"flower mood," it is designed as music and requires no thought of flowers to be understood.
No resemblance here, to the "Witches' Sabbath" of Berlioz's *Symphonie fantastique*, in
which one must cling to the image of the wild
spook to comprehend the musical content of the
score. The third movement is, like the second,
genuinely symphonic. A dream of the universe
took possession of Mahler's mind, and his soul
lovingly poured itself out in music. But as the
dream passed from flowers and animals to mankind, he longed for the word, and moved by the
mystery of human destiny changing between
grief and joy, he made Nietzsche's *Mitternachtsgedicht* the poetic theme for the nocturnal music
of the fourth movement. In the fifth movement,
again he wanted words for the joyful tidings of
the Angels. Certain lines in *Des Knaben Wunderhorn* had always moved him and lifted his
spirit:

Hast thou broken the ten commands?
Down on thy knees and pray to God!
Pray to God every day,
And heavenly joy shall come thy way.

From this angelic message, he worked out a solemn music, with clear-toned bells ringing, happy boys and women singing in chorus, and sinful humanity receiving the blessed tidings. In the final movement, words are stilled; what language can utter heavenly love with more power, more force, than pure music? The adagio, with its broad, solemn melodious line, is, as a whole, and despite passages of burning pain, eloquent of comfort and grace: it is a single sound of heartfelt and exalted feelings in which the whole giant structure finds its musical culmination. Mahler called the Third his "joyful wisdom." Essentially it communicates a joyous outlook on life and the universe.

This mood rises in the Fourth to a singularly exalted gladness. In the Second he had sung: "On wings I soar, for which I have fought": he

might, although in a more fantastic vein, have
said the same of the Third. And now he was borne
upward as in a dream: the earth was no longer
under his feet. The music of the Fourth tells of
this floating sensation; the themes of its final
movement connect with the angelic movement
of the Third and also, on the whole, continue
its inner mood. After his solemn works he felt a
longing for gladness, or rather for serenity. The
outcome was the idyllic Fourth, in which inward piety dreams a dream of Heaven. The
whole atmosphere, indeed, is dreamlike and unreal; the solemnity often audible in the Third is
hidden here behind a mysterious smile and whimsical humor. The Fourth is a fairy tale; the
power and pathos of its predecessors are translated into airy imponderability; the thundering
vision proclaimed by a prophet is now confirmed
by an angel's gentle voice. Earth has been left
behind and a blissful exaltation colors the music.
Here, however, the situation differs from that
of the Third: it comes from afar. The three
orchestral movements proceed without carrying

over the highly individual mood of their origin into more definite images. Even the *Kleiner Appell* of the first movement does not lead to any larger poetic vision. There is a hint of droll humor in the first movement and in the *Himmlisches Leben* (Heavenly Life), which strangely harmonizes with the loftiness of tone pervading the work. The scherzo is a kind of uncanny fairy tale; its demoniac solo for violin, like the charming trio, is in marked contrast to the rest of the work, and yet retains its lightness and its mystery. Of the andante, with its restful depth and lucid beauty, Mahler told me that when he wrote it he had a vision of a tombstone on which was carved an image of the departed, with folded arms, in eternal sleep. The words of the poem in the last movement depict the atmosphere that gave rise to the Fourth; its picture of childlike joys symbolizes heavenly bliss, and at the close music is hailed as the supreme joy; the humorous tone passes gently over into one of exalted solemnity.

Mahler's first four symphonies reveal a signifi-

cant part of his inner history. In them the power
of the musical language responds to the force
of the spiritual experience. They also have in
common a continuous interchange between the
world of sound and the world of ideas, thoughts,
and feelings. In the First the music reflects the
stormy emotions of a subjective experience; beginning with the Second metaphysical questions
demand answers and solutions. The reply is
threefold, and is given from a fresh standpoint
each time. The Second is concerned with the
meaning of the tragedy of human life: the clear
reply is its justification by immortality. Assuaged,
he turns, in the Third, to nature, and after trav-
ersing its cycle, reaches the happy conviction
that the answer is in "omnipotent love, all-
forming, all-embracing." In the Fourth he as-
sures himself and us through a lofty and cheerful
dream of the joys of eternal life, that we are safe.

Now the struggle to achieve a new vision of
the universe in terms of music is suspended.
Now full of strength and equal to life's demands, he is ready to write music as a musician.

His Fifth Symphony is a work full of power and sane self-confidence which turns its face toward life and reality. Its movements are a powerful funeral march leading into the agitated first movement; a scherzo of imposing scale; an adagietto, and a rondo-fugue. Nothing in my talks with Mahler, not a single note in the work, suggests that any extrinsic thought or emotion entered into its composition. Here is music. Passionate, wild, heroic, exuberant, fiery, solemn, tender, it covers the whole gamut of feeling. But it is "merely" music. And not even from afar do metaphysical questions cross its purely musical course. But the musician in him tried all the more eagerly to develop his symphonic craft, even to create new and higher forms. The Fifth demanded, in its heightened polyphony, a renewing of his style of orchestration. Here begins a new phase of his development, and we now have in the Fifth a masterpiece that shows its composer at the zenith of his life, his powers, and his craft. There is a certain sense in which the Fifth, Sixth, and Seventh belong together. Both of the

The Composer

latter are as unmetaphysical as music can be; in them the composer is concerned to expand the symphonic idea. However, the Sixth is bleakly pessimistic: it reeks of the bitter taste of the cup of life. In contrast with the Fifth, it says "No," above all in its last movement, where something resembling the inexorable strife of "all against all" is translated into music. "Existence is a burden; death is desirable and life hateful," might be its motto. Mahler called it his "Tragic." The mounting tension and climaxes of the last movement resemble, in their grim power, the mountainous waves of a sea that will overwhelm and destroy the ship; the work ends in hopelessness and the night of the soul. *"Non placet"* is his verdict on this world; the "other world" is not glimpsed for a moment.

The Seventh likewise falls into the absolutely musical, purely symphonic, group. These three works needed no words to clarify their conceptual ideas, and consequently no voices are used. For this reason, I cannot discuss them. I could never talk about the music itself, and there is no need to analyze it; analysis on these lines has long been available. Note, however, the reappearance of the seemingly long-buried Romantic, significant and humanly illuminating, in the three central movements of the Seventh. These three nocturnal pieces, steeped in the emotions of the past, reveal that the master of the superb first movement and of the brilliant rondo is again involved in that longing for fulfillment, that search for answers to his questions about life, which always haunted him.

At this crucial juncture, he came upon the Hymn of Hrabanus Maurus and turned all his highly developed symphonic powers to giving an answer to the most heart-searching of all questions, by placing in a full-scale musical context the *Veni, Creator Spiritus* and the belief in immortality voiced by Goethe in the final scene of *Faust*. This was his Eighth Symphony. No other work expresses so fully the impassioned "Yes" to life. "Yes" resounds here in the massed voices of the hymn wrought by a master hand into the temple-like structure of a symphonic movement; it peals from the *Faust* words and from the torrent of music in which Mahler's own emotion is released. Here, advanced in years, the seeker after God confirms, from a higher plane, the assurance which his youthful heart had poured out in the passion of the Second Symphony. In the later work the relation between idea and music is absolutely clear; from its beginning, the word is integral; and from its beginning, eternity is the issue of which the symphony is born, to which it is the reply.

Can the man who reared the structure of the Eighth "in harmony with the Everlasting," be the same as the author of the *"Trinklied vom Jammer der Erde"* (Drinking Song of Earthly Woe)—the man who slinks alone, in autumn, to the trusty place of death in search of comfort, who looks at youth with the commiserating eyes of age, at beauty with muted emotion, who seeks to forget in drink the senselessness of life and finally leaves it in deep melancholy? Is it the same master who, after his gigantic symphonies, constructs a new form of unity out of six songs? He is scarcely the same as a man or as a composer. All his previous work had grown out of his sense of life. Now the knowledge that he had serious heart trouble was, as with the wounded Prince Andrei in Tolstoi's *War and Peace*, breaking his inner hold on life. The loosening of all previous ties altered his entire outlook. *Das Lied von der Erde* is, in terms of the sentence of Spinoza already quoted, written *sub specie mortis*. Earth is vanishing; he breathes in another air, a new light shines on him—and so it is a wholly new work that Mahler wrote: new in its style of composition, new in invention, in instrumentation, and in the structures of the various movements. It is more subjective than any of his previous works, more even than his First. There, it was the natural "I" of a passionate youth whose personal experience obstructed his view of the world; here, while the world slowly sinks away, the "I" becomes the experience itself—a limitless range of feeling opens for him who soon will leave this earth. Every note carries his individual voice; every word, though based on a poem a thousand years old, is his own. *Das Lied von der Erde* is Mahler's most personal utterance, perhaps the most personal utterance in music. His invention, which from the Sixth on had been significant less in itself than as material for his formative hand, here achieves a highly personal stamp. In this sense, it is accurate to call *Das Lied* the most Mahlerian of his works.

"*Der Abschied*" (Farewell), title of the last song in *Das Lied*, might serve as rubric for the Ninth Symphony. Its first movement is derived from the mood of *Das Lied*, though in no sense musically related to it. It develops from its own thematic material into the kind of symphonic form which he alone could now create. It is a noble paraphrase of the "*Abschied*," shattering in its tragedy. The movement floats in an atmosphere of transfiguration achieved by a singular transition between the sorrow of farewell and the vision of the radiance of Heaven—an atmosphere derived not from imagination, but from immediate feeling. Its invention is as Mahlerian as that of *Das Lied*. The second movement, the old, familiar scherzo in a new form—this time the main tempo is broad—reveals a wealth of variations, with a tragic undertone sounding through the happiness: "The dance is over." The defiant *agitato* of the third movement shows once more Mahler's stupendous contrapuntal mastery; the last voices a peaceful farewell: with the conclusion, the clouds dissolve in the blue of Heaven. In design, movement, technique, and polyphony, the Ninth continues the line of the Fifth, Sixth, and Seventh symphonies. It is, however, inspired by an intense spiritual agitation: the sense of departure. And although it is also purely orchestral music, it differs from the middle group, is nearer to the earlier symphonies in its deeply subjective emotional mood.

In our art the new, challenging, revolutionary, passes, in the course of time, over into the known, accepted, familiar. The lasting validity of Faust's great thought is not due to the fact that he wrested new territory from the encroaching

sea; only when the new becomes the old do
thoughts and actions reveal their importance.
Mahler, an adventurer of the mind, left behind
him in music a certain stretch of newly conquered territory, but as the decades pass, his
works should no longer be expected to sound
sensational. Yet, strangely enough, they still
generate excitement; Mahler's feeling and unre-
stricted drive for self-revelation were far too
elemental in his music for it to become cozily
familiar and be taken for granted. The daring
spirit flames high whenever the notes are heard.
But should not the interpreter be distrusted
whose performance of the works of Bach, Beethoven, or Wagner conveys an impression of
easy possession? Have we not learned from
Mahler's conducting that it is possible to make
such works always sound as if they were being
performed for the first time? Adequate performances of Mahler's own works today will surely
reveal a Titan. Anything new in music and
the drama needs the protection of congenial interpretation.

There is, however, a gradual fading of the sound, and as time passes, the daring is bound to pale, to lose its edge, especially in lesser interpretations. This raises the question of how much daring and adventurousness really signify in a work of art. Mere daring, aimed at challenge and novelty, is certain to wear off; only together with profound and permanent values is it assured of lasting effect. If the works of these Promethean masters are rewarded with immortality, the reason lies in their creative power, depth of feeling, and, above all, beauty. For beauty is immortal; it can preserve the mortal charm of the merely "interesting" from decay.

So the supreme value of Mahler's work lies not in the novelty of its being intriguing, daring, adventurous, or bizarre, but rather in the fact that this novelty was transfused into music that is beautiful, inspired, and profound; that it possesses the lasting values of high creative artistry and a deeply significant humanity. These keep it alive today, these guarantee its future.

4

The Personality

EVERYONE who knew Mahler will recall
how often his expression would change suddenly from cheerfulness to gloom. It was as
though he was reproaching himself for having
lightly forgotten some sorrow. The root of
these fits of depression, which, though they
never ceased, were less frequent in his later
years, I did not, at first, discern; then I came to
realize that a profound sense of the misery of
this world would rise in icy waves from the
center of his being and overwhelm his spirit.
"What grim darkness underlies life," he said to

me once, deeply affected and his distracted
countenance still marked by the spiritual par-
oxysms from which he had emerged. He went
on to speak in broken accents of the tragic
dilemma of human existence. "Whence have we
come? Whither are we bound? Is it true, as
Schopenhauer says, that I willed this life before
I was conceived? Why do I fancy I am free,
when my character constricts me like a prison?
To what purpose is all this toil and suffering?
How can cruelty and evil be the handiwork of
a loving God? Will death at last reveal the
meaning of life?" Lamentation, astonishment,
horror would pour out, in a torrent of words like
these, as though a geyser had been turned on.
He never really found deliverance in his agon-
ized effort to find sense in human life. He was
distracted by ardent activity: he was helped
by his sense of humor to cast off the burden;
a vivid concern about intellectual questions
strengthened him and helped to still a nearly un-
quenchable thirst for knowledge and compre-

hension. Yet his spirit never knew escape from the torturing question—For What? It was the driving impulse of his creative activity. Each work was a fresh effort to find the answer, and even when he found it, the old, unassuageable longing would rise anew. His nature was such that he could not hold any achieved spiritual position; none had constancy. Impulse ruled his life and work, and so each spiritual gain had to be won afresh. This meant that everything— life, art, personal relationships—was new each day; it also meant that he was denied the blessings of a sense of systematic advance or the mastery and evaluation of experience. Each day with him saw the struggle and the sacrifice renewed. He could not have been taken as a model for the hero of a *Bildungsroman*; steady development and what Goethe calls a reasoned use of experience, thought, and achievement were denied him, were not in his nature. At heart he was a romantic, and a romantic governed by the favorable— or unfavorable—aspects of the hour.

At the same time, it would be entirely false to describe him as vacillating or unstable. Constancy was not in him; yet his course was defined and unalterable by any impulse. Nor would it be true to call him unhappy. Categories like happy and unhappy do not fit a man so richly endowed, so warm of heart, so eloquent of tongue. He knew the passionate uplift of spirit as well as deep sorrow. Such a gamut of feeling is a greater gift of the gods than happiness. In sorrow, his faithful companion on life's path, he knew the consolation of which Tasso speaks: "And, if man agonizes in silence, a God gave me the gift to speak my sorrow." He spoke it in a tongue of which he had supreme command: his sufferings and longings became music. Constantly born anew, they were constantly translated into works of art.

But Mahler knew and spoke not only of ecstasies of longing, of distress, of spiritual devotion. He was both ready and willing to "get outside himself," and richly endowed for communication on more serene levels. His soul's barometer was not set only to "stormy" and "changeable." Frost, storms, heat waves did occur; so did gentler skies, and the warmth and joy of sunshine. This is evident in many works, for example, the serene andante of the Second Symphony and the *"Rheinlegendchen,"* which he called a piece of captured sunshine. Smiles and sudden gay laughter suited his features as well as his nature, though the shadow always hovered near.

I have touched on the "nocturnal" element in his work. It was paralleled in his personality. It was the source of the very strong impression of something demoniac in him which made him interesting to everybody and terrifying to many. It remains one of Nature's mysteries that it is able to create a constitutionally sound human being combining such contradictions; a man who could be at one and the same time endowed with so much energy, brilliance of intellect, serenity, such dark vehemence, such whimsical humor, and continually be menaced by the dangerous depths within himself.

Because no spiritual experience, however hardly won, was ever his secure possession, I cannot, despite the religious cast of his mind, and its intermittent flights, call him a believer. Emotional excitement would carry him to transports of faith, but its serene assurance was not within his scope. The suffering of a creature touched too deeply; murder in the animal kingdom, the cruelty of man to man, the infirmities of the human frame, the continuous menace of fate —all this again and again shook the foundations of his belief. More insistent was the problem of reconciling the suffering and evil of the world with the goodness and omnipotence of God. If his music expresses, as it does, his longing and his questions, that music in its turn kept longing and questioning alive, and forever rekindled them. Music has, of course, an incomparable power of drawing us toward the spiritual. In the phrase of Nietzsche which I have already quoted, it scatters images like sparks; it also sows the seeds of faith. In its highest manifestations, it is

mysteriously related to religion. The divine service needs music to give the most solemn expression to piety. Music lends compulsive power to
the feeling of devotion in ecclesiastical texts and
to the religious scenes in biblical oratorios. Independently of all this, absolute music—for example, the andantes of Mozart or Beethoven—
produces, in its own right, an elevation and
lift of spirit otherwise accessible only through
religion.

This is not the place for a discussion of the
relation between religion and music. I merely
note their frequent association in visual art and
how naturally music appears in the works of
Bellini and kindred painters. Here the Giorgione "Concerto" comes again to mind. Not
angels, to be sure, are making here the lovely
music, filled with a happy sense of the goodness
of God, which sounds in Mozart's or Schubert's
melodies; here it is not the elderly, quiet viola da
gamba player of the picture who is the musician,
but rather the pious monk, whose soul burns

with ascetic fervor. Here is a human eye that seems longingly to search the heavenly distances: here are fingers that might produce tones like Beethoven's. Mahler's nature was of this order: he looks out from the earth, whose suffering is his, and seeks God. I stress the fact that his religious attitude is throughout rooted in the relationship between religion and music. Some musicians—and listeners to music—are unaware of its transcendental power; while steeped in music and genuinely musical, they are devoid of any kind of religious sentiment, or even awareness. Those, on the other hand, who strive to penetrate beyond the earthly veil find in music a support to and confirmation of faith.

Mahler's thoughts and aspirations strove toward that "other" world. Yet Goethe's phrase —"To the efficient man the world is not mute" —applies to him. Faustian as he was, and forever compelled to seek the ultimate meaning of everything that is, everything that happens, he was, at the same time, bound by a multiplicity of ties and interests to this earthly sphere and to the spiritual life within it. He was passionately interested in advances in the natural sciences. A physicist friend who kept him in detailed touch with the progress of research spoke eloquently of the keen and thorough understanding shown by his questions. His favorite reading was the philosophical aspects of science; Lotze's *Microcosmos* occupied him for a long time, especially in its development of the theory of the atom. A lasting impression was made by Fechner's *Zend-Avesta*, and he delighted in *Nana, or the Spiritual Life of Plants* by the same author. Needless to say, he was throughout his life deeply influenced by Goethe's general attitude to Nature and his prolific work in this field. But he was never merely on the receiving end. His own productive intelligence was constantly at work on problems arising out of his reading and contacts. I remember an occasion when he tried to interpret the law of gravitation as repulsion by the sun, and in conversation with a well-known physicist tried in his impassioned way to convince the latter by adducing other related cosmic ideas. Again, somebody said in his presence that when an earthworm was cut in two, two new units were produced, the back part growing a new head and thus an independent existence: "That," he cried, "is proof against Aristotle's doctrine of entelechy." He was far too sensible and far too well aware of the gaps in his scientific equipment to be dogmatic, but his lively interest in questions of the kind was not satisfied by the mere acquisition of knowledge. The vitality of his mind compelled him to wrestle with problems on his own, and he was delighted when, after meeting and overcoming instructed contradiction, he felt that he had touched a deeper level of understanding. In discussion the intuitive quality of his remarks invariably called forth the admiration of scientific friends.

When I first knew him, in Hamburg, he was completely under the influence of Schopenhauer. Nietzsche made a powerful but not a

lasting impression. He was attracted by the poetic fire of *Zarathustra*, but repelled by the core
of its intellectual content. Nietzsche's anti-
Wagnerism made him indignant, and later he
turned against him; the aphorist was bound to
antagonize the master of symphonic form. In his
later years he was taken by the philosophy of
Hartmann. But the sun in the sky of his spiritual
world was Goethe. He had a remarkable knowledge of his work, and, thanks to a unique memory, would quote endlessly from it. He was a
constant reader of Goethe's conversations with
Eckermann and others, and Goethe's discussion
of immortality with Falk was one of the foundations of his intellectual life.

Among German poets, Hölderlin was nearest
to him; poems like *"Patmos"* and *"Der Rhein"*
were sacred possessions constantly at hand. With
deep feeling he often quoted to me from the
splendid, enigmatic lines written by Hölderlin
after his mental disturbance. Among the mystics
he preferred Angelus Silesius; with him he felt a

close relationship, deriving comfort from such bold and exalted sense of nearness to God. His giving the name "Titan" to his First Symphony signalized his love of Jean Paul; we often talked about this great novel, and especially about the character of Roquairol, whose influence is noticeable in the Funeral March. Mahler would insist that an element of Roquairol, of his self-centered, self-tormenting, scornful and imperiled spirit, exists in every gifted individual, and has to be conquered before productive powers can come into play. He felt entirely at home with the witty and complex humor of Schoppe. *Siebenkäs* was a favorite work, and, he insisted, Jean Paul's masterpiece. In his younger days his heart was naturally given to E. T. A. Hoffmann, who attracted him by his glowing imagination, force, and humor, and especially by his "nocturnal" quality. Sterne's *Tristram Shandy* was among his favorites, also because of its humor. He often remarked that, but for the antidote of humor, the tragedy of human existence would have been unendurable. In the course of conversation he loved to refer to episodes like the opening of the will in Jean Paul's *Flegeljahre*, or to recall details of Dostoevski's *A Silly Affair*, each time laughing happily and loudly. His own sense of humor abounded in droll fancies, and his wit had a sharp edge. He also appreciated pointed remarks by others, if they were made spontaneously, and was often delighted by the most harmless witticism. On the other hand, he disapproved the telling of "funny" anecdotes or jokes: his face would go stony and for a while he would be out of temper as though pained by seeing fine fruits of fancy preserved in a tin. He loathed coarseness, and I cannot recall any remark of the kind made in his presence, far less by him. This aversion did not, of course, apply to the coarseness of a given period, as found in Shakespeare, Cervantes, Sterne, and others; then he took it as part and parcel of a work of art. A compelling affinity of mind bound him to the work of Dostoevski, who profoundly influenced his whole outlook. Indeed, what I have called his sense of the woe of the world is fully expressed in the conversation between Ivan and Alyosha in *The Brothers Karamazov*.

I have cited but a few examples of Mahler's endlessly diversified, comprehensive interest in things of the mind. Pictorial art came comparatively late into his life, and artist as he was in revealing the passion, the "nocturnal" in the realm of sound, the visual aspect never meant much to him. The one painter who deeply moved him was Rembrandt, a kindred spirit. Visual art was never a necessity of his life in the sense in which poetry and literature, science and philosophy, were indispensable to him.

It would be a mistake to see in the variety of Mahler's interests the mere dilettantism of a restless mind. The criterion of dilettantism is accumulation of knowledge without its assimilation. Mahler had a sure, selective instinct for the intellectual food that would strengthen him for the mission of his life. He was driven by the law of his nature to seek the ultimate meaning of the events, the actions, the pains of existence; his study was consciously directed toward equipping him for this task. In his exploration of the spiritual world the needle of his compass pointed imperturbably in one direction: upward. His learning thus became experience and was assimilated into his being; it had a steady metaphysical aim. His many-sidedness was of the surface; one would be nearer the truth if one spoke of the superb unity of a mind that brought an equal spiritual intensity to musical composition and to intellectual studies, and directed both by the light of a single aim.

True, there was no conscious system or method in his self-education; here again impulse was guide. While there is something magnificent in his conquest of the treasures of the mind, it failed to give him the definite outlook that might have stilled his restless heart. His style of life was set, the direction decided; but moved by impulse rather than by planned continuity.

Mahler's conversation was a perfect mirror of the multifariousness of his intellectual interests. It showed a man deeply absorbed in cosmic problems, poignantly aware of the sorrows of humanity, who pursued knowledge along every available path and sought release in creative work from the struggle within himself. The wealth and versatility of his intellect, his warmth of feeling and firmness of judgment, were matched by his inexhaustible choice of topics, the liveliness and sureness of his talk. Moreover, he never committed the common fault of not attending to his companion: he could listen as well as talk. And he was able and ready to give all of himself completely—a rare virtue. He never used his sagacity just to score easy dialectical victories —he was interested only in pertinent discussion of the matter at hand. Of course he loved a good argument and had unusual skill in putting his point of view in swift and telling terms. He also appreciated good, homely, leisurely talks, and liked to listen to lively and coherent recounting of tales—he himself was as interesting as a storyteller as he was stimulating as a listener.

I remember many a conversation that began in the afternoon in a *Kaffeehaus*, was carried on during long walks, and continued with unabated liveliness all through our supper. Then when it was time to say good-by, he would say that we had solved the seven problems of the universe, and so everything was settled.

His talent and taste for improvisation, so marked a feature of his interpretative work, lent the charm of endless surprise to his talk. Once as he was walking by the side of a mountain stream, a musician in his company sighed that musical possibilities were now exhausted; after Beethoven, Wagner, Bruckner, and so on, there was nothing left to be done. Mahler stopped in his tracks, and pointing to the water, exclaimed in tones of surprise: "Look, my dear friend!" "What at?" "The last wave!" This I had at second hand, but I remember his saying in reply to a remark that a certain new composition was interesting: "Interesting is easy, beautiful is difficult." His quickness of uptake, like his turn for the barbed phrase, sometimes produced remarks that were more puzzling than convincing, but he yielded to temptation only occasionally, and he soon returned to serious analysis of the topic under discussion. It was the particular charm of his conversation that, whatever the subject, it *was* conversation; even where the theme was serious or heavy, he would import something easy, enjoyable, unbuttoned. Then he was at his most lovable; his talk, however light, never degenerated into chat or, however serious, into a lecture.

Mahler's morals have been the subject of much misunderstanding. People who admired the artist often censored his character. To dispel misapprehensions of this kind it is only necessary to read his letters, and I urge anyone who wants to understand him to read them. In them the warmth of his heart, his attachment to his friends, and his outgoing sympathy speak with beautiful distinctness. Misconceptions were no doubt owing largely to the fact that, while fully able to share in the joys and sorrows of others and eager to help them, he was likely to regard the world with the absent-minded glance of the creative artist. A man whose immense gifts are concentrated on creative work cannot conduct his life on a plan of well-regulated ethical activity. When he realized a case of need he was always ready to help, and to make sacrifices in order to do so. He was full of affection—his music shows that. Yet, like many a creative spirit, he was likely to forget man while loving humanity. When he did see him, he was endlessly kind, but for the most part, his gaze was turned inward. I used to call his relation to his friends one of "intermittent loyalty." He could let long stretches of time go by in complete separation from them, physical and mental; the vacuum passed, he would be as warm and sympathetic as before.

Of petty faults he had none. Money had no

meaning for him. To earning or saving he gave no thought until, at forty-seven, he left Vienna with the future weighing heavy on his mind. His "ungrateful" programs show how little he was affected by the occupational diseases of vanity and desire for success. When he was invited to give a series of concerts in St. Petersburg, I voiced a doubt about how the audience would react to his programs. "I never thought of that!" he exclaimed. When, in response to my pleadings, he drew up a fresh program, he asked me: "Is that applause-pushing enough?" This droll expression registered his contempt for applause. Wholly dedicated to the work itself, he was without conceit; he found open praise unendurable. This of course went with a sense of his own strength and powers so secure that no opposition could shake it. Belittlement of his achievement did not affect him; he knew no envy of the success of others, when deserved, though undeserved and unworthy triumphs gave him a feeling of painful indignation. The worship of false gods often brought to his lips Schiller's words: "I saw the sacred wreaths of fame profaned by vulgar brows."

I have to admit, have indeed already admitted, that his outward demeanor left much to be desired, from the conventional, social standpoint. Kindly at heart, he could be harsh and biting, intransigent and swift to anger, cold and forbidding; but he was always sincere. Despite his commanding professional position, this child of nature never learned—and never wanted to learn —the unobliging obligingness, the smoothness of polite society. A commanding personality, he unconsciously demanded that others should fit in with him—and most of them did.

So far, the outline I have attempted to draw of his mind and spirit has been, so to say, vertical. It needs to be made horizontal; to be related to the course of time during which countless impressions have gone to build up my present clear picture, a picture often seen only in its general contour during the seventeen years of my contact with the current of his life under the changing climate of events. Save for the reservation that must be made in any attempt to reduce a living being to definition, the course of Mahler's development seems to me to be divided into three stages, which include within their temporal limits his creative work, his re-creative work, and his personality.

The first stage presents the young man, searching, suffering, uncontrolled; strong with the strength of youth, finding his creative element in the world of nature and folklore expressed in *Des Knaben Wunderhorn*. This takes him up to the termination of the Fourth Symphony (1900); in the re-creative field, it covers the first tumultuous years of his directorship of the Vienna Opera. The second stage shows a man at the zenith of his powers, his gaze, to a certain degree, on the "here" and "now," a conductor, carrying on a systematic battle with the world for the realization of his artistic aims, and a creator, influenced by Rückert and writing the symphonies from Five to Eight, inclusive. The third stage shows a loosening hold on the day-to-day world, a certain abnegation of the will to action, a redirection of gaze farther into the distance. As conductor he was, except for his performances of his Seventh and Eighth symphonies, withdrawn from my sight, being in America, while as a creative artist, stimulated by the Chinese lyrics, he was reaching fulfilment with *Das Lied von der Erde* and his Ninth Symphony.

The first stage was dominated by that central theme—the longing for God of a man tormented by the sorrows of the world—which I should call the "constant" element in his whole life. Closely related to this is his nearness to Nature. It provided an attitude akin to that of Faust when he says to the Deity: "Thou gavest me no chill astonished visit, rather permitted me to gaze into the secrets of thy bosom, as a friend. . . . Thou hast taught me to know my brothers in the still woods, in the air, and in the waters." But

Mahler transcended this, his relation to Nature was more elemental. In 1896 he wrote to the editor of a musical periodical: "It seems strange to me that most people, when speaking of 'nature,' have in mind only flowers, birds, the scent of the forest, etc. No one seems to know the great Dionysus, the God Pan." He, of course, knew him well; the first, Pan-like, movement of the Third Symphony shows this. At the same time, no Dionysiac sense of Nature, nor any devotion to creatures, could make him a pantheist, as the last movement shows. Originally, he had called this movement "What love tells me," and added the lines: "Father, look upon my pain, and let no creature die in vain." This is not a deification of Nature; still less is the adagio; it is personal religious confession.

Indeed, the great *moral* achievement of Mahler's life seems to me to lie in the fact that neither the torments of the creature nor the pangs of the human spirit caused him comfortably to shrug shoulders with the "*Ignorabimus*"

The Personality

→»-»»-»» • ««-««-««

of the philosopher, and turn away, withers unwrung, to look at what the world has to give
of beauty and happiness. In his gloomier moments, the words spoken in Mickiewicz's poem
"Funeral Rites," "Thou art not the Father of
mankind, but their Czar," might rise to his lips.
But the spasm was brief. He recognized the
misunderstanding implied. He was faithful to
the task laid upon him: to extract a divine significance from his suffering.

The second stage shows a highly limited adjustment to this world by the child of nature
and the seeker after God—this world, which,
all said and done, constitutes the atmosphere,
however problematic, of art. Works of art, conceived in solitude, yet demand for their realization great institutions and their public. Ten
years of unbounded devotion to such a great
institution, of the mutual interactions and the
contacts involved, could not but rub off some
of the intransigence and strangeness of an "original." Enough of the queer and aloof was left

to provide matter for daily astonishment to people. He would reply to friendly admonishment by saying: "A man's wild oats are often the best thing he has!" Or when a well-meaning official told him not to bang his head against a wall, he retorted: "Why not? It will make a hole in it one day." And yet it is plain that in the ten years of his directorship of the Opera, if he was not assimilated, at least he became acclimatized.

What of the seeker after God, in this second, "worldly" stage? The man who battled with the world and wrested its prizes had to pay it some attention. He held fast to that higher plane, it always gave him guidance, but it became overlaid by his worldly work. While it was still the source from which the Fifth, Sixth, and Seventh symphonies came, it seems less of a dominating influence on their course.

Toward the end of this stage, the metaphysical drive breaks through all barriers in a Faustian outburst; the Eighth was born, the "bearer of joy," as he called it. He hymns the *Creator Spiritus;* questioning and longing speak with renewed force, to be released and satisfied in the Goethean declaration of faith taken from the final scene of *Faust.* With this exalted recapitulation of his life's central theme the period of activity is over, and the third stage begins. Once again his gaze is turned away from the world. His heart is threatened; he has forebodings of death. The seeker after God faces a supreme crisis. He said, in a letter to me in July 1908: "If I am to find my way back to myself, I have got to accept the horrors of loneliness. I speak in riddles, since you do not know what has gone on and is going on within me. It is, assuredly, no hypochondriac fear of death, as you suppose. I have long known that I have got to die. . . . Without trying to explain or describe something for which there probably are no words, I simply say that at a single fell stroke I have lost any calm and peace of mind I ever achieved. I stand *vis-à-vis de rien*, and now, at the end of my life, have to begin to learn to walk and stand."

How did he surmount the crisis? The Chinese poems are at hand; he sings *Das Lied von der Erde*. When he was nineteen he closed a letter to a friend with the words: "Oh, beloved Earth, when wilt thou take the deserted one to thy bosom? Oh, Eternal Mother, receive a lonely, restless heart!" Now doomed to die, he ends his most individual work with the words: "The dear Earth blooms in Spring. Everywhere and forever blue tinges the horizons! Ever, forever! . . ." Loving greeting to the Earth was part of the nature of the young man, as of the aging one; now, under the shadow of his nearing end, it filled his whole soul. It also speaks from the Ninth, composed still later. And so he surmounted his last crisis in the spirit of the passage from Faust's monologue where, contemplating release by drinking the phial, he says:

The Personality
-》》-》》-》》·《《-《《-《《-

Forth to the open ocean leads my way,
Beneath my feet the flashing waters play,
To new shores I am called by a new day.

The glance at the "dear Earth" was now a
backward one; Earth at the leave-taking shows
a face of tender loveliness. The mystic meaning
of the following passage from a letter written
early in 1909 indicates the state of mind of one
who looks at life with the hand of death already
on his shoulder: "There is so much too much I
could say about myself that I cannot even try
to begin. I have gone through so much during
the last year and a half [i. e., since knowing of
his heart condition] that I can scarcely speak of
it. How can I attempt to describe such an overwhelming crisis? I see everything in such a new
light; I am so much in transformation that it
would not surprise me to find myself in a new
body (like Faust in the final scene). I am more
avid for life than ever, and find 'the habit of

being alive' sweeter than ever. The days of my life just now are like the Sibylline Books. . . . What nonsense it is to let one's self be submerged by the brutal whirlpool of life; to be false, even for a moment, to one's self and what is above ourselves. But I write at random; next moment, when I leave this room, I shall be just as silly as all the rest. What is it within us that thinks? What is it that acts?"

And now a magnificent and highly revealing sentence follows: "Strange—when I hear music —even when I am myself conducting it—I hear quite definite answers to all my questions, and am wholly clear and sure. Or, in reality, I seem to feel clearly that they are not questions at all." Hence came the new light in which he saw everything. After all his thinking, longing, struggling, he found the real consolation of his pain in music; in music, which as I have already sought to indicate, is a way to God closely akin to that of religion.

When asked what he believed in, Mahler of-

ten said: "I am a musician; that says everything."
If, as he suggests in the letter from which I
have quoted, he sometimes repined—went
"soft"—what was this but a sign of the toll
that the loftiest of men—and not least those of
his impulsive nature—have to pay for the common liability to physical illness.

What was indeed tragic was that toward the
end the acuteness of his feverish illness dimmed
the exaltation of his spirit. Until then he had
been sustained by the transcendental sense of
redemption of *Das Lied* and the Ninth Symphony. And that the questioning spirit had lived
on; that he still had wanted to learn, reminds one
truly of Tolstoi's beautiful legend of the three
pious old men, whom the bishop visits on their
island. Hundreds of times they let him teach
them the Lord's Prayer, but they could never
remember the words. Then, after they had
learned it at last, and long after the bishop's ship
had left their island, he saw them one night
walking the waves after him because, they said,

they had forgotten it again. And he, deeply moved, said to them: "You walked over the sea; what have you to learn?"

So it was with Mahler. He had and knew far more than what he asked, for in him was music, in him was love. Therefore, I believe the redeemed will have learned that his faithful seeking already contained the answer—and his longing will have been stilled.

Index

Aïda (Verdi), 20
Allgemeiner Deutscher Musikverein, viii, 3
Alyosha (*The Brothers Karamazov*), 158
America, 60, 63, 121; *see also* New York
Andrei, Prince (*War and Peace*), 140
Anselmus (*Goldner Topf*), 8
Aristotelian doctrine, 154
Arnim, Ludwig von, 105
Art of the Fugue, The (Bach), 117

Bach, Johann Sebastian, 117, 143
Beethoven, Ludwig van, 42, 67, 88, 92–3, 96, 103, 112, 125, 143, 151, 152, 161
Bellini (painter), 151

Berlin, 22–4
Berlin Philharmonic Orchestra, 22
Berlioz, Hector, 103, 131
Birth of Tragedy from the Spirit of Music (Nietzsche), 125
Böhler, Otto, 98
Boïeldieu, François-Adrien, 45
Brahms, Johannes, 117–18
Brentano, Clemens, 105
Brothers Karamazov, The (Dostoevski), 158
Bruckner, Anton, 67, 103, 113, 161

Cahier, Mme Charles, xiii
Cervantes, Miguel de, 30, 157
Charpentier, Gustave, 45
Cologne, 54

Index

>>>->>>->>>•<<<-<<<-<<<

"Concerto" (Giorgione), 8–9, 48, 151

Coriolanus (Beethoven), 93

Dalibor (Smetana), 35

Dâme Blanche, La (Boïeldieu), 45, 88

Dionysiac, 33

Dionysus, 168

Djamileh (Bizet), 35

Don Giovanni (Mozart), 46, 85

Don Quixote (Cervantes), 30–1

Dostoevski, Feodor, 157–8

Eckermann, Johann Peter, 155

"Ein Wunder ..." (Lohengrin), 60

Eugene Onegin (Tchaikovsky), 35

Faust, 142–3, 167, 172, 173

Faust (Goethe), 89, 138–9, 171

Fechner, Gustav, 153

Ferrier, Kathleen, xiii–xv

Fidelio (Beethoven), 46, 62, 93

Figaro, The Marriage of (Mozart), 46, 80, 82, 87

Flegeljahre (Richter), 157

Flying Dutchman, The (Wagner), 35

Franz Josef, Emperor, 48

Freischütz, Der (Weber), 44

Giorgione, 8–9, 48, 151

Gluck, Christoph Willibald von, 45, 85, 88

Goethe, Johann Wolfgang von, 138, 147, 152, 153, 155, 171

Goetz, Hermann, 45, 87–8

Goldner Topf (Hoffmann), 8

Götterdämmerung (Wagner), 16

Grimm, Jacob and Wilhelm, 105

Grinzing, 70, 73

Guttmann, Emil, 65

Halévy, Jacques, 45

Hamburg, 11–24

Hamburg Opera, 4, 5, 16; see also Hamburg

Hänsel und Gretel (Humperdinck), 5–7

Hartmann, Eduard von, 155

Haydn, Franz Joseph, 114

Henry, King (Lohengrin), 61

Hoffmann, E. T. A., 4, 8, 19, 156

Hölderlin, Friedrich, 155

Hrabanus Maurus, Hymn of, 138

Humperdinck, Engelbert, 7

Iphigenia in Aulis (Gluck), 46, 85

Ivan (The Brothers Karamazov), 158

Jean Paul, see Richter

Juive, La (Halévy), 45, 88

ii

Index

➤➤➤·➤➤➤·➤➤➤·◄◄◄·◄◄◄·◄◄◄

Kasper (*Der Freischütz*), 44

Klopstock, Friedrich Gottlieb, 127

Knaben Wunderhorn, Des, 105–6, 126, 131, 166

Krefeld Music Festival, viii, 54, 55

Kreisler (Hoffmann), 4

Kullmann, Charles, xiii

Leonora Overture, Third (Beethoven), 93

Lindhorst (*Goldner Topf*), 7

Lohengrin (Wagner), 34, 60–1, 78–80

Lohse, Otto, 11

Lotze, Rudolf, 153

Löwe, Dr., 25

Magic Flute, The (Mozart), 46

Mahler, Alma, ix

Mahler, Gustav, *passim*
Songs
"*Ablösung im Sommer,*" 108
"*Abschied, Der,*" 67, 141
"*Antonius von Padua Fischpredigt, Des,*" 18, 108
"*Aus! Aus!,*" 106
"*Es sangen drei Engel,*" 108
"*Hans und Grethe,*" 104
"*Himmlisches Leben,*" 107

"*Ich atmet einen linden Duft,*" 110
"*Ich bin der Welt abhanden gekommen,*" 110
"*Irdische Leben, Das,*" 108–9
Kindertotenlieder, xiii, 109
Klagende Lied, Das, 101, 105
Lied von der Erde, Das, ix, xii–xiii, 62, 67–8, 140–2, 167, 172, 175
Lieder eines fahrenden Gesellen, 18, 101, 105, 108
"*Nicht wiedersehen,*" 108
"*Revelge,*" 107, 116
"*Rheinlegendchen,*" 109, 149
"*Scheiden und Meiden,*" 108
"*Schildwache Nachtlied, Der,*" 107, 116
"*Selbstgefühl,*" 18, 108
"*Tambourgesell, Der,*" 107, 116
"*Trinklied vom Jammer der Erde,*" 139
"*Trost im Unglück,*" 106–7
"*Um Mitternacht,*" 110
"*Um schlimme Kinder artig zu machen,*" 18
"*Urlicht,*" 107
"*Verlorene Müh,*" 109
"*Wer hat dies Liedlein erdacht?,*" 109

iii

Index

-»»-»»-»»•«««««««

"*Wo die schönen Trompeten blasen*," 107

"*Zu Strassburg auf der Schanz*," 107

"*Zwei blauen Augen von meinem Schatz, Die*," 108

Symphonies

"Nordic," 104

First, x, 3–4, 18, 102, 108, 112, 114, 116, 120–2, 123, 125, 135, 140, 156; "Funeral March in the Manner of Callot," 3–4, 108, 120–2, 156; "Titan," 3, 156

Second, ix, 22–4, 62, 102–3, 108, 113–14, 115–16, 122–7, 132, 135, 139, 149; *Grosser Appell*, 23, 115, 127; *Urlicht*, 126

Third, viii, ix, 26–8, 32–4, 54, 55, 108, 114–16, 128–35, 168; *Das Gesindel*, 129; March, 114; *Pan erwacht: der Sommer marschiert ein*, 116, 128–9; *Südsturm*, 129; *Was mir das Felsgebirg erzählt*, 129; *Was mir die Blumen auf der Wiese erzählen*, 128; *Was mir die Liebe erzählt*, 128; *Was mir die Morgenglocken erzählen*, 128; *Was mir die tiere im Walde erzählen*, 128; "What the Rocks and Mountains Tell Me," 28, 129

Fourth, vii, 51, 53–4, 55, 109, 114–15, 132–5, 166; *Himmlisches Leben*, 134; *Kleiner Appell*, 115, 134

Fifth, v, 51, 54–5, 114, 116–19, 136–7, 142, 167, 170

Sixth, 51, 55, 113–14, 116–17, 136–7, 141, 142, 167, 170; "Tragic," 55, 137

Seventh, 51, 64, 113–14, 116–17, 136–8, 142, 167, 170

Eighth, ix, 51, 64, 65–7, 117, 138–9, 167, 170; "The Symphony of the Thousand," 65; *Veni, Creator Spiritus*, 66, 117, 138, 171

Ninth, ix, x, 62, 67, 68, 113–14, 116–17, 141–2, 167, 172, 175; "Brothers in Apollo," 117

Mahler, Otto, 21

Meistersinger, Die (Wagner), 13

Merry Wives of Windsor, The (Nicolai), 88

Metropolitan Opera (New York), 63

Mickiewicz, Adam, 169

Microcosmos (Lotze), 153

Miller, William, xiii

iv

Index

⤜⤜⤜⤜•⤛⤛⤛⤛

Mitternachtsgedicht (Nietzsche), 131
Mozart, Wolfgang Amadeus, 45, 49, 82, 85, 87, 88, 151
Munich, ix, 64, 66
Musikverein, Allgemeiner Deutscher, viii, 3
Musikvereinsaal (Vienna), vii
"Mystery Ensemble" (*Lohengrin*), 79–80

Nana, or the Spiritual Life of Plants (Fechner), 153
New York, 63, 64, 68, 71; *see also* America
Nietzsche, Friedrich, 125, 131, 150, 154–5
Ninth Symphony (Beethoven), 42, 92, 96

Oehmann, Martin, xiii
Onegin, Sigrid, xiii

Pan, 33, 129, 168
Paris, 23, 71
Parsifal (*Parsifal*), 127
"*Patmos*" (Hölderlin), 155
Patzak, Julius, xiii
Pears, Peter, xiii
Pfitzner, Hans, 45
Pollini, Bernhard, 4, 22, 25
Prague, 64

Rabanus Maurus, *see* Hrabanus Maurus
Rembrandt van Rijn, 158

"*Rhein, Der*" (Hölderlin), 155
Rheingold, Das (Wagner), 12
Richter, Jean Paul, 97, 156, 157
Ring des Nibelungen, Der (Wagner), 13
Roller, Alfred, 45–6, 83–5
Roquairol (*Titan*), 156
Rückert, Friedrich, 109–10, 166

St. Petersburg, 164
Schiller, Johann Christoph von, 165
Schönberg, Arnold, 56
Schopenhauer, Arthur, 146, 154
Schoppe (*Titan*), 156
Schubert, Franz Peter, 20, 103, 114, 151
Schumann, Robert, 104
Shakespeare, William, 157
Siebenkäs (Richter), 156
Silesius, Angelus, 155–6
Silly Affair, A (Dostoevski), 157
"*Singende Knochen, Die*" (Grimm), 105
Spinoza, Baruch, 140
Steinbach, 25–37
Stern Gesangverein, 22
Sterne, Laurence, 157
Strauss, Richard, ix, 99
String Quartet in F Minor (Beethoven), 42

v

Index

->>>->>>->>>•<<<-<<<-<<<-

Symphonia Domestica, (Strauss), 99

Symphonie fantastique (Berlioz), 131

Tales of Hoffmann, The (Offenbach), 43, 88

Taming of the Shrew, The (Goetz), 45, 87-8

Tasso, Torquato, 148

Thorborg, Kerstin, xiii

Toblach, 64, 65, 70

Tolstoi, Leo, 140, 175

Traviata, La (Verdi), 13

Tristan, 41

Tristan und Isolde (Wagner), 13-14, 46, 83, 84

Tristram Shandy (Sterne), 156

Urlus, Jacques, xiii

Variations on a Theme of Haydn (Brahms), 117-18

"*Venite inginocchiatevi*" (*Figaro*), 82

Verein der schaffenden Tonkünstler, 56

Vienna, 38-62

Vienna Opera, xv, 35, 62, 166, 170; *see also* Vienna

Vienna Philharmonic Orchestra, 23, 35, 42, 56

Wagner, Richard, 12, 13-14, 40, 79, 82, 86, 87, 88, 92, 96, 143, 161

Walküre, Die (Wagner), 46

War and Peace (Tolstoi), 140

Weber, Carl Maria von, 88

Weimar, 3

Weingartner, Felix, ix

Willer, Louise, xiii

"Witches' Sabbath" (Berlioz), 131

Zarathustra (Nietzsche), 155

Zemlinsky, Alexander von, 56

Zend-Avesta (Fechner), 153

A Note on the Author

BRUNO WALTER was born in Berlin on September 15, 1876. His musical career began on March 13, 1894, when he ascended the podium for the first time at the Cologne Opera House. In 1901 he went to the Vienna Hofoper at the invitation of its director, Gustav Mahler, remaining there for eleven years. He was general music-director in Munich from 1913 to 1922, and in the early twenties helped to found and develop the Salzburg Festival. In 1936 he returned to Vienna as director of the Staatsoper, a post he held until 1938. Dr. Walter made his English debut in 1909. From 1923 on he frequently conducted the New York Philharmonic and other American orchestras; he was also one of the notable conductors at the Metropolitan Opera. At the time of his death on February 17, 1962, he was living in California.

A NOTE ON THE TYPE

This book was set on the Linotype in JANSON, *a recutting made direct from the type cast from matrices made by Anton Janson. Whether or not Janson was of Dutch ancestry is not known, but it is known that he purchased a foundry and was a practicing type-founder in Leipzig during the years 1660 to 1687. Janson's first specimen sheet was issued in 1675. His successor issued a specimen sheet showing all of the Janson types in 1689.*

His type is an excellent example of the influential and sturdy Dutch types that prevailed in England prior to the development by William Caslon of his own incomparable designs, which he evolved from these Dutch faces. JANSON *is a highly legible type, and its individual letters have a pleasing variety of design. Its heavy and light strokes make it sharp and clear.*

The typography and binding were designed by

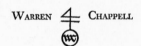

WARREN CHAPPELL

...er member exchange) training in which managers were instructed
...hat seems very similar to good old-fashioned human relations
...s.[59] Managers were taught the model underlying the training and
...instructed in how to interact effectively with their subordinates.
...pared to control managers who did not go through the training, the
...rdinates of trained managers showed a 19 percent improvement in
...activity that resulted in an estimated annual cost savings of over $5
...on. We cannot state conclusively why human relations succeeded in
...study and failed in so many others. Two possible reasons are that it
...mphasized specific communication skills rather than general styles
...dership and management and (2) was consistent with the organiza-
...l climate.

...e importance of higher management's support for human relations
...ng was demonstrated in a classic study conducted by Fleishman
...is colleagues at International Harvester.[60] Training was conducted
...rease the consideration behavior of first-line supervisors. Two years
...the program, only those supervisors with bosses who were highly
...derate and thus supportive of the goals of the training still showed
...r consideration. Trained supervisors whose bosses were low in con-
...tion were even less considerate two years after the training than
...ned supervisors. It appears that for the effects of leadership train-
...transfer back to the job, the nature and role of training in any
...zation should be consistent with the general philosophy of that or-
...tion. If, for example, a firm subscribes generally to the classical
...ucratic) model of management, it should not expect good results
...program designed to make supervisors more sensitive to the needs
...r subordinates. This type of program would place the supervisors in
...ult position. If, in fact, it were effective and the supervisors came
...ot a more considerate, people-oriented style, they would run the
...being judged weak and permissive by their superiors—a distinct
...in the eyes of bureaucratic management. On the other hand, if the
...g failed to take, it would have been money wasted.

...lack of success of many of the other human relations training pro-
...has led Fiedler to suggest that it is futile to attempt to change
...hip style. As an alternative, he proposes that leaders should be
... to *modify the situation* to fit their styles. Recently, he and his
...tes have designated a training package, *Leader Match,* which
...st that.[61] The Leader Match program consists of a self-paced pro-
...ed manual in which the trainee first completes Fiedler's leader-
...le, the least preferred co-worker (LPC) scale, and learns how to
...t the score. The trainee then learns to diagnose the situation in
...f leader-member relations, task structure, and position power.
...ainder of the program focuses on how the trainee can modify the
...n to fit his or her style of leadership. This is accomplished through
...of vignettes in which the trainee diagnoses the situation and then

program might constitute one such external event. In this case, an improvement in *after* scores compared to *before* scores could just as easily be attributed to trainees working hard to avoid layoff as to the effects of training per se.

A third problem in the before-and-after design is that the act of measuring the criterion before the training program might cause subsequent changes in the criterion measures. This *pretest sensitization* is more apt to occur with obtrusive measures, such as questionnaires or tests, than with unobtrusive ones, such as performance records. If trainees were pretested on their knowledge of how to operate a machine, for example, the test might spark their curiosity enough so that they familiarized themselves with the machine on their own. Consequently, gains in knowledge occurring over the course of training will have less to do with the training than with the pretest.

A fourth question that remains when improvements are shown in performance with a simple before-and-after design is whether performance is due to the training program or to improvements that would have *occurred naturally* without formal training. For instance, larger increases in performance can be expected when an employee is new to a job and has a lot to learn than when the employee is an old hand. If we find improvements in the performance of new employees following training, the simple before-and-after evaluation design does not allow us to eliminate the alternative explanation that employee performance improved simply as a result of job experience.

3. Experimental Design. In order to avoid the confoundings inherent in the other designs and to be sure that criterion changes are in fact due to the training program, we need to use an *experimental design* in our evaluation of the program. There are two essential characteristics of a true experimental design. First, as noted in Chapter 1, a *control group* is needed that is treated just like the experimental group except for training. They might be taken off the job and allowed to relax, read, or engage in some other activity unrelated to the specific training program. Or, if the object of the research is to evaluate a new program, they might be trained using the old methods. If the experimental trainees are aware that they are participating in an experiment, the control trainees also will be given this information. With a control group, one can legitimately make claims regarding the effectiveness of the training program on the basis of differences in terminal performance.

The second characteristic of an experimental design is *random assignment* of employees to the experimental and the control conditions. *Random* means that persons in a population have an equal chance of being assigned to the experimental or the control conditions. If people are assigned nonrandomly, one cannot ensure that differences on the criteria between the experimental and control conditions actually are due to training. For instance, if participants are selected for a program by asking for volunteers and those who do not volunteer are used as the control, any differences found between the experimental and control sessions might reflect differences between personal characteristics of volunteers and nonvolunteers. Given that training is associated with higher performance, an obvious confounding factor might be that those who volunteer are more motivated or more competent than those who do not volunteer.

A design that is far superior to a simple before-and-after design, then, is a before-and-after *design* with a *control* group and *random assignment* of persons to each group. This is only one of many available experimental designs—actually, the simplest possible arrangement.[54] There are other potentially troublesome extraneous factors and other designs appropriate to control for them. The point is, however, that a really meaningful evaluation requires experimental control of at least the major confounding influences.

The information from the evaluation phase—particularly that involving transfer to actual job performance—should serve as input to the planning phase for subsequent revision of the program. This "feedback loop" allows us to conceptualize the entire instructional model as a "closed-loop system," a type of system in which compensatory adjustments are made on the basis of output data in order to achieve a desired state. In the present case, this means that we should compare the ultimate results of training with the original objectives and see whether we have moved closer to or farther from these stated goals. We then consider how things might be changed—objectives, procedures, or evaluation—in order to bring results and objects into closer accord.

Specific Areas of Training

So far we have discussed general principles of designing, implementing, and evaluating training programs without going into specific types of training programs. The problems confronted in successfully implementing and evaluating a program, however, depend in part on what one is attempting to modify. The research and theory in each of the topics we have discussed have led to specific training interventions. It is illuminating to consider some of the successes and failures of training in each of these topical areas.

Motivation Training

Typically, psychologists have suggested that to increase the motivation of workers to work hard, we need to change the situation (e.g., provide rewards, set goals, enrich jobs) or hire people who already are motivated. Another alternative that seldom has been attempted by psychologists is to increase employee motivation through training. Perhaps psychologists tend to avoid such an approach because it smacks of success seminars in

which a charismatic speaker uses God, mother,
participants to strive for success, money, and fa
chologists who have attempted to compete with
Reverend Ike is McClelland, who designed ach
grams based on his need achievement theory (see

In McClelland's courses, participants are tau
act like a person with a high nAch" through tra
at skill in thematic apperception story-telling; t
make up answers that would be scored high on
plan realistic goals for themselves and, in follow-
progress in achieving their plans. Finally, an at
a group esprit de corps, with members providing
they seek to accomplish their plans.

In an ambitious application of this program
businessmen from a small city in India. Before
the participants had shown "unusual enterprise
the course, this increased to 50 percent. Accordi
thing clearly happened in Kilkinada: the own
started a chemical plant; a banker was so succe
cial loans in an enterprising way that he was p
branch of his bank in Calcutta."[56] Unfortunate
the subsequent studies evaluating nAch traini
ments.[57] The findings provide, at best, very ter
tiveness in improving job performance. There
ical questions related to nAch training.[58] Pre
in the Kilkinada study served voluntarily. We
ever, against the ethical implications of using
force this kind of change on employees, no ma
may believe it to be.

Leadership Training

One of the most common types of training in i
ing. The particular leadership style advocated
on the theoretical framework on which the tra
5). Human relationists have always argued
trained to adopt a highly considerate, partici
style. On the other hand, contingency theoris
designed either to help managers diagnose t
their style to fit it or to help them change th
into line with their style. Despite the million
on leadership training, such programs rarely
tive, regardless of the theoretical framewor
based.

Based on his VDL model, Graen and hi

selects which action to take. For instance, Fiedler's theory dictates that a high-LPC leader will be ineffective in a situation of low favorability (i.e., poor leader-member relations, low position power, unstructured task). The manual instructs the high-LPC trainee how to increase the favorability of this type of situation to match his or her style.

Several evaluations of the Leader Match program have been reported by Fiedler and his associates, and, predictably, their conclusion has been that the data unequivocally support its effectiveness.[62] Not everyone shares that assessment. In our view, the results are still too ambiguous to justify pronouncing the Leader Match an effective technique. Goldstein observed that although trained leaders in one study were rated higher in their performance than untrained leaders, a significant number of the trained leaders reported that they had not used the Leader Match materials in leading their subordinates.[63] In general, the results of leadership training are disappointing. It appears that leadership training programs have been designed too often on the basis of theories with uncertain validity rather than on an assessment of organizational needs. Given the present state of leadership theory, a much wiser approach would be to tailor the program to the specific needs of the organization and employees following the process presented in Figure 8–1.

Group Training

Although most training efforts are focused on individuals, organizations are collections of groups, and the effectiveness of the organization depends in part on how well people can work together (see Chapter 4). Another category of training, then, consists of programs that take place in a small-group setting, are concerned with interpersonal relations, and use experiences in the group as a focus of the training.

The more unstructured form of group training we will call *sensitivity training,* even though it has gone by a variety of names, including laboratory, T-group, D-group, L-group, and encounter group training. Sensitivity training is carried on in hundreds of different settings, from large institutionalized programs such as those offered by the National Training Laboratories in Bethel, Maine, to programs put on within individual firms. They differ in focus, trainer qualifications, type of participants (from the same or different firms, the same or different levels of management, etc.), and many other respects.[64] Regardless of the specific form it assumes, the objective is usually to train the participants in how to be sensitive or aware of themselves, of others, of their relations to others, and of the dynamics involved in social interaction.[65] The trainees meet in small unstructured groups under the nondirective supervision of a trainer (or therapist) and discuss themselves, each other, and what is going on in the group. The focus is on the social interactions that occur during the session itself: Specific events—comments, arguments, opinions, and so on—are analyzed in depth with the aim of understanding the social processes involved.

The basic premise underlying all forms of sensitivity training is that the group process somehow leads people to take an honest look at themselves in relation to others and, if what they see is maladaptive, to change their attitudes and behavior. One way this has been conceptualized is in terms of the Johari window, which was discussed in Chapter 4. In fact, the Johari window concept was presented by two participants in a sensitivity group (Joe and Harry) to capture the effects of the group training. According to their interpretation, the supportive environment of the group allowed them to drop the facades they used in relationships with others; and, in receiving feedback from others in the group, they became more aware of the blind spots in their relationships. The consequence was a widening of the open area and a reduction of the unknown area.

Another, more focused variety of group training is team building. *Team building* is a type of group training intended to improve the way in which work is accomplished through natural work groups by clarifying work roles within the group as well as improving supervisor-subordinate relations, problem-solving and decision-making skills, and the team's ability to handle conflict. Although team-building sessions often resemble sensitivity groups, there is a difference, at least in theory. The objective of a sensitivity group is typically to increase the individual's general understanding of human behavior through experiences in the group. In contrast, team building is focused more on developing the task or interpersonal effectiveness of an *intact* group. If we return again to the Johari window concept, the hope of team building is that team members will learn skills in open communications and leveling, with a corresponding decline in unwitting revelations and emotional contagion.

Controversy surrounds group training on two main counts—effectiveness and ethics. Are the results of sensitivity training or team building sufficiently positive to make it worthwhile? And, even if it is worthwhile, does the organization have the right to require its employees to undergo these types of training?

With regard to the issue of effectiveness, doubts exist as to whether either sensitivity training or team building can increase the effectiveness with which participants perform their organizational roles. In a review of the evidence on sensitivity training, Campbell and Dunnette report that few of the evaluative studies have been acceptable on scientific grounds.[66] Most have relied solely on internal change criteria (i.e., whether the trainee personally feels that he or she has improved). Those that have sought *external* verification of change (i.e., whether someone else feels the trainee has improved) have usually been poorly controlled. Overall, however, the findings provide some evidence that people do change—at least temporarily—as a result of sensitivity training. Unfortunately, it is not at all clear whether the change is predominately for the better. In one of the few really well-controlled studies, Underwood found that of 25 instances of reported change in trained managers, only 15 were in the direction of *increased* effectiveness.[67]

Similar to the research on sensitivity training, very few true experiments have been conducted to evaluate the effects of team building. In a recent review of this literature, Woodman and Sherwood could find only 1 of 30 studies that was a true experiment, and this study showed that team building did not improve performance.[68] There is some indication that team building can increase the satisfaction of group members and their perceptions of how effectively the team is performing, but at present there is no substantial evidence that team building improves organizational effectiveness. On the other hand, it has not yet been ruled out; it remains a possibility in need of further research.

Much of sensitivity training and team building rests on vague, conflicting, or tenuous theoretical notions. Hence, even if it works, we are at somewhat of a loss to explain why. Two conditions that are usually considered essential to most forms of group training, and particularly sensitivity training, are (1) an atmosphere of psychological safety that allows the trainee to display true feelings and emotions and (2) a degree of anxiety or tension that is reduced as the trainee develops deeper insights (thereby reinforcing the desired changes). The safer the atmosphere, however, the less tension one would expect to be generated. Moreover, safety is largely a matter of assurance that whatever one says within the group will stay there and not come back to haunt one on the job. Call the boss a SOB in a sensitivity session, and all is forgotten back on the assembly line. Some critics consider this an unrealistic expectation—that, as long as the participants are drawn from the same organization, psychological safety is problematical. If safety is not threatened, as in *stranger groups* where participants are drawn from different organizations, there is a greater question as to how much of whatever is learned will transfer back to the work environment. Thus, safety, tension, and transfer—all presumably key requirements for the success of the training experience—seem to operate at cross-purposes.

The second issue is the ethical one. The candor and personal orientation of the group interaction that occurs in group training (particularly sensitivity training) can be a very traumatic, anxiety-producing experience for some individuals.[69] This was put very aptly by Kirchner:

> Most people have taken many years to . . . build up their psychological defenses. While it can be very enlightening to find out that nobody loves you and that some people think that you have undesirable traits, this can also be a very shocking experience to individuals and not necessarily a beneficial one.[70]

The solution to the ethics problem would seem to be that of a voluntary participation requirement. Group training would be limited to individuals who volunteered to participate with full foreknowledge of what was in store—including the potential risks. Implementation of such a policy, of course, would require the full cooperation of the organization. It would be all too easy to use subtle forms of coercion and social pressure to fill up the rolls with reluctant volunteers.

Training Raters to Appraise Performance

As we discussed in Chapter 6, performance appraisals have often been rendered useless by leniency, halo, and other rating biases, and some attempts have been made to train raters to recognize these rating biases. In general, rater training has been shown to reduce halo and leniency. Unfortunately, training that reduces halo and leniency also has been shown to reduce the accuracy of ratings, perhaps as the result of replacing one bias with another.[71] The evidence seems to suggest that training should be focused directly on teaching raters to observe accurately and to judge ratee behavior rather than on avoiding halo, leniency, and other rating biases.

Training the Hard-Core Unemployed

As the consequences of Title VII of the Civil Rights Act, affirmative action, and changes in social values, there have been more efforts to provide economic opportunities to disadvantaged groups in the last two decades than in any other period of U.S. history. Training the hard-core unemployed has become a primary vehicle for providing these opportunities. Unfortunately, action has tended to precede understanding in this area, and many of the programs have been reported to have failed miserably. The apparent ineffectiveness of many of the attempts to train the hard-core unemployed is partly responsible for the dramatic reduction over the last few years in the support for such programs provided by the federal government.

Although widely seen as having failed, it is difficult to make any overall assessment because programs have varied greatly in content, method, and organizational backing. Moreover, few have been adequately evaluated. Nevertheless, some progress has been made in identifying desirable features for hard-core programs. While many of these generalizations are based on little more than expert opinion or experience with a single program, they are at least a start: They can serve both as hypotheses to be tested by more rigorous evaluative procedures when such are available and as an interim guide to program development.

The major content areas of hard-core programs have been *remedial education, specific job skills,* and *motivation or attitude change.* Specific programs have differed widely in the relative emphasis placed on these areas and in the techniques used to teach them. The following list of features summarizes key characteristics of programs that seem to have achieved a degree of success:

1.   The training should be carried out in conjunction with an actual *employment* program. Unless the trainee feels a job is assured when training is completed he or she will probably drop out.

2.   The job to which training leads should not represent a dead end. While some trainees might find low-level jobs suitable for their purpose, many like to feel that advancement is at least a possibility if they choose to work for it.

3.   Personal attention for purposes of providing knowledge-of-results reinforcement, encouragement, and counseling is important both during and after training. Trainees are likely to lack confidence and to be easily discouraged. Frequent reassurance by a trusted and sympathetic trainer or supervisor seems to help overcome these problems.

4.   Failure to consider motivational and attitudinal factors in the training seems to increase the drop-out rate. Exactly what sort of change procedure is most effective (role playing, group discussion, sensitivity training, etc.) has not been established. Just as important, however, exclusive concentration on these factors is also undesirable. Changing someone's attitude toward work without also giving that person the skills necessary to do the work can obviously produce frustration.

5.   Training should take into account the particular handicaps of the hard-core individual. For example, care should be taken to phrase instructions in terms that the trainee can understand. People from Spanish-speaking and black ghetto backgrounds often speak an entirely different version of the English language.[72] Many programs seem to have failed through a simple breakdown in communication.

Some programs designed with these general principles in mind seem to be working. The Lockheed Aircraft Company, for example, has reported low drop-out rates and on-the-job performance levels comparable to regular hirees for hard-core trainees enrolled in two such programs.[73] It appears, therefore, that "basic skills can be improved and that job training programs can pay off if they are carefully done, include lots of personal attention, and lead to a desirable job."[74] A great deal remains to be learned about optimal strategies for training hard-core individuals and for assimilating them into the work force.

One thing, however, is certain. Little progress can be expected so long as the organization considers the entire problem to be one of individual deficiencies and the solution to be exclusively that of individual change. It must also be considered an *organizational* problem: The organization, too, must be willing to make changes. Suppose, for example, a hard-core individual is hired and successfully trained. He must then apply what he has learned within a work context that includes a boss and fellow workers, all of whom may resent his presence or treat him with suspicion and disdain. If he is to accommodate this very new and potentially threatening environment, the boss and fellow workers must also be trained. Special managerial skills must be acquired by his supervisor; tolerance, understanding, and new social habits must be learned by his peers (role playing and group discussion might be effective means of accomplishing such training). The organization might also need to consider revising some of its rules—for example, penalties for tardiness, dress codes, requirements for promotion. In short, adapting the individual to his new environment must be viewed as a *system* project—not just hard-core training.

Essential Characteristics of Organizational Development (OD)

The field of organizational development (OD) is a very loose conglomeration of techniques and models and, in its broadest application, could include everything that we have discussed in this book. French, Bell, and Zawacki and other proponents, however, claim that OD is "not just anything done to better an organization" but that it is "a process of planned, system change that attempts to make organizations (viewed as social-technical systems) better able to attain their short- and long-term objectives."[75] Although there is a wide spectrum of approaches that go by the OD label, at least three characteristics are often used by proponents to describe OD:

1. Systemwide Change

Unlike training interventions, which primarily focus on individual change, OD interventions typically have as their long-range objective the modification of an entire organizational system. System usually means the whole organization, although it sometimes is used to refer to a subsystem, such as a department. The organization and its subsystems are viewed as complex systems with specifiable goals that operate in a constantly changing environment (see Chapter 2). The goal of OD is to improve the ability of the organizational system to cope with this environment.

2. Humanistic Assumptions

Most advocates of OD approaches are firm believers in the humanistic view of organizations and management (see Chapter 2). Because most organizations still function to a great extent according to the bureaucratic model, it is not hard to imagine the general direction that OD-fostered change usually takes. Very frequently it ends up as an effort to get the whole organization to adopt the tenets of Theory Y.

3. Planned Change

Another characteristic of OD is that, ideally, it consists of planned change. OD begins with a diagnosis of organizational needs for change, followed by a planned and systematic implementation of the change, and an evaluation. Changes implemented in an OD project ideally consist of long-term projects that undergo continuous monitoring and revision.

Miles and Schmuck have presented what they consider to be a frequent sequence of events in OD projects.[76] First, middle or top management of an organization becomes interested in OD, often as the result of the manager's personal attendance at a sensitivity training session. An OD consultant is invited into the organization and, through a series of initial meetings, specifies the boundaries of the project and its goals and procedures. The consultant collects data on the organization through interviews, observations, and questionnaires. Then, together with the organizational members, the consultant identifies key problem areas, diagnoses the causes of these problems, and specifies possible remedies. The first "intervention" is often in the form of survey feedback sessions in which data collected in earlier phases are fed back to the group and discussed. This survey feedback may take place in the context of training in communication skills or group functioning. Other interventions may come out of these sessions, including those listed in Figure 8–4. According to this scheme, OD interventions can be described along three dimensions. One is according to the problem that they address, the focus of attention, and the specific activity prescribed. These activities range from the more "soft," people-oriented approaches such as traditional training, process consultation and coaching, and confrontation meetings, to "harder," more task-oriented approaches such as data feedback, problem-solving sessions, plan making, OD task force, and techno-structural (e.g., sociotechnical) interventions. According to Miles and Schmuck, in actual practice these intervention modes overlap and flow into each other.

After each intervention, additional data is collected to evaluate the intervention and to plan future action. By this point, the hope of many OD consultants is that the culture of the organization will change in the direction of becoming "more open, trusting, collaborative, self-analytical, and inclined to take risks." It is also hoped that OD activities will become institutionalized and that the consultant's presence will no longer be needed for the continued success of the program.

The OD program outlined here is more of an ideal than it is the typical project. It is rare that any large-scale attempt at change progresses so smoothly or is so successful that it is institutionalized. Nevertheless, the

FIGURE 8–4   Miles and Schmuck's OD Intervention Classification Scheme

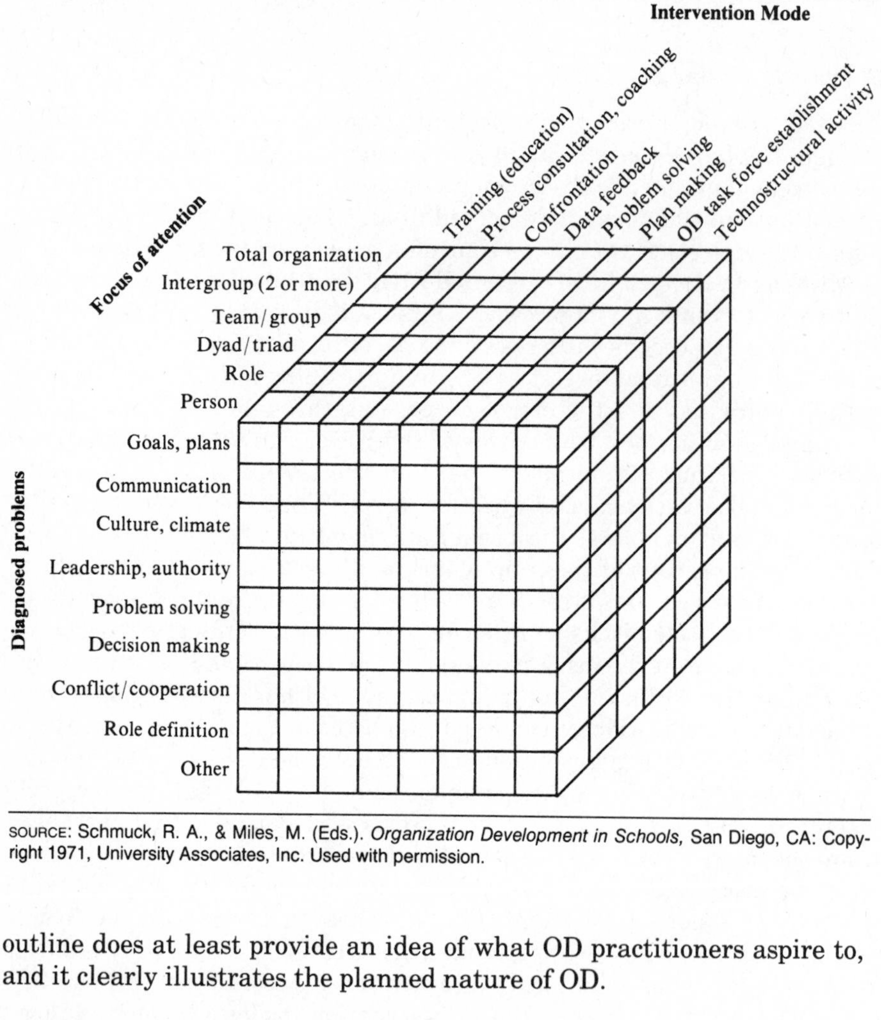

SOURCE: Schmuck, R. A., & Miles, M. (Eds.). *Organization Development in Schools,* San Diego, CA: Copyright 1971, University Associates, Inc. Used with permission.

outline does at least provide an idea of what OD practitioners aspire to, and it clearly illustrates the planned nature of OD.

Organizational Climate and OD

Because the ambition of OD programs is to change the whole organization or at least a major part, it is important to be able to monitor changes in the individual, group, and structural components of the organization. But how do we measure such broad and wide-ranging effects? A useful construct for conceptualizing such comprehensive changes in an organization is *organizational climate* or *culture.* There is little discernible difference in the definitions of climate and culture, although the latter appears to be the more popular term in recent years. The primary difference is that the research on climate tends to be quantitative and frequently employs structured questionnaires, whereas the research on culture is more qualitative and consists mostly of case studies of individual organizations. Because climate measures are commonly used devices for diagnosing organizational ills and measuring the success of OD interventions, we will focus on the climate research.

Organizational climate is the relatively stable characteristics of the organization that distinguish it from other organizations and influence the behavior and attitudes of its members. In a sense, climate is to the organization as personality is to the individual. Just as people have a characteristic style of doing things, whole organizations also appear to have styles that characterize their typical mode of operation. For example, PepsiCo has a high-pressure, competitive climate in which beating out its chief competitor, Coca-Cola, appears to be the chief obsession. This competitive orientation spills over into internal operations, as managers are pitted against each other to see who survives. J. C. Penney Company, on the other hand, appears to have a highly paternalistic climate in which pleasing the customer is stressed.[77] In stark contrast to the PepsiCo emphasis on acquiring more profits, one Penney store manager purportedly was called on the carpet by the president for making too much profit at the expense of the customer. Although most researchers agree that there is something that we can call organizational climate, they differ on what the specific defining features are and how they should be measured. Some argue that the climate concept should include primarily *objective* features measured objectively. Others feel it should reflect *subjective* features— notably the perceptions of its employees. In this case, measurement would have to be entirely via questionnaire. An abbreviated version of one standard questionnaire for measuring such features, The Profile of Organizational Characteristics, is illustrated in Table 8–1.[78] This particular instrument is based on Likert's notion that organizations can be categorized as falling into one of four categories, namely Exploitative Authoritative (System 1), Benevolent Authoritative (System 2), Consultative (System 3), and Participative (System 4).[79] Reflecting the humanistic assumptions of most OD consultants, System 4 is usually presented as the "ideal" climate.

Indicative of the systems nature of OD, a common hypothesis underlying many OD interventions is that a change in one part of the organizational climate is only likely to succeed if the interventions are consistent with the overall organizational climate. For example, attempts to move the organization toward a System 4 mode on the goal-setting dimensions of the profile in Table 8–1 might fail if the company remained a System 1 organization on the other dimensions.

Another hypothesis often implicit in OD interventions is that satisfaction and performance will improve to the extent that the climate matches a System 4 profile. Thus, a climate measure such as the profile questionnaire often is used to track the effects of an OD intervention. One example of such a use is presented in Table 8–1. The two profiles found in this table came from an evaluation of the effects of placing all employees in a manufacturing organization, including blue-collar workers, on salary as the first step in a major job enrichment project.[80] The change seemingly was successful in moving the organization from a System 2 climate to a climate having both System 3 and System 4 elements, although there is likely some degree of rating halo contained in these profiles. A more wide-ranging OD intervention, the Weldon experiment, is described by Katz and Kahn.[81] In this experiment, an attempt was made to change the climate of the Weldon company to conform to the System 4 climate of the Harwood company, with which it had merged. The OD project included the whole gamut of techniques illustrated in Figure 8–4: changes in the technology, personnel practices, and organizational structure, the firing of some workers, sensitivity training, and joint problem-solving meetings between workers and their supervisors. Surveys of the managers in the company, using the Profile of Organizational Characteristics, revealed a rather large shift in the profile of the company toward System 4. Additionally, the company appeared to show equally dramatic improvements in performance on such dimensions as return on capital and production efficiency. In both these examples, the companies seemed to change for the better as the result of changes in the climate. However, as is usually the case in OD studies, there was no control organization against which to compare the effects of the interventions. It is difficult, therefore, to pinpoint the exact cause of the improvements. Nevertheless, both studies illustrate the usefulness of climate measures in diagnosing organizational ills and in providing at least crude evaluations of the effects of the OD interventions aimed at correcting these ills.

There has been considerable debate on several issues related to the measurement of climate. There is some question as to whether climate measures really measure anything other than job satisfaction (see Chapter 3). Another issue is whether climate questionnaires measure characteristics of the organization as much as they do personal orientations and biases of the respondent. In support of the latter position, it is frequently found that organizational members disagree considerably in their response to the same climate measures.

This is not to say that climate is a useless concept or that efforts to measure it should be discontinued. Rather, it suggests that if we are to use organizational climate to diagnose needs for change or to evaluate the effects of changes, we need a clearer definition of organizational climate and better ways to measure it. Guion feels that the major problem in the past has been the tendency to describe the attributes of organizational climate in terms of how employees feel about the organization rather than how it actually is or how it appears to them.[82] As a consequence of this misplaced emphasis, he argues, we have developed measures of people rather than of organizations. It makes no sense, therefore,

TABLE 8–1 Profile of an Organization's Climate before and after Placing All Employees on Salary

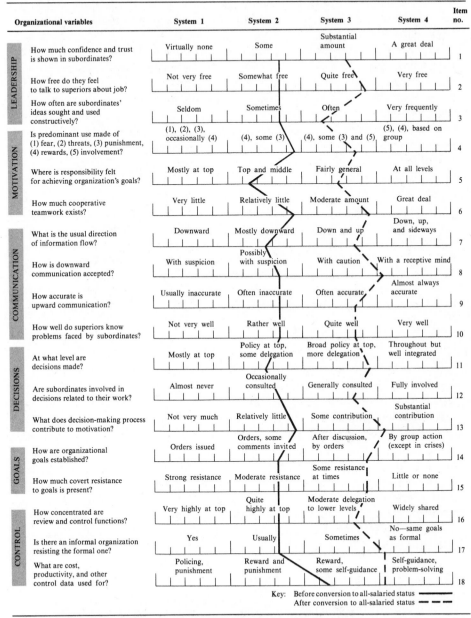

Organizational variables	System 1	System 2	System 3	System 4	Item no.
LEADERSHIP How much confidence and trust is shown in subordinates?	Virtually none	Some	Substantial amount	A great deal	1
How free do they feel to talk to superiors about job?	Not very free	Somewhat free	Quite free	Very free	2
How often are subordinates' ideas sought and used constructively?	Seldom	Sometimes	Often	Very frequently	3
MOTIVATION Is predominant use made of (1) fear, (2) threats, (3) punishment, (4) rewards, (5) involvement?	(1), (2), (3), occasionally (4)	(4), some (3)	(4), some (3) and (5)	(5), (4), based on group	4
Where is responsibility felt for achieving organization's goals?	Mostly at top	Top and middle	Fairly general	At all levels	5
How much cooperative teamwork exists?	Very little	Relatively little	Moderate amount	Great deal	6
COMMUNICATION What is the usual direction of information flow?	Downward	Mostly downward	Down and up	Down, up, and sideways	7
How is downward communication accepted?	With suspicion	Possibly with suspicion	With caution	With a receptive mind	8
How accurate is upward communication?	Usually inaccurate	Often inaccurate	Often accurate	Almost always accurate	9
How well do superiors know problems faced by subordinates?	Not very well	Rather well	Quite well	Very well	10
DECISIONS At what level are decisions made?	Mostly at top	Policy at top, some delegation	Broad policy at top, more delegation	Throughout but well integrated	11
Are subordinates involved in decisions related to their work?	Almost never	Occasionally consulted	Generally consulted	Fully involved	12
What does decision-making process contribute to motivation?	Not very much	Relatively little	Some contribution	Substantial contribution	13
GOALS How are organizational goals established?	Orders issued	Orders, some comments invited	After discussion, by orders	By group action (except in crises)	14
How much covert resistance to goals is present?	Strong resistance	Moderate resistance	Some resistance at times	Little or none	15
CONTROL How concentrated are review and control functions?	Very highly at top	Quite highly at top	Moderate delegation to lower levels	Widely shared	16
Is there an informal organization resisting the formal one?	Yes	Usually	Sometimes	No—same goals as formal	17
What are cost, productivity, and other control data used for?	Policing, punishment	Reward and punishment	Reward, some self-guidance	Self-guidance, problem-solving	18

Key: Before conversion to all-salaried status ——————
After conversion to all-salaried status — — —

SOURCE: Davis, L. E., & Cherns, A. (Eds.). (1975). *The Quality of Working Life.* (Vol. 2). New York: The Free Press, a Division of Macmillan, Inc. Copyright © 1975 by Louis E. Davis and Albert Cherns. Reprinted with permission.

to use such measures to help explain how people feel or act at work; this would amount to saying they are satisfied because they are satisfied. What we need are independent measures that reflect the real or perceived attributes of the work atmosphere. These should define organizational climate.

In a review of the research on this topic, James and Jones go a step farther than Guion and propose a distinction between climate regarded as an organizational attribute and as an individual attribute.[83] They would reserve the term *organizational climate* for the former concept and substitute a new one, *psychological climate,* for the latter. A perceptual measure would qualify as an index of organizational climate only if it could be shown to vary systematically with situational, rather than individual, variables. This is not, however, an easy condition to verify. Probably the most significant point developed by James and Jones is that even if the notion of climate is redefined as they suggest, the task of defining the boundaries of the concept still remains. What, for example, distinguishes the variables, dimensions, and constructs that we use to define organizational climate from those that we use to define other situational characteristics? Does climate include something like span of control (see Chapter 2) or doesn't it? Because research to date has been more concerned with measuring climate than with specifying what it is, boundary definition is the most pressing immediate problem.

Summary of Organizational Development

What can we conclude regarding OD? The whole approach is loosely defined, wide ranging, and idiosyncratic. There is probably no adequate way to test its overall worth empirically, although facets of it could certainly be evaluated. There have been attempts to evaluate individual OD interventions, but most of these studies were poorly designed and subject to a host of alternative interpretations. Furthermore, the primary indicator of most OD interventions, organizational climate, is somewhat vague in its conceptualization and measurement. For all its limitations, however, there is one thing it offers—assuming that it is carried out in a conscientious and thorough manner—that none of the other interventions do: the promise of organizationwide, planned, evaluated change. Considering the alternatives, this is no trivial advantage.

CONCLUSIONS

Personnel training consists of all those procedures through which an organization attempts to change the attitudes, skills, knowledge, or interpersonal relationships of individuals within the work force. Although the usual strategy is to change individuals to fit existing job demands, training can also be used as a means of bringing about change in the organization itself (as in OD). As it exists today, training is a very costly enterprise. Paradoxically, it also tends to be lightly regarded, poorly planned, infrequently evaluated, and, in all likelihood, less effective than it might be.

Although *learning* is the critical process in training, very little of what we know about the learning process has been applied to the design of training programs. In fact, there is a growing suspicion that many of the variables shown to be important for learning in simple laboratory setting share little relevance for training. Even if they are relevant, it is difficult to translate these learning principles into training conditions. Nevertheless, a few concepts still seem worth considering. The concept of *reinforcement* appears to be important, although probably not in the laboratory sense of automatically "stamping in" a prior response. People do, however, tend to repeat behaviors that lead to reward and to avoid those that result in punishment. Thus, training conditions should be arranged so that desired behaviors are clearly related to satisfying consequences (praise, test scores, knowledge of results). This seems to promote learning both through motivation and information: It increases one's desire to learn and makes it easier to recognize what one must do to get rewarded.

Other conditions that influence learning include *meaningfulness* of the material to be learned and various conditions of practice (*part* versus *whole*; *massed* versus *distributed*). It is always a good idea to organize whatever is to be learned in a way that makes sense to the learner. However, the program by which it should be *practiced* depends on characteristics of the material (and possibly the learner as well). Complex, difficult material that is not highly meaningful is learned more easily by most people if it is practiced by the part method in a *distributed* fashion.

Learning is valuable in the training situation only to the extent that it transfers positively to the job itself. The only way to establish how well a training program has accomplished this objective is through experimental research comparing people who have been trained with those who have not on *relevant job criteria*. However, high positive transfer is most likely when the training program incorporates key elements of behavior, or general principles, that characterize the job itself. Careful job analysis is necessary for the tentative identification of these features. Some theorists have argued that the design of training programs should be guided more by such analytic considerations, particularly organization and sequencing of component tasks, than by traditional learning principles.

It is possible to spell out, at a very general level, the necessary ingredients for a successful training program. First, the specific behavioral objectives of the program must be identified, based upon careful analysis or organizational goals, tasks, and people. The idea is to assure that the real training needs are identified and then translated into specific terms: What sort of changes are needed in whom and on what specific tasks? Second, a *training environment* must be created that is conducive to achievement of these goals. The major decisions involve the identification of appropriate *learning conditions* and *training media*. Third, procedures for evaluation must be built into the program design. Provisions must be made for pretesting, monitoring, and posttesting each trainee's performance. Moreover, transfer must be measured using relevant criteria of on-the-job performance. In evaluation of both terminal performance and transfer, it is important that experimental designs be used that control such extraneous factors as pretraining proficiency and the Hawthorne effect. Finally, results of training must be compared with the original objectives to see whether revisions are necessary. Essential as all four of the above steps are, few of the programs in effect today show evidence of having considered them. Little wonder that so many programs are ineffective, irrelevant, and even maladaptive.

A host of specific techniques have appeared as training media. Often they have been overpromoted and oversold, creating a succession of fads in the training field. It should be obvious from the above discussion that the particular medium is but one small part of the overall training picture. Its value depends a great deal upon how well it meshes with the other parts—how suitable it is for the behavioral objectives, the people, the material, and the situation to which it is applied. Although some tentative information is available regarding which techniques are suitable for what, much remains to be learned. One can be certain of the usefulness of a technique only through empirical verification—which, of course, is another reason why evaluation is such a critical part of any program. The point is, we cannot simply assume that a technique will work because it should or because it has worked for someone else.

The most commonly used approach is on-the-job training. This can include several formally distinct techniques such as job rotation and coaching. More frequently, it is a rather haphazard business. The trainee is typically assigned to a more experienced worker and told to learn what he or she can. Unless the experienced worker happens to like training people and knows something about how it should be done, the trainee might wind up poorly trained at a relatively high cost to the organization. It is, however, a hidden cost in that it doesn't involve a direct outlay of money for an exclusively educational activity. Instead, it takes the form of prolonged development, reduced output for an experienced worker, and possible accidents or equipment damage. Properly done, of course, on-the-job training has the advantage of minimizing any transfer problem.

Off-the-job techniques range from the standard classroom methods of lecturing and group discussion to such innovations as programmed, personalized, and computer-assisted instruction. Each of these methods has strengths and weaknesses, although direct comparisons among them have been more notable for similarities than differences in obtained performance. As a rule, the various individualized methods produce about the same level of terminal performance as the more conventional methods but at a considerable savings in time. Audiovisual techniques are particularly useful for certain kinds of material (such as detailed manual operations) and for provision of expert instruction where none is available. Simulation offers high positive transfer, at least in theory, in exchange for a relatively costly training environment. Most of these techniques suffer from insufficient or inadequately designed evaluation efforts. Thus, we are a long way from a complete understanding of what each is good for—and why.

There seems to be a fairly wide consensus that, as a rule, organizations could be doing a more effective and efficient job of training people. The main failure, it appears, is the reluctance of management to authorize proper planning and evaluation efforts on the assumption that the needs are obvious and effectiveness is inherent in the program. Nothing could be farther from the truth. Without planning, the training is likely to be irrelevant to the real needs of the organization; without evaluation, it is likely to be totally useless. Training must be considered as but one of a whole host of interrelated system functions. To be effective, it must be consistent and compatible with management philosophies, selection policies, job descriptions, performance evaluation procedures, and many other facets of the system. Considered in isolation, it is doomed to failure.

Training failures have, in part, given rise to another approach to organizational change that follows a model of planned change—organizational development (OD). OD represents an orderly approach to the problem of initiating change in organizations. It involves planning, implementation, and evaluation activities, just as should any training program. By and large, it seeks to change the organization by changing the opinions and attitudes of people—usually managers—in the direction of the participative management philosophy. It may also, however, involve changing other aspects of the organization as well. Thus, it is a systems approach.

NOTES

1. Hinrichs, J. R. (1976). Personnel training. In M. Dunnette (Ed.). *Handbook of industrial and organizational psychology*. Skokie, Ill.: Rand McNally.
2. Wexley, K. N. (1984). Personnel training. *Annual Review of Psychology, 35,* 519–551.
3. Lusterman, S. (1977). *Education in industry*. New York: The Conference Board.
4. Ibid.
5. Goldstein, I. L. (1974). *Training: Program development and evaluation*. Monterey, Calif.: Brooks/Cole Publishing.
6. Campbell, J. P. (1971). Personnel training and development. *Annual Review of Psychology, 22,* 565–602.
7. Goldstein. *Training*.
8. McGehee, W., & Thayer, P. W. (1961). *Training in business and industry*. New York: John Wiley & Sons.
9. Folley, J. D., Jr. (1969). Determining training needs of department store sales personnel. *Training and Development Journal, 23,* 24–27.

10. Goldstein. *Training,* p. 28.

11. McGehee, W. (1958). Are we using what we know about training? Learning theory and training. *Personnel Psychology, 11,* 1–12.

12. Gagne, R. M. (1962). Military training and principles of learning. *American Psychologist, 17,* 83–91.

13. Komaki, J., Heinzmann, A. T., & Lawson, L. (1980). Effects of training and feedback: Component analysis of a behavioral safety program. *Journal of Applied Psychology, 65,* 261–270.

14. Nemeroff, W. F., & Cosentino, J. (1979). Utilizing feedback and goal setting to increase performance appraisal interviewer skills of managers. *Academy of Management Journal, 22,* 566–576.

15. Gagne, Military training and principles of learning, 83–91.

16. Campbell. Personnel training and development, 565.

17. Folley. Determining training needs; Buchler, R. E. (1969). Job-related behavior rating scale. *Training and Development Journal, 23,* 14–21.

18. Bass, B. M., & Vaughn, J. A. (1966). Training in industry: The management of learning (pp. 131–132). Belmont, Calif.: Wadsworth.

19. Hunt, D. M., & Michael, C. (1983). Mentorship: A career training and development tool. *Academy of Management Review, 8,* 475–485.

20. Roche, G. R. (1979). Much ado about mentors. *Harvard Business Review, 57,* 17–28.

21. Stumpf, S. A., & London, M. (1981). Management promotions: Individual and organization factors influencing the decision process. *Academy of Management Review, 6,* 539–549.

22. Randolph, W. A., & Posner, B. Z. (1979). Designing meaningful learning situations: A contingency decision-tree approach. *Academy of Management Review, 4,* 459–467.

23. Skinner, B. F. (1961). Teaching machines. *Scientific American, November, 3.*

24. Carroll, S. J., Jr., Paine, F. T., & Ivancevich, J. J. (1972). The relative effectiveness of training methods—Expert opinion and research. *Personnel Psychology, 25,* 495–510.

25. Bugelski, B. R. (1971). *The psychology of learning applied to teaching.* Indianapolis, Ind.: Bobbs-Merrill.

26. Ibid., p. 162.

27. Miner, J. B. (1961). Management development and attitude change. *Personnel Administration, 24,* 21–26.

28. Atkinson, R. C., & Wilson, H. A. (Eds.). (1969). *Computer-assisted instruction: A book of readings.* New York: Academic Press.

29. Campbell. Personnel training and development, 565.

30. Holt, H. O. (1963). An exploratory study of the use of a self-selection instruction program in basic electricity. In J. L. Hughes (Ed.). *Programmed learning: A critical evaluation.* Chicago: Educational Methods.

31. Nash, A. N., Muczyk, J. P., & Vittori, F. L. (1971). The relative practical effectiveness of programmed instruction. *Personnel Psychology, 24,* 397–418; Welsh, P., Antoinetti, J. A., & Thayer, P. W. (1965). An industrywide study of programmed instruction. *Journal of Applied Psychology, 49,* 61–73.

32. McKeachie, W. J. (1974). Instructional psychology. *Annual Review of Psychology, 25,* 186.

33. Goldstein. *Training.*

34. Edwards, D. D., Hahn, C. P., & Fleishman, E. A. (1977). Evaluation of laboratory methods for the study of driver behavior: Relations between simulator and street performance. *Journal of Applied Psychology, 62,* 559–566.

35. Williams, B. H., Roscoe, S. N., & Williges, R. C. (1972). *Synthetic flight training revisited.* (Tech. Rep. ARL-72-21/AFOSR-72-10). Savoy, Ill.: Aviation Research Laboratory.

36. Neuhauser, J. J. (1976). Business games have failed. *Academy of Management Review, 1,* 124–129.

37. Bugelski. *Psychology of learning.*

38. Argyris, C. (1980). Some limitations of the case method: Experiences in a management development program. *Academy of Management Review, 5,* 291–298.

39. Berger, M. A. (1983). In defense of the case method: A reply to Argyris. *Academy of Management Review, 8,* 329–333.

40. White, S. E., Dittrich, J. E., & Lang, J. R. (1980). The effects of group decision-making processes and problem situation complexity on implementation attempts. *Administrative Science Quarterly, 25,* 428–440.

41. Kidron, A. G. (1977). The effectiveness of experiential methods in training and education: The case of role playing. *Academy of Management Review, 2,* 490–495.

42. Bandura, A. (Ed.). (1974). *Psychological modeling: Conflicting theories.* Hawthorne, N.Y.: Aldine Publishing.

43. Goldstein, A. P., & Sorcher, M. (1974). *Changing supervisor behavior.* Elmsford, N.Y.: Pergamon Press.

44. McGhee, W., & Tullar, W. L. (1978). A note on evaluating behavior modification and behavior modeling as industrial training techniques. *Personnel Psychology, 31,* 477–484.

45. Latham, G. D., & Saari, L. M. (1979). Application of social learning theory to training supervisors through behavioral modeling. *Journal of Applied Psychology, 64,* 239–246.

46. Decker, P. J. (1979). Modesty and caution in reviewing behavior modeling: A reply to McGehee and Tullar. *Personnel Psychology, 32,* 399–400.

47. Randolph & Posner. Designing meaningful learning situations in management.

48. Kolb, D. A. (1980). Experiential learning theory and the learning style inventory: A reply to Freedman and Stumpf. *Academy of Management Review, 5,* 445–447.

49. Freedman, R. D., & Stumpf, S. A. (1978). What can one learn from the learning style inventory. *Academy of Management Journal, 21,* 275–282.

50. Eden, D., & Ravid, G. (1982). Pygmalion versus self-expectancy: Effects of instructor- and self-expectancy on trainee performance. *Organizational Behavior and Human Performance, 30,* 351–364.

51. Dossett, D. L., & Hulvershorn, P. (1983). Increasing technical training efficiency: Peer training via computer-assisted instruction. *Journal of Applied Psychology, 68,* 552–558.

52. Kirkpatrick, D. L. (1977). Evaluating training programs: Evidence versus proof. *Training and Development Journal, 31,* 9–12.

53. McKinney, A. C. (1957). Progressive levels in the evaluation of training programs. *Personnel, 34,* 72–77.

54. See, for example, Campbell, D. T., & Stanley, J. C. (1963). *Experimental and quasiexperimental designs for research.* Skokie, Ill.: Rand McNally.

55. McClelland, D. C. (1974). That urge to achieve. In D. A. Kolb, I. M. Rubin, & J. M. McIntyre (Eds.). *Organizational psychology: A book of readings.* Englewood Cliffs, N.J.: Prentice-Hall.

56. Ibid., pp. 152–153.

57. Durand, D. E. (1975). Effects of achievement motivation and skill training on the entrepreneurial behavior of black businessmen. *Organizational Behavior and Human Performance, 14,* 76–90; Timmons, J. A. (1971). Black is beautiful—Is it bountiful? *Harvard Business Review, 49*(6), 81–94.

58. Jackson, K. W., & Shea, D. J. (1972). Motivation training in perspective. In W. R. Nord (Ed.). *Concepts and controversy in organizational behavior.* Santa Monica, Calif.: Goodyear Publishing.

59. Scandura, T. A., & Graen, G. B. (1984). Moderating effects of initial leader-member exchange status on the effects of a leadership intervention. *Journal of Applied Psychology, 69,* 428–436.

60. Fleishman, E. A. (1955). Leadership climate, human relations training, and supervisory behavior. *Personnel Psychology, 6,* 205–222.

61. Fiedler, F. E., Chemers, M. J., & Maher, L. (1976). *Improving leadership effectiveness: The leader-match concept.* New York: John Wiley & Sons.

62. Fiedler, F. E., & Mahar, L. (1979). The effectiveness of contingency training: Validation of leader-match. *Personnel Psychology, 32,* 45–62.

63. Goldstein, I. (1980). Training in work organizations. *Annual Review of Psychology, 31,* 229–272.

64. Buchanan, P. E. (1971). Sensitivity, or laboratory, training in industry. *Sociological Inquiry, 41,* 217–225.

65. See, for example, Campbell, J. P., & Dunnette, M. D. (1968). Effectiveness of T-group experiences in managerial training and development. *Psychological Bulletin, 70,* 73–104.

66. Ibid., 211–212.

67. Underwood, W. J. (1965). Evaluation of laboratory method training. *Training Directors Journal, 19,* 34–40.

68. Woodman, R. W., & Sherwood, J. J. (1980). The role of team development in organizational effectiveness: A critical review. *Psychological Bulletin, 88,* 166–186.

69. Hartley, D., Roback, H. B., & Abramowitz, S. I. (1976). Deterioration effects in encounter groups. *American Psychologist, 31,* 247–212.

70. Kirchner, W. K. (1965). Book review of A. J. Marrow's *Behind the executive mask.* In *Personnel Psychology, 18,* 211–212.

71. Bernardin, J. J., & Buckley, M. R. (1981). Strategies in rater training. *Academy of Management Review, 6,* 205–212.

72. Goldstein. *Training.*

73. Hodgson, J. D., & Brenner, M. H. (1968). Successful experience: Training hard-core unemployed. *Harvard Business Review, 46,* 148–156.

74. Campbell. Personnel training and development, 587.

75. French, W. L., Bell, C. H., & Zawacki, R. A. (Eds.). (1978). *Organization development: Theory, practice, and research.* Plano, Tex.: Business Publications.

76. Schmuck, R. A., & Miles, M. B. (Eds.). (1971). Improving schools through organizational development: An overview. Reprinted from Richard A. Schmuck and Matthew B. Miles (Eds.), *Organization development in the schools.* San Diego, Calif.: University Associates. Used with permission.

77. Ritchie, J. B., & Thompson, P. (1984). *Organization and people: Readings, cases, and exercises in organizational behavior* (3d ed.). St. Paul, Minn.: West Publishing.

78. Davis, L. E., Cherns, A. B., & Associates. (1975). *The quality of working life: Vol. 1. Cases and commentary* (pp. 274–275). New York: Free Press.

79. Likert, R. (1961). *New patterns of management.* New York: McGraw-Hill.

80. Davis et al. *Quality of working life.*

81. Katz, D., & Kahn, R. L. (1978). *The social psychology of organizations.* New York: John Wiley & Sons.

82. Guion, R. M. (1973). A note on organizational climate. *Organizational Behavior and Human Performance, 9,* 120–125.

83. James, L. R., & Jones, A. P. (1974). Organizational climate: A review of theory and research. *Psychological Bulletin, 81,* 1096–1112.

9

External Relationships

Our perspective on the organization has thus far been exclusively *inward-looking*: We have considered only those aspects of its operation that involve its own features and those of its members. While it is true that an important function of any organization is keeping a group of people constructively occupied and meeting various needs, this is clearly not its ultimate purpose. To survive, it must also have some impact on society *outside* its own boundaries. Similarly, modern systems theory recognizes that the organization draws from and is profoundly influenced by outside forces.

Although we do not intend to explore all or even most of these "boundary-spanning" relations in this text, the present chapter introduces the reader to three externally oriented topics that are particularly relevant to I/O psychology: the *consumer, engineering,* and *organized labor* domains. The first two, which were described briefly in Chapter 1, are "officially" recognized as part of the I/O field, whereas the third is an important topic in personnel management that has not yet received the attention it deserves from psychology. Our field has been much more concerned with the way employees are managed internally than with external organizations, such as labor unions, to which people often feel a considerably stronger affiliation. Naturally, principles of human motivation, leadership, group process, and so forth apply to organizations generally—labor unions or professional societies as much so as employers. However, the fact that unionized employees are under the dual control of union and employee systems presents some special problems that we shall introduce under the heading of *union-management relations*.

CONSUMER PSYCHOLOGY

All organizations—industrial, charitable, nonprofit, governmental, or whatever—exist to provide society with some combination of goods and services. Each, therefore, has a product and a target population that, in the broadest sense, "consume" that product. Thus, in addition to the obvious marketplace relationships, the congregation of a church is the primary consumer population for its theological or spiritual product; children under the age of 18 are the primary consumers of the educational product offered by the public school system; and the ordinary citizen consumes the roads, medicare programs, wars, income tax laws, and all the products of government organization.

Consumer psychology is concerned, very broadly, with people as consumers of goods and services. Its central objective, therefore, is explaining consumer behavior; for example, describing what sort of choices people make, under what circumstances, and for what reasons. What determines whether or not a person will buy a new car? If he or she does decide to buy one, what determines whether it will be a Ford, Plymouth, Jaguar, or VW? Factors of many different kinds are considered in dealing with such questions, including marketing factors, advertising effects, economic conditions, and population characteristics.

Naturally, there are several principal reasons for seeking this knowledge, and each represents a distinct emphasis within the field. Foremost among these is the *marketing and advertising* emphasis. Organizations would like to be able to anticipate consumer behavior patterns and to influence consumer choices in directions favorable to their products. For obvious reasons, this has long been the dominant emphasis.

A second identifiable emphasis stems from purely scientific goals. Consuming goods and services is, after all, an important aspect of human behavior and, as such, is worthy of study in its own right. This orientation is of more recent origin and still represents but a small part of the field. The growing popular interest in consumerism, however, may serve to stimulate more research on the consumer qua consumer.[1] It has certainly stimulated a number of areas of political and legal activity that, together, have improved the consumer's lot.

A third emphasis, which is even smaller, concerns the relationship between what consumers think or do and general economic trends. This perspective, which is sometimes called *economic psychology*, has been championed for years by George Katona and his associates at the University of Michigan Survey Research Center. Katona's group has been able to show, for example, that durable good expenditures in the United States and western European countries can be predicted several months in advance on the basis of consumer attitudes.[2]

In the pages to follow we will encounter illustrations of each emphasis—the reader should have no difficulty recognizing them. Our discussion will not, however, be organized around the *objectives* of consumer research. Instead, it will focus on what consumer psychology *is*: the variables and relationships that presumably govern human consuming behavior. We shall begin, therefore, with a crude overview of the whole constellation of relevant concepts.

Overview

Consumer psychology may be looked upon as an attempt to describe how people behave as consumers as a function of several classes of interacting factors or variables. An illustration of the kinds of variables and relationships that have been emphasized appears in Figure 9–1. Starting with the *environment*, we have *marketing* and *product* variables, which include everything that a product is and everything that is done to make it accepted by, attractive to, satisfying for, or available to the consumer. The influence of such variables, together with that of *social* and *cultural* factors, operates directly upon the consumer, helping to shape perceptions, beliefs, wants, attitudes, and knowledge of the consumer regarding the product through a combination of *cognitive* and *affective* processes. These, plus the more enduring *trait* characteristics, in turn, play a major role in the *behavior* exhibited by the consumer: preferences among products, actual or intended choices, timing of purchases, tendency to try new products or stick with old ones. Finally, the consequences of consumer behavior are seen both in the individual, as he or she experiences satisfaction or dissatisfaction with the choice, and in the general economy as it responds to the aggregate of such decisions. Of course, these fairly direct consequences also may contribute to further changes in both the person and the environment: people may come to see the product differently; marketers may change their strategies.

This simple diagram is intended only as a means of guiding the reader through the diverse content of the consumer field; it does not represent a comprehensive model of consumer behavior. Various models of the latter sort have been proposed and, as the one illustrated in Figure 9–2 shows, they present an extremely complicated picture.[3] We shall not attempt to explore all the components and functions suggested by such models. Many of them are quite speculative anyway. Nevertheless, they do serve to illustrate several important points. First, consumer behavior is not simply determined. Therefore, a great deal of the attention of both marketers and researchers is directed toward processes or relationships that are quite peripheral to the act of purchasing. For example, the goal of many advertising campaigns is to increase consumer *awareness* of a product or to create more positive *attitudes* toward it in the belief that more favorable *person states* will produce increased sales. Similarly, both scientists and marketers study population trends with an eye toward shifts in the definition of markets. One current trend is the rapid growth in the older segment of our population: the over-55 *gray market*, as it is called, already numbers over 45 million in the United States and is growing at

FIGURE 9–1   Classes of Variables Involved in Consumer Psychology Considered in Its Broadest Sense

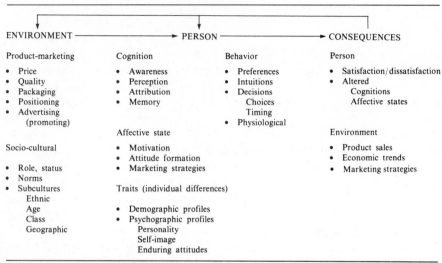

ENVIRONMENT ──────────► PERSON ──────────► CONSEQUENCES			
Product-marketing	Cognition	Behavior	Person
• Price	• Awareness	• Preferences	• Satisfaction/dissatisfaction
• Quality	• Perception	• Intuitions	• Altered
• Packaging	• Attribution	• Decisions	Cognitions
• Positioning	• Memory	Choices	Affective states
• Advertising		Timing	
(promoting)		• Physiological	
	Affective state		Environment
Socio-cultural	• Motivation		• Product sales
	• Attitude formation		• Economic trends
• Role, status	• Marketing strategies		• Marketing strategies
• Norms			
• Subcultures	Traits (individual differences)		
Ethnic			
Age	• Demographic profiles		
Class	• Psychographic profiles		
Geographic	Personality		
	Self-image		
	Enduring attitudes		

twice the rate of the overall population.[4] The reason for studying such groups is that they are believed to represent somewhat homogeneous patterns of needs, attitudes, and buying habits. As we proceed through the chapter, we will encounter many other cases of this kind in which the link between the object of study and actual consumer behavior is either remote or assumed.

A second point suggested by Figure 9–2 is that the consumer field has no unified body of theory. Rather, each of its various facets draws upon its own set of concepts and principles. For example, one of the more prominent theories deals exclusively with the relationship between *attitudes* and *behavioral intentions*. Another looks only at how people process advertising messages. Still another considers the way in which they go about choosing among relatively comparable product alternatives. As the material in this section unfolds, the reader would do well to refer back periodically to see where in the total picture each concept belongs. For this purpose, our simplified Figure 9–1 should suffice.

The third point implied by Figure 9–2 is that there are many junctures in any model of consumer behavior where measurement is required. Quite often, these measures leave something to be desired: The researcher must settle for what he can get rather than what he would like. Consumer behavior is itself difficult to quantify and even more difficult to relate unambiguously to causal measures. Some advertisers have expressed considerable disenchantment with traditional ways of quantifying such things as the effectiveness of an ad or the size and composition of a media audience.[5] In the words of one frustrated executive: "For a

FIGURE 9–2 Engel and Blackwell Consumer Behavior Model

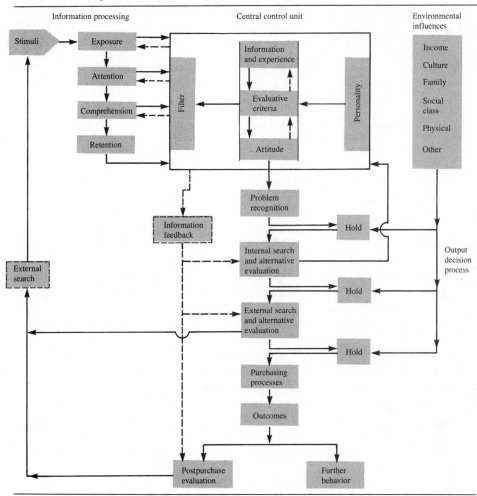

Information processing   Central control unit   Environmental influences

SOURCE: Engel, J. F., Kollat, D. T., & Blackwell, R. D. (1973). *Consumer Behavior* (2d ed.), (p. 58). New York: Holt, Rinehart & Winston.

business that is almost totally centered on what goes into a selling idea, we seemingly by design measure everything but the message in its selling habitat."[6] Because of these difficulties, we will be obliged to look closely at methodology.

The moral of this brief overview, then, is that consumer behavior results from many *interacting* causal factors. When we look at particular variables and relationships, as indeed we must to make the discussion manageable, we must recognize that we are dealing with *artificial* segments. Advertising does not operate completely independently of the name and price of a product; neither is this combination of factors likely to have the same impact on one market segment as on another. With this word of caution, it is perhaps safe to proceed with our illustration of variables, theories, and methods that together comprise the field of consumer psychology. Our attention will be limited primarily to the *person* segment of Figure 9–1 rather than trying to cover the vast literatures on marketing and advertising research and practice.

Uses of Person Information

Much attention has been given to the *description* of consumers for the purpose of predicting how they will behave in the marketplace or how they will respond to marketing variables. There are several distinct ways of approaching this task. First, in the tradition of scientific psychological inquiry, one may examine the *general principles* relating human mental processes or states to consumer behavior. How do the laws of selection attention or learning or motivation affect a person's reaction to a commercial message? How does a person's intelligence or need for dominance affect which brand is chosen? This, of course, is an *internal state* emphasis.

Second, one may take an *individual difference* orientation, attempting to segment the population into more or less homogeneous consumer clusters on the basis of relatively stable *traits*. This has been done on the basis of *demographic* features (age, sex, income, education level, ethnic group, etc.), *psychographic* features (personality traits, firmly held beliefs and attitudes including those regarding one's self, etc.),[7] and *involvement* or *benefit* profiles (i.e., similar patterns of association with or utility for particular kinds of messages, or product features).

Consumer segmentation has itself been used several different ways. For example, market research is often aimed at comparing the consuming tendencies of different market segments (ages 18–25, urban blacks, housewives, commuters, etc.). Advertising campaigns are frequently pitched to a particular market segment based upon assumed (or demonstrated) common features of that population. Advertising media (magazines, television, radio, billboards) sell exposure on the basis of particular audience composition as well as overall reach. One would hardly want to buy time on a daytime TV soap opera to sell carpenter's tools or auto parts, or a spot on a football telecast to sell women's cosmetics. In other words, market segmentation is used both in the *study* and attempted *manipulation* of consumer behavior.

A third way in which person variables are used is through application of general psychological *theories* to marketing decisions. Assumptions are made about human motivation or perception in the development of products and advertising appeals. Probably the most notable (or notorious) illustration of this approach is the use of psychoanalytic theory in advertising. Freud's psychoanalytic theory held that much of human conscious experience and behavior is the overt expression of unconscious motivational processes. Thus people buy things or respond to marketing appeals not for the obvious values offered but to satisfy deeper, hidden, perhaps even *suppressed* motives. Coffee is not drunk for taste, thirst satisfaction, or stimulation but because it represents companionship. Cigarettes provide oral gratification. Automobiles signify initiation into adulthood. Naturally, if one subscribed to such ideas about consumer motivation, one would direct a marketing appeal to these hidden motives. Fortunately, the popularity of this *depth* approach has waned considerably since reaching its zenith in the 1950s. One still sees ads in which the obvious intent is to exploit hidden motives through the use of sexual symbols. More often, however, when sex is used to sell, it is done blatantly— nothing hidden about it.

Each of these three uses of person variables merits closer inspection. Since theoretical issues permeate both of the other orientations, we shall organize the discussion around illustrative affective, cognitive, and individual difference topics.

Affective States

1. Motivation. As we saw in Chapter 3, the fact that behavior happens at all, and is directed toward specific ends, is frequently attributed to internal *motive* states. Consuming is clearly directed behavior. Therefore, it isn't surprising that those interested in either understanding or manipulating consumer behavior should look to motivational concepts just as do those who try to explain effort expenditure. If people are driven to seek out or to choose those products, experiences, and conditions that are most likely to satisfy existing needs, then it is obviously useful to know what those needs are. Moreover, since learning plays a big part in the definition of specific motivators, it is also useful to know how needs can be shaped or even created.

Early psychoanalytic theories, as we said, turned out to be difficult to test in either the laboratory or the marketplace and hence were of little practical value. It has proven considerably more profitable to take expressed (or directly inferred) need states at face value, superficial though they may be. In some of our rapidly growing cities, for example, citizens are becoming increasingly annoyed with the inadequacy of public services such as fire and police protection and transportation. Were they asked, they would probably express a strong need for improvements. Now, we could take this simple expression either as an indication that people wanted better services or as a symptom of some complex web of underlying frustrations and insecurities. Were we interested in promoting a tax increase we could direct our appeal either to the surface needs that we can describe, or the hidden ones at which, even if they exist, we can only guess. The tendency today, as we said, is to go with what we can measure.

Of course, it is an oversimplification to suggest that motives are either hidden or tied to specific and obvious goal objects. Within the limitations of our measuring instruments (usually questionnaires), it is possible to search for dimensions of human motivation that have considerably greater generality. To continue the previous example, we might find that there is a general *anxiety* component underlying all three of the expressed needs: The "average citizen" feels vulnerable and helpless in the face of what is perceived as a growing threat to security. Were this the case, we might consider an appeal addressing the anxiety and promising alleviation contingent upon the tax increase. Some very effective—as well as reprehensible—advertising campaigns have centered around the creation or intensification of anxieties.[8] We will probably never know how much psychological damage has been visited upon the American teenager by ads aimed at increasing their already excessive concern over personal appearance and peer acceptance.

Consumer psychology thus invokes the concept of motive or need states chiefly to help predict how messages or consumables will be received by the relevant public. Not surprisingly, therefore, the emphasis has been upon fairly specific motive *content*: identifying what particular groups of people need, want, or prefer under specified conditions (e.g., in the store, in the present economy, while relaxing with friends).

For this reason, the principal method used to identify and measure need states has been the self-report questionnaire as administered through large-scale *survey research projects*.[9] Of course, such direct methods always run the risk of "social desirability" bias (i.e., intentional distortion due to the respondent's unwillingness to admit to unseemly motives), and there is still a segment of the motivation research community that probes for unconscious motives using all sorts of esoteric approaches: psychoanalytic *depth interviews*; *projective techniques*; small-group discussion sessions (*focus group interviews*); and *physiological* responses (such as the pupillary response, which presumably indicates a person's level of interest in a stimulus by the extent to which the pupils in the eyes dilate).

In Chapter 3 we learned that current theories of work motivation emphasize *process* rather than content, trying to explain how motivation serves its energizing and directing functions. We also learned that most of these theories (i.e., path-goal, VIE, goal-setting, and equity models) rely heavily on cognitive elements such as *expectations* and *beliefs*, and that needs or incentives are only part of the story. Analogous models have been applied to consumer behavior as well.

Two general kinds that can be distinguished are those with a *communication* emphasis and those with a *decision* emphasis. As an example of the former, McGuire's model suggests that a message (such as an advertisement) passes through a hierarchy of processes on its way to a possible influence on the consumer's behavior (such as a product purchase).[10]

First, it has some chance of influencing *cognitive* processes (being attended to, perceived, comprehended); if comprehended, it has a chance of influencing *attitudes* toward the target (concept, product); if the attitude is affected, it may affect *behavior*. Motivation would presumably serve to affect the odds at each step in the process. A message about something desired would more likely be received, viewed favorably, and responded to than a neutral message.

From the *decision-theory* standpoint, consuming behavior is viewed as a conscious choice among options, each of which, from the viewpoint of the potential consumer, consists of an aggregate of expected consequences. What a person is willing to do (e.g., how much he is willing to pay) in order to acquire something, or whether he will choose that something in preference to another, is dictated by his weighted composite of its desirable and undesirable features. Using this logic, the issue becomes one of measuring the features (attributes), the weights, and the rules by which the consumer arrives at his composite—and his decision.[11] Motivation, then, becomes translated into the concept of *utility*. To the extent that we can model the processes by which individuals or groups arrive at utility judgments, we move that much closer to understanding how their motivational systems work, and to being able to predict their choice behavior. If, for example, we could show that there are only five relevant considerations in a person's utility for coffee, that perceived quality is weighted more heavily than the other four combined, and that the aggregate utility is a simple linear combination of the five weights, we would have a fairly good idea of what motivates her to buy a particular brand. We would also realize that it would be fruitless to use price as an inducement to buy a brand that she considered of lesser quality, although she might be persuaded by price to try a brand that she saw as less desirable for one of the other three reasons.

One could perhaps argue that neither the utility concept nor the communication model really belongs in a discussion of *motivation*. Our reason for mentioning them here is simply to show that *process* models (other than the old psychoanalytic kind) have a place in modern consumer psychology even though the *content view* has been the chief vehicle by which *motivation* concepts per se have been applied.

2. Attitudes. Like a motive, an attitude is an hypothesized internal state used by theorists to help explain human behavior. In fact, the two concepts are very closely related if one takes the broad view of motivation that we have. The main difference is that attitudes necessarily have a cognitive component (whereas motives can be hidden) and they are object-oriented (*pulling* rather than *pushing* behavior). Also, they are usually seen as less directly linked to action than are motive states. Attitudes have a distinct *object of reference* and involve some degree of positive or negative *affect*.[12] If, for example, a person were said to hold a strongly negative attitude toward the Democratic party, we would expect that person to believe certain unfavorable things about the party, to have generally bad feelings whenever confronted with it, and to show some inclination to vote against Democrats. Thus many theorists look upon *beliefs, feelings,* and *action tendencies* as the main components of attitudes.[13]

For purposes of our present discussion, we have chosen to classify attitudes under the *state* as well as the *trait* categories. This is because they can vary considerably in permanence: some, such as the political kind, tend to be firmly entrenched and stable; others, such as attitudes towards brands of toothpaste, are more easily replaced. Both ends of the continuum are important to the marketer but for different reasons. Permanent attitudes (traits) constitute a basis for market definition and segmentation; the more unstable ones (states) constitute a target for potential influence and change.

Naturally, our present interest in attitudes, like motives, stems ultimately from the action-tendency component: Will they or will they not buy the product? Although theorists disagree on questions of how directly and consistently beliefs and feelings generate action, most recognize that there is at least some relationship between these components. Thus if one can measure what people believe and how they feel about something — and how strongly — it should be possible to make some prediction about their behavior toward that object. Similarly, one wishing to change their behavior might seek ways to change their beliefs and feelings. This is, of course, a greatly oversimplified statement of modern thinking on how attitudes affect behavior; still, it captures the essential logic of most of the applications and research in the consumer field. Attitudes are measured, and attempts are made to appeal to or change them, in the belief that they do, in fact, have an action-tendency component.

It is important to recognize that products have many attributes, each of which may be the object of somewhat independent attitudes. Further, attributes may differ in *relevance* (or importance or motivational potential) for the consumer as a function of a lot of other factors. For example, gasoline economy was for years a far less relevant attribute for most car buyers than horsepower, styling, comfort, or initial purchase price. Even though people might have had a positive attitude toward low fuel cost, it was of little consequence in their car purchasing behavior. With the threat of fuel shortages and the drastic increases in gasoline prices that occurred during the late 1970s, however, attitudes toward fuel economy became extremely salient. People began buying small, fuel-efficient cars. This response, coupled with a worldwide glut in the oil market that stabilized prices, rekindled the consumers' demand for comfort, styling, horsepower, etc., which in turn produced the current return to popularity of larger cars. If one wishes to predict (or influence) buying behavior on the basis of attitudes, therefore, one must be careful to weight all the salient attributes. It is at this point that the attitude and motivation concepts merge into *utility* measurement.

Far and away the most influential view on how attitudes influence consumer behavior is Fishbein's model,[14] which incorporates elements of the multiattribute utility notion together with a social motivation component to predict behavioral *intentions*. In its simplest form it is expressed:

$$B \sim I = (A_B)W_1 + (SN)W_2$$

Where the intentions (I) are seen as closely, but not perfectly, linked to actual behavior (B); A_B, the attitudinal component, is a weighted average of the expected personal consequences of that behavior; SN, the social motivation component, is the product of normative beliefs and compliance motivation, and the W terms are empirically determined weights. In other words, the idea is that a person's measured intention to act (e.g., buy a product, vote for a candidate) is determined by what he thinks it will get for him plus the combination of how society views that act and how important social approval is to him. If, for example, you were an auto worker in Detroit, you might consider a Japanese car your best buy (an attitude based on your expected return on investment). However, you know that society (the people whose opinions you care about) frowns on buying foreign cars, and you are not exactly thrilled at the prospect of being snubbed at work, ridiculed at the union hall, and having your windshield smashed whenever you park your car (i.e., you care a *lot*). Therefore, when the consumer survey lady comes around, you tell her that it is your *intention* to buy a Pontiac. But shortly thereafter, you are laid off. So instead, you take your life savings, buy a Toyota, and head for Tennessee, the site of the new Toyota-GM plant (intentions do not *always* foretell behaviors).

Much research has been generated by Fishbein's model with somewhat mixed results.[15] On the one hand, the weight of evidence seems to support its general ability to predict intentions. On the other, questions have been raised concerning the independence of the attitudinal and social components, the validity and usefulness of an *intentions* measure, and various other technical aspects of the model. At this point, it seems fair to say that few other theories have contributed as much—directly or indirectly—to our understanding of the relationship between attitudes and consumer behavior.

Attitudes are generally measured by one form or another of self-report devices (such as a questionnaire), which, as we saw in Chapter 3, are all subject to various kinds of bias. The most troublesome, from a practical standpoint, are *social desirability* errors—answers that reflect how the respondent thinks he *should* respond rather than what he really *believes*. Fishbein's model, of course, treats this as a formal element in the prediction of intentions, not as a source of measurement error. If, however, one is trying to measure attitudes per se, the social factor is a problem no matter what status we give it.

Despite the measurement problems, attitudes are at times reasonably predictive of consumer behavior particularly when "the attitude is specific rather than general, . . . the connection is direct, . . . and the attitude can lead to one and only one behavior."[16] Achenbaum, for example, found close agreement between consumer ratings of product quality and incidence of usage, as illustrated in Figure 9–3.[17] He also reported that, as one might expect, the attitudes of people who never tried a product tend to be clustered around an average rating in the shape of a normal distribution.

Others have shown that market shares of various brands and shifts in these shares are also predictable to an extent from prior attitude measures.[18] So, as we saw earlier, are overall trends in consumer spending. The Michigan Survey Research Center has been able to anticipate both aggregate and individual tendencies to spend or save discretionary income on the basis of answers to six attitudinal survey questions: (1) how well off the family is compared to the previous year, (2) how good it expects its financial situation to be during the coming year, (3) its one-year expectations regarding business conditions, (4) its longer-range economic outlook, (5) its appraisal of buying conditions for household goods and clothing, and (6) its expectations regarding prices. The effect, however, is not a simple one in that attitudes are more predictive under some conditions than others. Particularly good prediction is obtained, for example, when the economic environment is unstable and people hold widely different opinions about its future.[19]

Research on attitudes and consumer behavior ranges far beyond the mere demonstration that the two are correlated, as we saw in the case of Fishbein's model. Many studies have also been done to test specific theoretical notions about the way attitude systems *change*. For the most part, this research has been concerned with the implications for advertising and marketing of *communication processes* (how people are persuaded on the basis of information) *need fulfillment* (what roles attitudes play in satisfying basic needs), and *structure* (how attitudes are organized).

As an example of a communication issue, consider the case of *subliminal advertising*. Introduced in the 1950s as an effective way to manipulate attitudes, stimulate motives, and influence behavior—all without conscious awareness—the technique aroused a storm of controversy. The early studies suggested that messages to "buy popcorn" or "buy Coke" flashed on a movie screen so briefly that people could not report having seen them nonetheless resulted in increased sales of these products during intermission. If, in fact, one could exercise control in this fashion, there would be justifiable cause for alarm, for consumers would be at the

FIGURE 9-3   Relationship between Attitudes and Usage for Selected Brands of Consumer Products: A. Cigarette Brand, B. Deodorant Brand; C. Gasoline Brand; and D. Laxative Brand

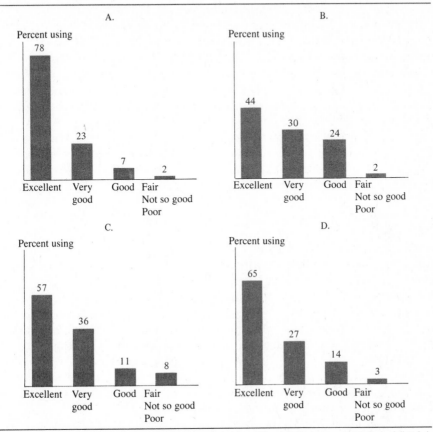

SOURCE: From Achenbaum, A. A. (1968). Knowledge is a thing called measurement. In L. Adler & I. Crespi (Eds.) *Attitude research at sea (pp. 113–115).* Chicago: American Marketing Association.

mercy of unscrupulous advertisers, despots, or anyone else with a special interest to promote and an access to the electronic media.

Fortunately, the early claims have never been substantiated. Admittedly, few of the experiments on subliminal perception—pro or con— have been adequately controlled. Still, the weight of evidence suggests that if viewers can be influenced subliminally it is probably a very trivial effect—certainly far less efficient than direct, conscious appeals. And, even if it did work, advertisers realize that its potential benefits would not be worth the public outcry that its use would generate. As an ironic postcript to this story, recent work in the area of human cognition has demonstrated fairly convincingly that information presented at exposures too brief to permit any measurable indication of conscious awareness *can* influence subsequent mental events.[20] How this happens is still a puzzle. But the fact that it can restores subliminal influence on a theoretical, if not practical, possibility.

A theoretical notion concerning the organization or structure of attitude systems that has had some popularity in the consumer context is *cognitive dissonance*, which we encountered in Chapter 3. The reader will recall this concept as the hypothesized desire people have to be consistent in their thinking. When situations arise in which they find themselves holding conflicting attitudes about the same object, as when a product they consider inferior is recommended by someone they admire, they are likely to change one or both attitudes to resolve the dissonance. For example, the admired person may be conceded to be misinformed about the product (and therefore somewhat less admirable than before), or the product may be reevaluated as somewhat less inferior than originally thought.

One common dissonant situation is that in which a consumer must choose between two virtually equivalent products. Since her attitudes toward them are about the same but she must behave as though one were distinctly better, she tends to alter her attitudes in the direction of her decision following the choice: The chosen alternative is seen as more favorable; the rejected one as more unfavorable than before.[21] A closely related situation arises when the consumer buys something without much inducement or product information. Once again, her choice is not easily justified cognitively, and dissonance is hypothesized to result.[22]

Dissonance theory has stimulated a great deal of research within the consumer field, most of it aimed at defining dissonant situations (as in the above illustrations) and their possible role in attitude change.[23] It is difficult to draw any sweeping generalizations from this research for reasons discussed earlier: There are so many ways for a person to reduce dissonance that it is hard to say how the individual consumer will handle the problem in any given situation. Recently, however, improved ways of measuring dissonance have appeared that may greatly enhance the theoretical and practical value of the concept.[24] In any case, it is useful to know that consumer decisions involving cognitively comparable alternatives (which is probably more often the rule than the exception in everyday purchases) are likely to generate a condition that sets the stage for some kind of attitude change. With this in mind, it should be possible to design better studies to answer specific marketing questions.

All things considered, attitude variables, particularly when combined with motivational and perceptual considerations, offer considerable promise for the practical understanding of consumer behavior. It is becoming quite clear, however, that attitude-behavior relationships are not simple enough to justify the assumption that measuring how people *feel* about a product is tantamount to indicating whether or not they will *buy* it. Despite this fact, attitude measurements constitute the *only* criterion for marketing decisions in many instances.

Cognitive Processes

Other, more narrowly focused person conditions also have a bearing on consumer behavior (often in conjunction with motives, attitudes, and the like). These include all the cognitive processes involved in acquisition and storage of information—notably attention, perception, and retention. People do not merely absorb information about products randomly and passively. They attend selectively to what is presented and perceive mainly that to which they attend. Factors that determine the focus of attention, the manner in which attended material is perceived, and the likelihood that it will be remembered include both characteristics of the material and conditions within the person.

We cannot hope to do justice here to the vast quantity of research on these basic processes. Together they constitute much of the content of modern experimental psychology. We shall only take note of the fact that people actually take in very little of the potential stimulus information in their environment, they do so very selectively, and they modify or adapt what they do take in to fit a particular set of needs, moods, attitudes, and stored background information. It has been estimated, for example, that although the average consumer is *potentially* exposed to around 1,500 advertisements daily, he or she only perceives about 76 (of which, only about 12 produce behavior).[25]

What a person sees, then, and how well he remembers it depends a great deal upon his motivational and cognitive states. If he is hungry, he will be more likely to notice food ads or to perceive an ambiguous figure as a food object. If he is set, or cognitively prepared, to notice how quietly a particular automobile rides, he will probably perceive it as quiet. Much of what he *remembers* about an advertisement or product is also determined by the way in which it fit into his cognitive system at the time he originally experienced it. Most people, for example, are familiar with the taste of cola drinks. Promoting 7UP as the *Un-cola* served to emphasize a contrast but also assured that people would remember the contrast since it was integrated into an existing conceptual system.

Traits and Individual Differences

Market Segmentation.   It is obvious that few, if any, products and services appeal equally to everyone. Similarly, there are few ways of promoting products and services that have an equal chance of *reaching everyone*. At every stage in the marketing process, therefore, the seller must decide to whom the primary appeal will be directed. The *target population*, or *primary market*, must be identified and described as completely as possible. Once this is done, many other aspects of the marketing strategy fall into place.

Suppose, for example, that a cosmetics manufacturer decided to develop a skin cream for teenage girls. Knowing that soft, clear skin is highly valued by this group, the manufacturer would try to develop a product that would actually help soften and clear the skin and would then advertise it in media that are known to have a large audience in this age range (*Seventeen* magazine, rock music radio stations, and so on), using a message designed to appeal to this particular population ("be nice to look at," "nice to touch," "kissable," "popular," and so on) and a price geared to teenage budgets. If the manufacturer later discovered that the product might be well received by older women who like to see themselves as remaining forever young, he would approach this new market through other media (*Woman's Day* magazine, daytime television), using a different message (mother-daughter look-alike ads) and possibly an increased price. The point is everything one does in the development and marketing of a product is influenced to some extent by data and assumptions about a distinct target population. It is important, therefore, to consider how market segmentation is accomplished and how valid or meaningful are the assumptions made about segments thus identified.

Market segmentation is, of course, nothing more than classification of consumers on the basis of individual difference characteristics that are believed to be related to buying (or other consuming) habits. As noted earlier, both *demographic* and *psychographic* factors may be used for this purpose. The demographic characteristics of *age, sex, income*, and *geographical location* are the traditional bases for classification. Marketers have come to recognize, however, that there is often considerable variation in the psychographic makeup of any purely demographic segment and that the more subjective factors may be equally indicative of behavioral tendencies. Thus, it has been argued that *attitudes, motives, values, usage patterns, aesthetic preferences*, and the like should receive equal consideration. Going even farther, Yankelovich[26] contends that markets should be segmented according to the relevance of particular factors—demographic or psychographic—for particular marketing problems. In other words, one set of distinctions may be important for the toothpaste market, another for the clothing market, and still another for the automobile market. The decision as to how consumers should be classified would thus be made only after careful study of consumer behavior patterns for a particular product category, not on the basis of prior assumptions.

There seem, then, to be two rather different ways to look at market segmentation. On the one hand, we can try to identify groups of people who are *generally similar* in their consuming patterns (e.g., middle-income, suburban whites buy a lot of the same kinds of things). On the other, we can start with a particular *product category* and through market research try to discover what characteristics distinguish users from nonusers or frequent from infrequent users. The trend in recent years has definitely favored the latter approach. Market research has come to rely less and less on preconceived notions about consumer clustering (demographic or psychographic) and increasingly on empirical classification derived from consumer preferences or choices with the help of sophisticated statistical methods. For example, analysis of the importance or value that individuals attach to various aspects of multiattribute choice alternatives permits estimations of their *involvement* with specific product categories. One can then segment the market for those products in terms of *high-* versus *low-involvement* consumers, a classification that has proved very useful for a variety of advertising and marketing problems.[27]

It would be fruitless to try to enumerate all the characteristic patterns of consumer behavior that have been described for various market segments, although such compendia are readily available.[28] Several illustrations will serve the present purpose. Britt has studied drive-in theater audiences and found that they differ markedly from the general population.[29] As a rule, they have better jobs, higher income, more education, more children, more home ownerships, more cars, more major appliances, and more conveniences.

Considerable interest has been shown in recent years in the "Negro market"—undoubtedly because blacks account for large portions of the total sales of certain products (nearly half of all the Scotch whisky and grape soda consumed). Among other things, it has been learned that blacks spend more money on clothing and less on food than do whites.[30] Of the foods they do buy, cooked cereals, cream, rice, syrup, and frozen vegetables are represented far more heavily than is true for white buyers.[31] Although blacks appear similar to whites in package design preferences, young blacks react very negatively toward advertisements in which blacks are not adequately represented.[32]

One rather different way in which consumers have been classified is in terms of their propensity to *innovate* or try new products. It is important to identify and appeal to such people when introducing a new product because they are believed to play a major role in its ultimate success or failure. The thinking is that the innovators provide an initial sales base and, more important, set the trend that others will follow. Since on the order of 90 percent of the new products introduced fail to gain consumer acceptance—and not necessarily because they are objectively inferior—the importance of reaching the innovative segment is obvious.[33]

Innovators are usually defined arbitrarily as the first 2½ percent or 10 percent of the potential adopters of an item. So defined, this segment has been reported to differ from followers on many dimensions: They are younger, more affluent, better educated, and more mobile demographically; psychologically, they are more venturesome, higher in risk preference, less dogmatic, and prone to group things into broader rather than narrower categories.[34]

While the evidence does, therefore, support the idea that consumers differ in innovative tendencies, there is little justification for segmenting them into distinct categories—innovators and followers. Jacoby favors a concept of *innovation proneness*, a behavioral continuum along which people vary just as with any other trait.[35] Viewed in this fashion, the whole topic of consumer innovation might be considered under the heading of *internal states* rather than *segmentation*.

Unquestionably, one *can* define market segments in ways that relate consistently to consumer behavior. The trick is in finding out which are the most relevant defining characteristics, how they might be measured, and how useful the resulting classification is for the problem at hand. Now that the debate has moved from the realm of speculative theory to empirical modeling, useful—if not final—answers are becoming commonplace.

Personality.   Probably the most comprehensive way of describing human cognitive, affective, and behavioral tendencies, as we saw earlier, is in terms of personality traits or attributes. The assumption is that a person's characteristic mode of response to various life situations (*personality*) is measurable along a few basic dimensions (dominance, sociability, responsibility, manifest anxiety, and so on). If this is so, it is reasonable to suppose that personality should provide a handy means of summarizing psychographic profiles; hence, an individual's personality trait measures should predict product preferences, willingness to try new products, and other indexes of product acceptance.

Research on this point has produced discouraging results.[36] A few studies have shown weak relationships between trait profiles and specific product usage; for every positive instance there seems to be at least one corresponding negative instance. Kaponen, for example, found that, as measured by a popular personality inventory, male smokers were higher than average in need for sex, aggression, achievement, and dominance; lower in compliance, order, self-depreciation, and association.[37] Using another inventory and another population of smokers, Tucker and Painter found no differences.[38] They did, however, find differences in the case of certain other products. Headache remedies were used most frequently by people who scored low in ascendency and sociability. Ford and Chevrolet owners showed small personality profile differences in one study,[39] but not in another.[40] Even where there were differences, they were not nearly as predictive as *demographic* differences.

It is possible, of course, that personality is more important than it has seemed but that the effect has been masked by other factors. The reader will recall that, at best, personality measures leave much to be desired. Moreover, most of the leading indexes were designed for purposes other than predicting consumer behavior. And even if the measures were adequate, most of the studies themselves have been suspect. Worthing, Venkatesan, and Smith made an effort to correct these flaws in a study involving some 20 diverse products (radios, razor blades, beer, deodorant, and the like).[41] Using an instrument (*Jackson's personality research form*) designed in part for the study of consumers, and an analytic procedure capable of handling some of the complexities inherent in a multifactor design, these investigators were able to show significant differences between male users and nonusers on 21 of 100 product-trait combinations. In the case of beer drinkers and cigarette smokers, differences appeared on all five traits: affiliation, aggression, dominance, exhibition, and social recognition. Users of other products, such as radios and electric shavers, differed from nonusers on none of these traits. For the majority of products, differences were limited to several of the trait categories. Women, however, showed far fewer consumer profile differences than did men.

One instrument designed specifically for market research purposes describes consumer personality in terms of three main dimensions: *compliant, aggressive,* and *detached* scales (*CAD*). The original studies carried out using CAD were among the more successful, suggesting that the problem of inappropriate measures may indeed have been the chief stumbling block in previous research.[42] Recently, however, it has been shown that even the CAD scales have serious deficiencies: Reliabilities are not very high (mostly in the .30–.60 range), the measures show little convergence with other scales designed to measure similar constructs, and the internal structure is not as clear as originally hoped.[43]

All things considered, then, we are forced to conclude that if overall personality, as usually measured, makes a difference in consumer decisions, it is probably a rather minor one,[44] one that is easily masked by more powerful transient states and situational factors. There are undoubtedly countless Mercedes personalities driving around in Fords, Plymouths, and VWs. This does not mean that the search for, and use of, psychographic information is a useless exercise. Just because we cannot show reliable relationships between overall profiles and purchasing behavior does not rule out the possibility that some measurable individual differences may be salient for some products, as noted earlier.

Current Status

In many respects, consumer psychology is the most diffuse, least coherent of the subfields within industrial-organizational psychology. Its objectives are both scientific and applied; its theory and methodology are drawn from a wide assortment of other specialty areas from psychoanalytic theory to attitude measurement to the laboratory study of attention. Much of the salient research is conducted by people other than psychologists within the context of specific marketing problems (segmenting markets, setting media rates). The only central theme in all of this is a common concern for people as consumers of goods and services.

To understand a person as a consumer, or to influence what is consumed, one must consider a staggering array of potentially relevant variables. Only a few of these have been explored in any systematic fashion using acceptable scientific procedures and, of these, only a small sampling was presented here. Most of the findings have been limited to a specific product and set of market conditions. The global theoretical glue necessary to bond these isolated facts together and permit broader generalizations is sadly lacking. Theory and research seem almost to proceed independently in many cases. Thus marketers often find themselves in the position of having to choose between someone's unverified theory of how the consumer operates and someone else's market research data that may or may not apply to their own marketing problems. If their problems are important enough, they may carry out their own marketing study, thereby adding other items to our inventory of isolated facts or fairly limited models.

What is particularly discouraging in all this is that the topic of consumer behavior has all but disappeared from the research literature in I/O psychology. A promising upsurge that seemed to be developing in the early 1970s was not sustained. The good news, however, is that market and advertising research does seem to be growing in both quantity and sophistication as reported in such excellent publications as the *Journal of Marketing Research, Journal of Advertising Research*, and *Journal of Consumer Research*. It remains to be seen how much of this work will find its way into the mainstream of psychological theory, and how much advances in psychology will affect the future direction of this research.

ENGINEERING PSYCHOLOGY*

Person-Machine System Design: The Concept

Suppose you were asked to assemble a team of experts to design something—say, a new kind of wrench, or a space shuttle, or a 50-story office building. What kinds of specialists would you choose? Probably you would start with engineers or architects, the traditional design professions. Next you might add an expert user—in this case, perhaps, an auto mechanic, astronaut, or realtor—to contribute practical insights. Depending on your background and orientation, you might also include marketing specialists, lawyers, and a host of other professions. But the chances are you would never think to recruit a *psychologist.*

You would not be alone in this oversight. Design teams have tradition-

*Adapted from Chapter 10, Engineering psychology. In E. M. Altmaier & M. E. Meyer (Eds.). (1985). *Applied specialties in psychology* (pp. 239–273). New York: Random House, Inc. Reprinted by permission of Random House, Inc.

ally been more concerned with the cost, efficiency, reliability, and attractiveness of their creations than with the characteristics of the people who must use them. And it is in the latter domain, the scientific description of human capabilities and tendencies, that psychology has something to offer. There is an important contrast in the design philosophies involved here. The traditional approach might be called "machine-oriented" in that its aim is to construct something that works properly irrespective of the user. In fact, according to this philosophy, the less a design relies on people the better, since everyone knows that "to err is human." If a machine has met the predetermined design criteria and people have trouble using it, well, the human is obviously at fault.

The more enlightened approach holds that people and machines are partners, not antagonists. Together they constitute *systems* for accomplishing things—usually work. Each has a legitimate role to play, and it is the designer's job to strive for an efficient, reliable, and safe combination of human and nonhuman components. If a particular design results in a lot of errors or accidents, one does not bemoan the stupidity of the human operator; one tries to isolate the design features that contribute to the problem. Perhaps the only solution is more automation, which in essence designs the human out of the system. But in many, if not most, instances, a careful analysis will suggest a less radical solution: an improved information display, communication link, control device, or even training program. This more "user-oriented" view is generally referred to as the *person-machine system* philosophy. It calls, naturally, for an understanding of the strengths, operating limits, and tendencies of all components, including the human ones.

A useful way of depicting the person-machine philosophy is to trace the flow of information and/or energy through the various components of an abstracted system, as shown in Figure 9–4.

We assume that the object of the system is to achieve or maintain some desired state, such as keeping your car on the road and within the speed limit. The relevant information comes to you, the human component, in either literal or "processed" form via machine elements known as *displays* (e.g., the scene through your windshield and speedometer, respectively). You use various *sense systems* to pick up this information and transform it into impulses that undergo a series of transformations as they traverse your *nervous system* (including your brain) and eventually deliver instructions for corrective action to an appropriate set of *muscles*. At this point, the transition is made from person to machine, and from information to energy transfer as the muscles execute the action via *controls* (e.g., the steering wheel, accelerator, and brake). Thereupon, a sequence of machine processes ensues similar to that for the person, and the car's position and speed change. You pick up the new state of affairs as before, decide whether it meets the criteria that you have stored in your memory, and the entire cycle is repeated. Finally, the whole process takes place within an *environment* that can greatly affect how well some or all

FIGURE 9-4   Illustration of the Primary Route of Information Flow through the Person-Machine System

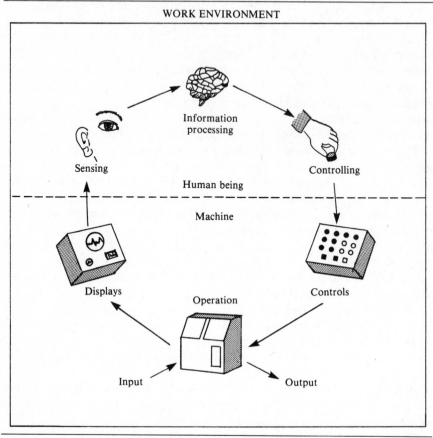

WORK ENVIRONMENT

Information processing

Sensing

Controlling

Human being

Machine

Displays

Operation

Controls

Input

Output

SOURCE: Chapanis, A. (1976). Engineering psychology. In Marvin D. Dunnette (Ed.). *Handbook of industrial and organizational psychology.* Skokie, Ill.: Rand McNally. (By permission of the editor.)

of the components function: flooding might interfere with machine operation, fog or alcohol with person operation and so on.

This is, of course, a greatly simplified picture of what happens in most systems, but it is sufficient to illustrate the logic and the main principles involved in the person-machine design philosophy. First, it emphasizes the importance of understanding both human and nonhuman components with an eye toward integrating them into an effective combination. A breakdown anywhere in the flow can cause problems. Second, it suggests that there are usually many alternative ways to allocate functions to achieve a given result (a principle sometimes referred to as *equipotentiality*). For example, your car might be equipped with "cruise control," a device that takes the functions of monitoring speed, computing corrections, and executing control action away from the human subsystem and puts them into a machine subsystem. Or, you might have a broken speedometer, which would make you responsible for computing speed in your head—a function, it turns out, for which you are not particularly well suited.[45] Much of the problem of system design reduces to questions of what functions should be assigned to which components.

Third, Figure 9–4 emphasizes some particularly vulnerable points in the system, notably those where person meets machine (known in the trade as person-machine *interfaces*). Misreading or ignoring human factors at these critical junctures has lead to some costly and tragic design flaws, as we shall see in the next section. And finally, the illustration implies that it makes more sense to consider human factors in the initial design of a system than after the cry of "human error" has gone up. Unfortunately, even though designers today are showing a greater interest in human factors than they have in the past, the typical application is still an after-the-fact correction. Far too seldom is the total system considered in the initial planning stage.

Some Graphic Illustrations

The present section describes and illustrates a branch of psychology that is concerned explicitly with the human factors aspect of design. As we noted in Chapter 1, it is called *engineering psychology* and is part of a larger field, usually referred to as *human factors engineering* (or simply *human factors* or *human engineering*), which deals with a full spectrum of human design considerations (e.g., medical, physiological, anthropometric, as well as psychological). Before proceeding further, it might be well to establish that such a discipline is, indeed, necessary for the design of modern systems, and that the need is likely to grow rather than diminish as systems become more complex. So far we have made the case only in rather abstract terms. Let us now look at a few concrete examples to contrast what can happen when human factors are and are not properly recognized.

1. The Three Mile Island Accident

One of the most serious peacetime nuclear accidents occurred at Three Mile Island in Pennsylvania on March 28, 1979. Accounts in the popular media pointed to a whole succession of "human errors" leading up to and exacerbating the disaster: failure to detect critical information, misinterpretation of what was detected, poor decisions based on that misinterpretation, more misinterpretation, and so on. Closer analysis, however, revealed an appalling lack of attention to human factors principles in the design of the plant and its operator tasks. Displays were poorly arranged and hard to read; key information was obscured or missing; tasks were designed in ways that are known to cause people problems in times of stress.[46] While no one can say for sure that good human factors design would have prevented the accident, it is obviously a real possibility. Consequently, the Nuclear Regulatory Commission has begun a major project to work toward improvement in this aspect of existing and future plants.[47]

2. Power Presses

Since the earliest days of modern industrialization, one of the most widely used pieces of manufacturing equipment has been the manually controlled power press—a device that brings tremendous force to bear on a "point of contact" to stamp, cut, or shape metal parts. It has also been proved to be among the most dangerous, for it is equally adept at stamping out human parts such as fingers, hands, and arms. Since the danger is "open and obvious," however, it was many years before adequate safeguards were developed; and even today, guarding is not mandated as a condition of sale for presses in the United States (although it is in most European countries). The problem, of course, has always been a failure to appreciate fully the human factors aspects of power press operation. Most of these tasks are repetitive and dull, features that are known to induce inattention and carelessness in human operators.[48] Most also put a premium on quantity of output, a feature that encourages operators to take shortcuts and risks—as in using one's fingers to clear material when it jams or binds on one of the plates. The only effective solution to this problem, short of complete automation, is a design principle that removes from the human subsystem the option of performing the clearing and activating tasks concurrently. This principle, *fail-safe* design, lies at one end of a continuum of approaches to safeguarding, which is anchored on the other with simple *warnings*. The underlying difference, of course, is the extent to which responsibility for safety is vested in human consciousness as opposed to a machine element. Where a particular system belongs on this continuum requires careful consideration of human cognitive processes and the relative costs involved—not only of the design but of its predictive consequences. Warnings are cheap, but they will not prevent power press accidents. Fail-safe devices, on the other hand, will prevent such accidents but are costly. While one could justify the cost to prevent serious bodily injury, one would have greater difficulty doing so as a deterrent, for example, to illegal parking.

3. Computer Software Design

It is obvious that we are in the midst of a "computer revolution." In one short decade, we have seen "intelligent machines" develop from a relative novelty reserved for the most complex operations in the largest organizations and requiring the services of sophisticated technicians, to a commonplace fixture in the office, school, and home. Naturally, the technological advances that have permitted massive improvements in "hardware" capability—ever smaller, cheaper, and more powerful systems—have played a major role in this transition. Equally important, however, has been the evolution of "software" capabilities—the instructions and logic through which the machine's immense potential is put to constructive use in addressing an ever-widening array of tasks.[49]

Among the more dramatic advances in software design have been a host of improvements aimed at increasing the "usability" or "user friendliness" of computer systems. Rather than forcing the user to learn bizarre new languages, such as FORTRAN or COBOL, in order to communicate with the machine, the computer was taught to recognize the languages that *people* speak. Rather than allowing the machine ruthlessly to penalize the user for even the tiniest of errors, the machine was made to be more tolerant (e.g., to recognize instructions despite minor infractions in spelling, vocabulary, or syntax). "Menu-driven" programs were developed to relieve the user of having even to remember all the available processing options and commands.

A moment's reflection will identify a common prerequisite to all these software improvements: an understanding of how the *human* processes information. One cannot design a program to understand human language unless one knows what the language is (i.e., its vocabulary, syntax, even its semantics); or to correct human errors unless one knows what those errors are and how common they are; or to aid in storage and retrieval unless one knows how human memory is organized. One needs to understand human strengths, limitations, and tendencies—the essence of the person-machine system philosophy. In some areas, such as vocabulary, our knowledge of the human is sufficient and implementation is easy. In others, such as retrieval of information from large, multidimensional data bases, there is still a lot to be learned, and it is to these issues that engineering psychology directs its attention.[50]

A recent project on display features is a good example of this research. The question addressed was, how should the information from data bases like airline and hotel reservation records be displayed to the clerks who handle these reservations in order to maximize speed of processing and minimize the chance of error (misquotation of price or availability, double-booking, etc.). After an exhaustive survey of the feasible ways to organize such material on a display screen (i.e., to identify *formatting dimensions*) and a review of what is known about human perceptual tendencies, Tullis conducted a series of experiments in which he had subjects perform simulated clerical operations under the various formatting conditions.[51] He measured both the speed and accuracy of their performance as a function of six formatting dimensions (the overall density of items, use of spacing, etc.) and found that he could predict how well they would do with about 80 percent accuracy. As a result, it is now possible to specify in advance how any particular alphanumeric display design will fare at the hands of the typical user in any look-up task simply by measuring how it rates on these six dimensions and applying the Tullis model!

4. A Household Color-Coding Problem

Recently, one of the authors replaced a defective fan motor in his home air conditioning unit with the factory-authorized replacement part. The warehouseman gave assurance that the hook-up was identical to that for the original motor. Upon unpacking it, however, the author discovered a slight difference in the color of the wires (the usual mode of designating the various leads): the green, white, black, and yellow of the original motor were replaced with green, *brown*, black, and yellow in the new one. "No problem," he thought "since all the others are the same, brown must simply have been substituted for white." After an hour or so of pain and suffering under a 100-degree Houston sun, the new motor was mounted, wired up, and running. For about 15 minutes! Another hour of pain and suffering and a very irate amateur serviceman was on his way back to the warehouse with one "defective" new motor and some very dark thoughts concerning the manufacturer. Of course, the motor checked out just fine. Puzzled, the warehouseman dug through a pile of old manuals and eventually found the wiring diagram. White had been changed to yellow, and yellow to brown several years ago! Thus the hook-up caused the motor to run backwards (which the author had failed to notice in his excitement over the fact that it ran at all), it overheated, and that eventually activated the automatic shutoff, which is designed to protect the motor from burning itself out.

This incident, though trivial in the greater scheme of things, is by no means an isolated illustration of poor design in everyday household products. Manufacturers have neglected human factors in this area as much—if not more so—than in the design of power plants and military systems. Only recently, with the growing incidence of product liability litigation, has much thought been given to the user—and that mainly with respect to *safety*.[52] One does not have to look far to find many examples of products that are unnecessarily difficult to use, easy to misuse, or impossible to maintain. Returning to our illustration, one can only wonder what considerations went into the change in color coding (a sale on brown wire, perhaps?). Certainly, anticipation of the problems created for the potential user was not among them. On the other hand, anticipating a common threat to the welfare of the *machine* component, the designers saw fit to build in an overload switch. Here we see a classic case of the traditional "machine-oriented" philosophy. By contrast, good human factors design would have dictated against *any* coding change. Were one absolutely necessary for economic or other reasons, every effort should have been made to minimize the confusion (e.g., preserve as much as possible of the original code—green, black, and yellow—and indicate "brown replaces white" in a conspicuous place on the brown wire or motor). At the very least, an explanation of the code should have been affixed to each unit so that the installer would not have had to depend on an informed and cooperative distributor or an easily lost instruction sheet for the necessary information.

Four examples cannot, of course, do justice to the full scope of design problems to which engineering psychology either has made or could make an important contribution. They do, however, provide some insight into the diverse forms that such a contribution can take and the kind of benefits to be expected. Inputs range from little more than "common sense" (which, nonetheless, traditional designers seem rather prone to overlook) to specialized information on how people perceive things, make decisions, or react under stress. Potential benefits range from reducing inconvenience to improving performance; from saving time or money to saving limbs or lives; from making our everyday existence a little more pleasant to reducing the chances of a nuclear holocaust.

Focal Areas of Research and Application

In the preceding pages, we have touched upon a variety of human factors issues in the course of exploring what engineering psychology and those who practice it are all about. Now it is time to consider such issues a bit more systematically and in a little greater depth.

A convenient way to organize this material is in terms of the general flow of information through the system (See Figure 9–4) with particular emphasis on the human functions involved. While we know it is a gross oversimplification, classification in terms of *input, central processing, output,* and *work environment* issues has proven useful. Thus we shall examine a few of the problems involved in detecting and interpreting signals (the display-person interface); in "mentally" processing or transforming the information (human information processing functions); in choosing and executing responses (the person-control interface); and in functioning under various stresses and strains imposed by the task setting.

Problems in Detecting and Interpreting Signals

It almost goes without saying that humans can be of little use to the system unless they are able to pick up key information about the system's mission: its current status, the desired state, feedback from corrective action, or some combination thereof. Although accurate and timely reception of signals conveying such information is not a sufficient condition for system performance, it is certainly a necessary one. Therefore, good human factors design requires that we know what characteristics of signals affect human receiving proficiency as well as how the two are functionally related. Of course, the better we understand the basic ways in which human sensing and receiving systems work, the easier time we have identifying potentially important signal or display properties.

There exists at this point a great deal of pertinent information on both the fundamental properties of sensory and perceptual systems and the desired features for signals and displays to have.[53] We know, however, that the best designs cannot be determined completely without considering how the person must use the information: task and display variables often have an interactive effect on system performance.

S-R Compatibility

A good example of this interaction may be seen in a study of five different coding (display) schemes used in combination with five different system tasks.[54] Subjects were required to count, identify, verify, locate, or compare items on a maplike display when the items were presented as numerals, letters, geometric shapes, configurations, or colors. As shown in Figure 9–5, people generally performed well with numerical designations and not so well with configural ones. But within different tasks, the best code was not always the same: color was best for location but relatively poor for identification; shape was good for verifying and counting but not so good for either locating or identifying. It is because such interactions are common, a phenomenon known as *S-R compatibility*,[55] that it is desirable to test any proposed set of display options in either the actual system or a simulation of it before finally implementing them.

Despite all we know about presenting information to people, many practical issues still remain. One such problem, which involves the detection or identification of infrequent events, is known as the *monitoring* or *vigilance* problem.

Vigilance

Technological advances have made it increasingly rare for human operators to deal with anything but highly processed input signals. In fact, in many cases their principal function is to monitor largely automated processes for the occasional malfunction or the unanticipated occurrence that cannot be incorporated into the program. Sometimes, the to-be-reported events are well defined and easily identifiable; in other cases, their characteristics are not known precisely in advance, so identification involves an element of judgment. Very often the consequences of missed signals, misinterpreted (or falsely reported) signals, or delays in reporting signals are most severe. Consider, for example, the Three Mile Island situation, the anesthesiologist monitoring the vital signs of a patient, the air traffic controller watching for potential mid-air collisions, or the missile warning officer surveying a CRT for evidence of nuclear attack. It is,

FIGURE 9–5   Relative Performance on Five Different Tasks as a Function of the Type of Code Used to Convey the Information (Points Are Connected Only to Facilitate Task Comparisons—the Shape of the "Functions" Has No Meaning)

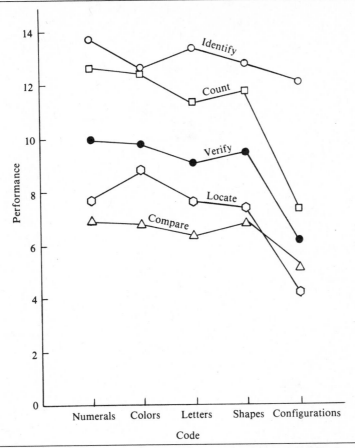

SOURCE: From *Human factors engineering and design* by E. J. McCormick & M.S. Sanders. Copyright, © 1982 McGraw-Hill Book Company. Used with permission of McGraw-Hill Book Company.

in fact, because of the critical nature of mistakes that we do not care to relinquish complete control over certain situations to machines.

The problem is that people are generally not very good at maintaining their proficiency over prolonged periods of watchkeeping.[56] As illustrated in Figure 9–6, it has been shown repeatedly in a wide variety of studies that a substantial "vigilance decrement" occurs after as little as an hour on the job. Recognizing this problem, researchers have explored the phenomenon from many different angles hoping, on the one hand, to gain a better understanding of the human processes responsible for it and, on the other, to formulate human factors recommendations to help overcome this threat to system performance.

FIGURE 9–6   Decrements in Monitoring Performance Reported in Two Different Studies Using Four Different Tasks

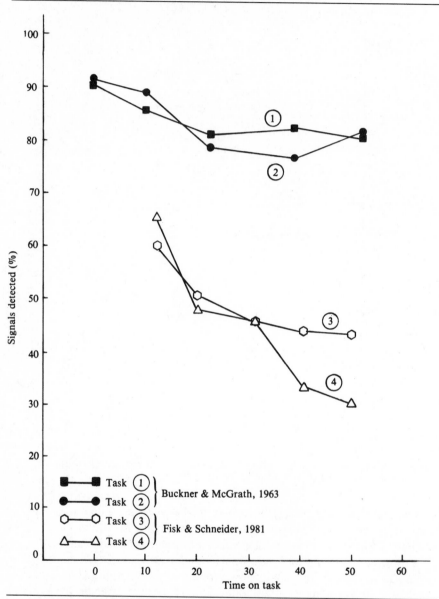

SOURCE: Adapted from sources cited and included in the list of references.

Progress has been made on both fronts. One approach that has proven particularly useful in analysis of the problem derives from a general theory of signal detection (TSD or *theory of signal detectability*). The basic premise of TSD is that devices for distinguishing between the occurrence

FIGURE 9–7 Illustration of the Conceptual Elements of the Theory of Signal Detectability Using Hypothetical S and $S + N$ Distributions and a Rather Conservative Decision Cutoff (i.e., One that, for the Assumed Distributions, Requires Nearly a 3/1 Likelihood Favoring the Presence of a Signal)

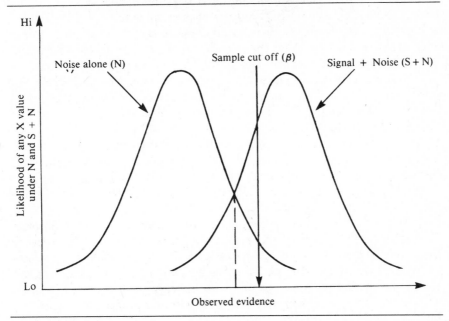

Noise alone (N)   Sample cut off (β)   Signal + Noise (S + N)

Hi

Likelihood of any X value under N and S + N

Lo

Observed evidence

of signals (which always appear in conjunction with some level of background "noise") and nonsignals (i.e., the "noise" alone) operate by transforming the evidence available at any given time into a likelihood estimate (i.e., the "odds" that the observation at hand came from a distribution of evidence generated by "noise" alone versus one generated by "signal plus noise").

As you can see from the hypothetical case in Figure 9–7, as the observed evidence (point on the X-axis) shifts from left to right, the odds (indicated by the relative position of that point on the two curves) move from strongly favoring the N-*alone* to strongly favoring the $S + N$ interpretation. If our signal detection device isn't allowed to respond with "odds" but must tell us whether or not it thinks a signal is present, it must pick some point on the X-axis (i.e., some odds level) above which it will say "signal" and below which it will say "noise". This is called a decision *criterion* or β. All other things being equal, an ideal device would choose the point where the curves cross (dashed line) as its β, since this criterion will be as accurate when it says "signal" as when it says "noise." In the case shown (arrow), however, the point chosen is conservative, suggesting that the device considers false alarms more serious than missed signals. Naturally, anything that brings the $S + N$ and N distributions closer together will increase the overlap and therefore move the odds for whatever β is chosen closer to even, making the decision tougher. Separation, then, increases discriminality and is indexed by a measure called d', which should be independent of β.

When people are serving as monitors, they are behaving as signal detection devices. Using a TSD analysis, it is possible to estimate what criterion they are using as their internal decision criterion (β) and how well they are able to distinguish the two distributions (d' or pure discriminability). The advantage of this sort of analysis is that it allows one to pinpoint where in the human receiving process any variable has its principal effect, and that, in turn, suggests what might be done about it. If, for example, a vigilance decrement represented a progressive relaxation in β, one would take steps to maintain the operator's decision standards (possibly through training). If, instead, ability to distinguish signal and nonsignal conditions (d') deteriorated over the watch, the solution might be to increase the signal's distinctiveness. As it turns out, both kinds of effects can occur under certain task conditions,[57] and both potential remedies have been used together with a number of others.

The TSD model is not, of course, the only way to look at monitoring performance. One team of researchers, for example, suggested recently that vigilance declines only if the task requires expenditure of "mental effort."[58] Some monitoring tasks, it seems, can be performed almost "automatically," and on these, people hold up very well. Nevertheless, the TSD approach has proven both theoretically and practically useful in a host of human performance contexts—monitoring is just one of them.

Problems in Central Processing

The aspect of human performance that has received more attention than any other over the past few decades is the set of cognitive or "mental" operations that people use to transform input signals into a form appropriate for the task at hand. How do they encode the information they have received? Store it for later use? Retrieve it when needed? Combine it with other information? Filter out competing or irrelevant signals? What are their capacity limits in these functions, and what happens when capacities are exceeded?

Much of the research on these processes has been carried out at a very basic level. That is to say, tasks and experimental conditions have been designed principally to isolate cognitive *structures*—the elementary mental operations that people apply fairly consistently to a rather narrow range of problems. Posner and McLeod[59] distinguish the structural approach from studies of cognitive *traits* (the individual's typical mode of dealing with all kinds of problems), *states* (mode of dealing with them at a particular time), and *strategies* (typical mode of dealing with a narrow range of problems). Since the cognitive tasks imposed by real-world systems rarely involve simple structures, and successful performance undoubtedly depends upon trait, state, and strategy considerations as well, it is often difficult to translate cognitive-process principles into human factors recommendations. For this reason, we shall not venture into the vast body of literature on cognitive structures except, once again, by illustration. The reader will recognize that the concept of *S-R compatibility* that we discussed earlier is one such principle. Several others involve the idea that human processing capacity is limited, and that tasks differ in terms of demands placed on that capacity.

Mental Workload

Much of our understanding of cognitive structures comes from studies in which a subject's speed and/or accuracy in responding to inputs is measured as a function of systematic variations in task conditions. The logic behind this approach is that any information-processing activity involves a series of mental operations, each of which takes time and adds a potential for error. Greater delays and more errors imply more processing steps. If the experimenter is clever in choosing task conditions, the function attributable to specific steps (structures) such as encoding, central processing, response selection, and response execution can be isolated.[60] One implication of this logic is that a highly compatible S-R pair requires fewer steps than an incompatible pair.

It turns out, however, that the processing picture is much more complicated than this because, for one thing, not all "steps" happen in *serial* order: some work in *parallel*.[61] Another complication is that people seem to have a limited amount of total processing capability (*capacity*), and how they allocate it is somewhat under their control.[62] Thus, for example, investing a lot of attentive effort in a difficult encoding operation (say, trying to decipher a garbled message) might make you forget a phone number you were about to dial or fail to see an important warning on your CRT. And finally, there is growing evidence that not all kinds of processing operations draw on a common store: some, in fact, may be so "cheap" in capacity demand that they are virtually automatic (e.g., driving a car under nonstressful conditions).[63]

What all this means is that it is virtually impossible to specify the human capacity for handling information in any absolute sense. But the capacity question is one of the most important practical issues in human factors today. Despite the fact that, as we saw earlier, people are not as directly involved in system control as they once were, they are far from inactive. Very often, mental effort has been substituted for physical effort. Even though overt action may be called for less frequently and, when taken, may just involve pushing a few buttons, the mental activity leading up to that act may be intense, and the potential consequences, catastrophic.

So, we have a problem. Many tasks to which people are being assigned require them to process more and more information under greater and greater pressure, but we have no handy means of predicting when their capacity is about to be overtaxed, nor have we a convenient way to express the total workload under which they are operating. Both of these aspects of the problem, however, are being actively pursued by engineering psychologists today.

Attempts to quantify mental workload have produced a number of physiological, subjective, and performance measures.[64] Unfortunately, they do not agree as well as they should if they were all measuring the same construct, and little is known about the specific mental processes that underlie them. Still, some have proven of considerable practical value for particular task settings.

POC Functions

Progress is also being made in the measurement of human capacity for dealing with particular kinds of tasks. The way this is generally done is by having subjects perform multiple tasks singly and in combination, and measuring their performance under single- and multiple-task conditions using some typical index such as reaction time or processing rate. The extent to which proficiency on each single task drops off as others are added (or to which combined performance falls short of what one would get by combining the component single-task scores) is taken as an index of the capacity limitation. In this way, one can compute a "performance operating characteristic" (POC) that describes the extent to which pairs of tasks draw upon the same mental resource.

In one such study, for example, Wickens[65] and his associates plotted POC functions for all combinations of four common tasks: tracking, classification, line judgment, and auditory running memory. These tasks were chosen because they typify activities that are believed to use somewhat distinct stores of mental capacity. As shown in Figure 9–8, the results generally supported their expectations. That is, the pairs that are supposed to be most distinct (hence to produce the least dual-task decrement) are plotted in the upper-right portion of each graph (i.e., in the direction of 0 decrement on both tasks). Those involving similar activities (e.g., LL, LC, CC, TT) were generally below the midpoint. Pairing two classification tasks (CC) turned out to have a large and equal effect on both; pairing line judgment with classification (LC), however, hurt classification proficiency much more than it did line judgment.

Judgment and Decision Making

In citing death and taxes as the only sure things in life, Mark Twain may have been guilty of overstating the case, but not by much. Few situations that we face are totally predictable; very few tasks we perform require

FIGURE 9–8 Reduction in Performance on One Task Resulting from Its Concurrent Pairing with Another

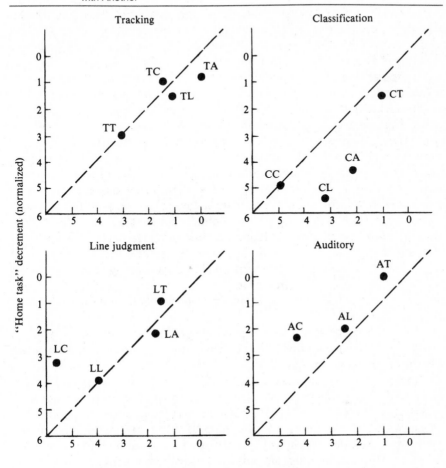

Paired task decrement (normalized)

Note: Each point represents a pair; nine pairings of four different tasks are shown (some twice). No decrement in either task would be plotted at 0-0; the dashed lines represent all points of equal decrement in both members of a pair. Pairing a task with itself (TT, LL, CC) necessarily results in a point on that line.

SOURCE: From *Human Factors*, 1981, *23*: 221–229. Copyright 1981 by the Human Factors Society, Inc., and reproduced by permission.

absolutely no judgment of future prospects, contingencies, or relationships. Take, for example, the simple case of loosening a "frozen" bolt. An inexperienced mechanic, if strong enough, will increase the applied torque until the bolt either comes free or breaks off. An experienced one will stop short of the breaking point recognizing, from a combination of stored information and sensory output, that the chances of a successful outcome are dropping off fast while those of a disastrous outcome are becoming prohibitive.

In the long run, of course, system performance reflects the quality of a host of such judgments and decisions. Broken bolts add up to wasted time and money; misinterpreted intelligence data adds up to events such as the Bay of Pigs and the surprise in Iran. It is therefore important to understand how people process the information that they use in making decisions under conditions of uncertainty, to determine how good the resulting decisions are, and to explore ways to make them better.

Until a few decades ago, the only scientists interested in such matters were the economists. They tended to see people as rational, decision-making entities, who, though perhaps imperfectly, operate to maximize their marginal expected profit or utility. Since the laws of probability define rationality in risky situations, the economic view assumed that such rules also serve as a model for human judgment. As we saw in Chapter 2, however, at least one prominent economist, Herbert Simon (who, it happens, is also a psychologist), disputed this view. He argued that the rationality assumption is untenable—that people and organizations tend to settle for the first acceptable option that comes along rather than trying to maximize profit, utility, or anything else. Thus "rationality," in the strict classical sense, is a poor starting point for an account of human decision behavior.

Somewhat surprisingly, when psychology finally became interested in human decision behavior, it was the classical economic view—not Simon's—that dominated. The assumption was that, yes, people do act rationally, seek to maximize utility, and try intuitively to apply the right rules. The only problem is, they are limited in what they can do mentally (see the previous section) and they also have certain biases. Therefore, the proper approach to understanding and predicting human decision behavior is (a) to rescale "objective" quantities, such as probabilities and dollars, into "subjective" ones, such as uncertainty and utility values and (b) to determine how far (and in what way) people go wrong in their efforts to apply the optimization rules.[66]

Not all the work during the 1950s and 1960s, however, was in the economic tradition. Several investigators adopted a more descriptive approach.[67] Like Simon, they were not inclined to view human decision behavior as an approximation to any rational model; rather, they used statistical methods (regression analysis) to infer from actual judgments or choices what "policy" a person was, in fact, using. This work, too, has resulted in practical applications. For example, through a procedure known as "bootstrapping," a decision maker's policy is "captured" (or described statistically), a model of it is created, and the model is used in making subsequent choices.[68] The advantage of this approach is that it allows the human's value system to be applied in decision making more consistently than is humanly possible.

Early in the 1970s, Simon's original argument was rediscovered and given additional impetus through a series of studies by Kahneman and Tversky.[69] What they showed was, in essence, that behavior often does not even approximate normatively optimal rules. Rather, people seem to rely on handy rules of thumb or "heuristics," which, while not the best they could do, probably have served them reasonably well in the past, or so it seems to them. After all, they rarely get the kind of feedback that would indicate the existence of a better way.[70]

The Tversky and Kahneman work has led to a whole decade of descriptive research—attempts to identify the kinds of biases heuristic processing yields and to understand some of the causal factors. From a practical standpoint, attempts have also been made to find ways to reduce the biases.[71]

All of the major lines of decision research, then, have increased our understanding and led to suggestions for improving the performance of the decision system. At the present time, however, concern seems to be growing over the fact that specific task conditions may have a lot to do with how the decision maker approaches various problems.[72] The project for the 1980s, therefore, seems to be one of teasing out and organizing these (often subtle) task influences.

Problems in Executing Responses

Despite the trend toward automated and semiautomated control, there will probably always be system tasks that require skilled movements of one sort or another. Thus, while it is no longer the central issue that it once was, how people execute skilled movements still concerns engineering psychologists. Today, they share that interest with researchers from other fields (notably physical education).

Research in this area has generally taken one of two forms: (1) attempting to describe, analyze, or model the movement pattern produced by the human controller in relation to a time-varying input signal and (2) attempting to analyze the processes involved in discrete movements. The former has tended to favor use of so-called tracking tasks, in which the controller attempts to follow as closely as possible a programmed course by moving a wheel, joystick, or other control device. The target and response signals are usually displayed either separately (*pursuit* tracking) or as to-be-corrected error (*compensatory* tracking) on a CRT display, much in the fashion of modern video games; performance is measured in terms of various error indexes (time-on-target, average error, "lead" or "lag" error, and so on). Discrete movement research, on the other hand, has tended to use fairly simple tasks such as "aiming," in which the subject moves a stylus from a "home" position to a "target" position as quickly as possible on command. Success in hitting the target and travel time (measured from leaving the home position to contacting the target) are common measures of performance.

The great appeal of the laboratory tracking task lay in its close

resemblance to real-world vehicular control. In fact, it allowed researchers to incorporate any sort of machine dynamics they wished in order to
study human proficiency or the relative merit of different design features
under realistic control conditions. A host of studies was carried out on everything from display features to control "feel" to the dynamic properties
of the task itself.

While this work was undoubtedly useful in many aspects of system design (and still is), it never produced the insight into human control processes that many had hoped it would. Today, the tracking task is still
widely used in research on other issues, such as stress effects; as a way of
studying basic motor processes, however, it has been largely replaced by
simpler tasks. Just the opposite trend has characterized research on discrete movement. One example drawn from the many issues being studied
within this general framework should serve to illustrate the point.

Open-Loop versus Closed-Loop Processes

It has generally been assumed that any skilled movement results from
two kinds of processes: a preplanned "program" that, once initiated, follows its course without further adjustment (as in a ballistic missile or a
thrown football); and a controlled aspect, in which status information is
monitored and in-course adjustments are made. The former is referred to
as an *open-loop* process; the latter, as a *closed-loop* process. The issue involved is essentially how much of a role the two kinds of processes play in
various types of skills.

Today, the predominant view favors the "motor program" emphasis,
the idea being that the key to most skills lies in building up and refining
prototypic sets of instructions that are delivered to muscle groups as required by the task.[73] Evidence for this position includes studies in which
the nerves that convey the main feedback by which the closed-loop control could be exercised are effectively anesthetized. Despite "breaking the
loop," the skill survives.[74] It is difficult, however, to eliminate all feedback information, so even such an apparently conclusive test can be ques-
tioned. One of the central issues yet to be resolved is the minimum time
required to process feedback. If, as some suggest, it is very short, the possibility of closed-loop control in even rapidly paced skills (such as typing
or playing the piano) becomes more tenable. Probably the most plausible
view is that response patterns are selected in accordance with a motor
program, but errors in execution can be detected (and minor corrections
made) without changing the whole pattern.

Problems in the Work Context

Human performance in a system is not just a matter of task characteristics and basic information-processing functions. Simple input-output relationships never tell the complete story. For one thing, people learn;

thus the most carefully defined functions can change with experience. The student in a driver's education class not only is less proficient than a seasoned taxidriver, he or she probably uses an entirely different set of control functions. For another thing, individuals differ a great deal in ability and personality—enduring traits that can greatly affect performance, as we saw in earlier chapters (especially Chapter 7).

And finally, a person's proficiency may vary as a function of his or her physiological or mental *state*. Alcohol affects one's ability to control an automobile (as well as other functions); biorhythms may affect one's ability to put forth sustained effort;[75] and the feeling of intense pressure or great physical discomfort can reduce one's ability to work effectively. Engineering psychology has paid some attention to learning issues (chiefly as they relate to training procedures) and almost none to individual traits. But it has concerned itself a great deal with states, particularly as they are induced by the environment or context within which human operators find themselves. Therefore, we shall end our excursion into the problem areas of the field with a brief look at this amorphous set of issues.

Stress

A common way in which environmental influences are organized conceptually is through the notion of *stress*. A *stressor* is anything that affects a person's general state of arousal. Temperature conditions can do it; workload (mental or physical) can do it; noise can do it; an obnoxious officemate can do it—a lot of things singly and in combination. *Stress*, then, is the biological and psychological reaction of the organism to stressors. This sounds rather circular, and indeed it is an extremely difficult concept to pin down. Its main justification rests on the evidence that a variety of different conditions seem to bring about a very similar, nonspecific response pattern.[76]

The effects of stress are also many and varied. So far as task performance is concerned, the relationship is generally regarded as having an inverted-U shape: too much or too little stress hurts performance. One way this seems to happen is by limiting our capacity to attend to things, as we saw earlier. Whether this same function describes the equally important matter of the person's subjective feelings has not been clearly established, although some argue that without the perception, there can be no stress.[77] Instances are commonplace, however, in which an operator will express discomfort but continue to perform at a high level (we shall examine one of these in a moment). Finally, one must consider the long-term consequences: people can suffer mental and physical problems from prolonged stress (it is even listed as one of the major contributing factors in heart disease). (See Chapter 3 for a discussion of stress in the workplace.)

The practical problem from a system design standpoint, of course, is that of measuring stress effects for particular stressors and for their various combinations. Without some such index, plus a general idea of what constitutes tolerable (or even desirable) and intolerable ranges of stress, we are hard pressed to set design standards. This is why the "mental workload" issue is prominent today—and, as we saw, no single measure of that has yet emerged. One of the reasons this task is so difficult is that people differ tremendously in stress tolerance; moreover, conditions at work are but one set of life's stressors. Thus the best level for me and my life situation may be a poor one for you. Another is the fact that there are so many potential stressors, and the interactions among them are not simple. Adding two of them to a situation may be worse than either alone, the same, or even better in some cases.[78]

Thermal Conditions

One set of potential stressors about which volumes of research literature have appeared is that defining the operator's thermal environment (hot, cold, humidity, air velocity, clothing insulation, etc.). Unlike mental workload, both physical and physiological measurements are well developed here: what the body does under various conditions is described in quantitative terms and is fairly well understood. Also fairly well established are a number of task performance functions. The surprising thing revealed by these data is how resistant performance is to seemingly miserable conditions. One must work at least three hours at temperatures above 86° F. before performance declines at all (see Kantowitz and Sorkin, 1982), and it takes almost 100° F. for 43 minutes to disturb performance on mental tasks.[79]

What is not so firmly established is how people react subjectively to these conditions. Not that the topic has suffered from neglect; thermal comfort has received much the same treatment at the hands of the heating, refrigeration, and air conditioning (ASHRAE) research community as has physiological response. Precise functions have been developed relating the distribution of comfort measures to all combinations of physical parameters.[80] And from these "comfort equations" have come standards that are in general use throughout the worlds of engineering and design.

The only problem is, these neat, orderly functions misrepresent reality. In fact, they illustrate quite nicely the cardinal sin in design that engineering psychology and human factors engineering were sent to save the world from: the neglect of *psychological* variables. In the case of the "comfort equations," the only predictors are *physical*—despite the fact that the measure being predicted is entirely subjective. Even the scale that defines "comfort" is mislabeled: it is actually a measure of perceived warmth or coldness. There is growing evidence, however, that how warm someone feels (and thus how much the thermal environment is stressful)

FIGURE 9–9   Mean "Thermal Sensation Votes" Obtained under the Original (T_1) and Shifted (T_2) Conditions for Groups Subjected to Actual and "Psychological" Temperature Changes (Adjustment Was in Terms of Several Variables Used as Covariates)

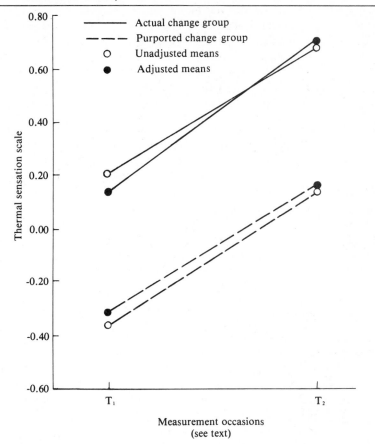

depends on psychological as well as physical conditions.[81] In one study, for example, the comfort-scale responses of students were obtained in two large classes: one in which the temperature was shifted by 5° F. without their knowing it; the other in which they were told it had been shifted, but it wasn't. The results showed exactly the same perceived change in comfort regardless of whether the manipulation was physical or psychological (see Figure 9–9).

UNION–MANAGEMENT RELATIONS

Much of our discussion in this book has been from a managerial perspective: motivating workers, managing groups, selecting and placing personnel, and so forth. This does not reflect any particular pro-management or antiunion bias on our part but accurately reflects the fact that, in their research and theorizing, industrial and organizational psychologists have neglected unions. This one-sided approach may be changing, however, as evidenced by the increasing number of studies on unions that have appeared in the literature in recent years. In the present section, we will review some of this work as well as provide a general introduction to how unions operate.

The Importance of Unions to Understanding and Changing Organizational Behavior

It is important to consider unions for several reasons. First, many of the ideas we have discussed in this book have no chance of success unless they are both permitted and actively supported by the union that represents employees. For example, job enrichment, which we discussed in Chapter 3, in theory can increase worker motivation to achieve organization goals, but attempts to implement it can run head on into the restrictions on job redesign that are found in many labor contracts. To enrich jobs may even require a renegotiation of the contract, or at least the full cooperation of union officials, something not considered in the Hackman and Herzberg models of job enrichment. Similar restraints exist for many of the other interventions that we discussed in this book. Another reason that it is important to study unions is that they are organizations in their own right. After all, the name of the discipline is Industrial and Organizational Psychology, not Managerial Psychology. Thus, it is just as legitimate to understand how the theories and techniques we have discussed can be applied to unions as it is to understand how they can be used in General Motors, Du Pont, and other profit-oriented organizations (e.g., how to increase commitment of the rank-and-file to the union, how to develop effective union leaders, how to motivate the rank-and-file to work hard to achieve union goals, how to manage union groups, and so forth).

As indicated earlier, industrial and organizational psychologists have tended to avoid these issues. In part, this is due to their own personal disinterest in unions and to the fact that management is often subsidizing their research. It is not entirely by choice, however, that psychologists have neglected unions. Historically, union leaders have tended to distrust psychologists. Consequently, they have seldom sought the assistance of industrial and organizational psychologists and are frequently unwilling to cooperate in their research. Their distrust is understandable if we consider the history of the union movement in the United States.

A Short History of Unions in the United States

Unions exist primarily to improve the socioeconomic status and the working conditions of their members and, as such, are self-interest groups as defined in Chapter 4. The first unions in the United States were local craft societies made up of skilled workers who organized on a local basis to bargain for better wages and hours. It wasn't until after the Civil War, however, that serious attempts were made to organize workers on a national level. Many of these early attempts failed largely because of the active attempts by employers to prevent unionization. These attempts included *lockouts*, in which employees who attempted to unionize were fired and prevented from entering work premises, and *blacklisting*, in which lists of employees involved in union organizing were circulated among employers. As national unions were struggling for recognition in the first three decades of this century, industrial and organizational psychology was emerging as a profession and an academic discipline. This new field of psychology was supported and fostered by some managers of business organizations who saw personnel and human relations techniques as tools that could be used not only to improve productivity but also to prevent unions.[82] Even today it is not uncommon to see management consultants promoting their services with the claim that they will reduce the likelihood of unionization. It is not surprising, then, that "industrial psychology" is a dirty word to many union leaders.

Despite all the attempts to weaken them, powerful and stable national unions formed in the late 19th and early 20th centuries. Among the first was the American Federation of Labor, which was founded in 1881 and had Samuel Gompers as its leader. Membership in the AFL rose from 350,000 in 1899 to 1,675,000 in 1904. In the years of the Great Depression, a series of federal laws finally gave legitimacy to unions and led to an explosive growth in union membership. In particular, the National Labor Relations Act (Wagner Act) guaranteed employees "the right to self-organization, to form, join, or assist labor organizations, to bargain collectively through representatives of their own choosing, and to engage in concerted activities, for the purpose of collective bargaining or other mutual aid or protection." Another important piece of legislation, the Fair Labor Standards Act of 1938, provided for a minimum wage, regulated child labor, and provided for time-and-a-half pay for work that exceeds 40 hours a week. Not all employees are covered under the FLSA. Professional and managerial employees, for example, are exempted; hence the common distinction between *exempt* and *nonexempt* employees. With the protection of the federal government, unions grew from fewer than 3 million members in 1933 to over 10.5 million before World War II. The major AFL-CIO unions and changes in their membership from 1970 to 1983 are depicted in Table 9–1. Although unions represent a powerful force in our society, they still constitute a minority of workers. Union membership has never amounted to more than one third of the total work force and has declined in recent years to less than one fifth.

Why Do People Want Unions and Why Do They Join?

The reasons for joining a union are as many and varied as the reasons for joining any group or organization. The most consistent finding is that

TABLE 9–1 Changes in Union Membership (1971–1983)

Labor Organization	1971	1975	1979	1983
Total*	13,177ˣ	14,070	13,621	13,758
Automobile, Aerospace and Agriculture (UAW)	(x)	(x)	(x)	1,010
Bakery, Confectionery and Tobacco†	152	149	131	125
Boiler Makers, Iron Shipbuilders	121	123	129	119
Bricklayers	121	143	106	103
Carpenters†	714	712	629	609
Clothing and Textile Workers (ACTWU)†	440	377	308	253
Communication Workers (CWA)	415	476	485	573
Electrical Workers (IBEW)	760	856	825	820
Electronic, Electrical and Technical	283	255	243	192
Engineers	300	300	313	345
Firefighters	101	123	150	142
Food and Commercial Workers (UFCW)†	1,036	1,150	1,123	1,007
Garment Workers (ILGWU)	363	363	314	258
Government, American Federation (AFGE)	286	255	236	204
Graphic Communications†	220	198	171	154
Hotel, Restaurant and Bartenders	300	421	373	340
Ironworkers	157	160	146	140
Laborers	475	475	475	444
Letter Carriers (NAL)	151	151	151	175
Machinists and Aerospace (IAM)	754	780	664	596
Musicians	236	215	206	131
Oil, Chemical, Atomic Workers (OCAW)	149	145	146	124
Painters	160	160	160	150
Paperworkers Int'l[2]	245	275	262	241
Plumbing and Pipefitting	228	228	228	228
Postal Workers	169	249	245	246
Railway, Airline, Steamship Clerks[2]	161	167	127	120
Retail, Wholesale Department Store[2]	122	120	122	110
Rubber, Cork, Linoleum, Plastic	169	173	158	108
Service Employees (SEIU)[2]	406	490	537	589
State, County, Municipal (AFSCME)	458	647	889	959
Steelworkers	950	1,062	964	707
Teachers (AFT)	194	386	423	456

Note: X: Not applicable. *Includes other AFL-CIO affiliated unions, not shown separately. †Figures reflect mergers with one or more unions since 1971. For details see source. [2]Thousands.

SOURCE: U.S. Department of Commerce. (1985). *Statistical abstract of the United States 1985* (105th ed.) Washington, D.C.: U.S. Government Printing Office.

employees desire a union because they are dissatisfied with some facet of their jobs: the organization, the supervision, the pay, the working conditions, and, to a lesser degree, the work itself.[83] The union is seen as a vehicle for redressing past inequities and of generally bettering one's situation. People are also more likely to join unions if there are norms (see Chapter 4) to support unionization. Youngblood and his associates found that persons who were inclined to sign an authorization card to allow a union certification election and to vote for the union in such an election were those who perceived that their parents and co-workers favored a union.[84] In fact, the perceived opinions of others toward the union were more strongly related to union vote intentions than to job satisfaction, the perceived instrumentality of the union for satisfying personal needs, and a variety of demographic characteristics such as sex, race, and occupational status.

Although there are many things we still do not understand about why people join unions, the research that has been conducted has at least dispelled two common misconceptions. There is little empirical support for the existence of a "union type." Thus attempts by management to screen employees on the basis of their propensity to join a union are futile. Also, people do not appear to join because they are "brainwashed" by outside organizers. Rather, it is because they see the union as instrumental to achievement of their personal goals and because there is social support for doing so.

Rules Governing the Formation of Unions and the Negotiation Process

If employees want to join a union, their attempts to organize are protected under the National Labor Relations Act.[85] This act created the National Labor Relations Board (NLRB), a federal agency appointed by the president of the United States to enforce the labor laws. Under its rules, if 30 percent or more of a group of employees sign a petition in favor of unionization, an election is held under the supervision of the NLRB. What constitutes the appropriate group, or bargaining unit, is generally decided by the NLRB. If the majority of these workers then cast ballots for a union to represent them, the union is certified as their exclusive bargaining agent. The union then negotiates a contract, which will govern the relationship between the management and the employees represented by the union.

There are several types of contracts.[86] Under a *union shop contract*, all employees must become members of the union. As of 1983, a total of 19 states had *right-to-work* laws, which forbid this type of contract. Under a *sole bargaining agent* contract, the union is the recognized agent for all employees but union membership is not required. Other contracts require employees who benefit from the union contract to pay some fee to the union but membership in the union is not required. Regardless of type, union contracts typically include provisions covering (1) basic wages and hours, (2) seniority rules governing the order with which employees are laid off, rehired, promoted, and transferred, (3) work rules applying to rest periods, safety procedures, discipline, and discharge, (4) fringe benefits such as vacations, pensions, and insurance, and (5) procedures for handling grievances and disputes during the term of the contract.

In the typical negotiation process, the union and management begin by presenting and arguing the merits of the principles underlying their respective demands.[87] Hard bargaining then proceeds, first on noneconomic demands and then on the cost items, including wages and fringe benefits, until each side presents its final offer. If these are close, agreement may be reached by splitting the difference. If a resolution cannot be achieved in this manner, a neutral mediator (arbitrator) may be called in to assist the two sides in reaching an agreement. Some contracts include arbitration as a specific "last resort" provision. In one form of arbitration, the arbitrator considers both sides and then makes a judgment that both management and the union are compelled under the contract to accept.

If there is no provision in the contract to prevent it, the last resort in a negotiation process is a strike by the union or a lockout by management. Strikes and lockouts are illegal during the 60 days following the time either the union or management first notifies the other that they wish to modify or terminate the contract. During a strike, management may replace strikers, except in cases involving unfair labor practices. After the contract is negotiated and the strike is over, however, management is required to reinstate striking employees. Throughout the collective bargaining process, each side is required to bargain in "good faith" under the NLRB act. Although what constitutes bad faith is not altogether clear in many cases, actions such as stalling tactics, sudden shifts in position, refusal to furnish data to the other side, and refusal to sign once an agreement is reached all have been considered by the NLRB as signs of bad faith bargaining.[88]

The Grievance Process

Once the union and management agree to a contract, this does not mean that all disputes cease. It is only natural that disagreements will arise during the period of a contract, and almost all union contracts provide for a process to settle these disputes. This process is called the *grievance procedure*, and it serves at least two important functions: (1) as an avenue through which conflicts that arise between workers and supervisors can be resolved and (2) as a means of clarifying those parts of the contract that are ambiguous or incomplete.

Under the typical grievance provision, an employee must first take his or her gripes to the *shop steward*. The *shop steward* is elected by workers in a department, division, or job, and it is her duty to try to settle disputes that arise on the job when a worker is unable to reach a satisfactory agreement with his supervisor. There are several options available to the steward: She may simply pass the complaint on to a designated *grievance committee* for adjudication, she may advise the grievant to abandon his complaint, or she may try to pursue a resolution of the grievance informally with the supervisor involved. If by whatever means the steward fails to achieve a resolution, then the next step is for the grieved employee to take his complaint directly to the grievance committee. This body, which usually consists of four or so members elected by the union membership, then meets with management representatives and presents the case of the grievant. If this also fails, the matter may finally go to outside arbitration. Here, a neutral umpire (a judge, a lawyer, or a professional arbitrator) hears both sides of the grievance and renders a binding decision.

A question of interest to both management and the union is just what variables are related to the filing of grievances. Fleishman and Harris reported leadership style to be the contributing factor: supervisors high in initiation of structure tended to have employees with higher grievance rates, particularly when the supervisors were low in consideration.[89] Ash found some evidence that younger, more unstable employees were most likely to file grievances.[90] In both of these studies, however, the relations were quite weak. According to Dalton and Todor, the characteristics of the shop steward, not the individual employees, are most predictive of the grievance rates for a department. In one study, they found that the higher the shop steward's need for dominance, the higher the number of grievances filed.[91] In a second study, these same investigators found that the less committed shop stewards were to the company and the less satisfied they were in their jobs, the more grievances they filed.[92]

Union–Management Relations

The relationship between a union and its management is inherently an adversarial one, insofar as each side is out to improve its own position and to increase its power relative to the other. Adversarial relationships are not necessarily destructive, however, and there is considerable variability in the quality of union-management relations across organizations. In some organizations, the union and management relationship is extremely poor and marked by continual bickering and strife. In others, the relationship may be one of collaboration, harmony, and mutual respect. Most union-management relationships probably fall in-between. Indeed, Derber, Chalmers, and Edelman found that in the typical unionized company, the union and management had moderately favorable feelings about joint collaboration, a moderate level of union influence, a moderate amount of joint problem solving, and a low use of work stoppages or threats by the union to achieve objectives.[93]

Brett suggests that two general areas need to be examined when considering the quality of union-management relationships: the relationships characterizing collective bargaining and the relationships characterizing the administration of the contract.[94] Things to look for when evaluating the collective bargaining relationship include the duration of negotiations (the longer they continue, the poorer the relationship), whether the membership ratifies the contracts produced through bargaining, the frequency and duration of strikes, the frequency with which mediators and arbitrators are required, and the frequency with which intervention on the part of government representatives is required. In the administration of the contract, one should examine the frequency of grievances, how far the grievances go before they are settled, the frequency of unauthorized or wildcat strikes, absenteeism, sabotage, turnover, slowdowns, and the frequency with which outside intervention is needed to settle contract disputes.

As noted by Brett, just because union and management show little conflict does not mean that the relationship is a functional one.[95] All other things equal, however, unions and management seem better off if their relationships are harmonious than if they are marked by costly strikes and slowdowns. The most important consideration is probably how predictable or structured the relationship is. Both management and unions probably can live with conflict, and it can even benefit them if the conflict is structured and follows the rules. Just as a boxing match can be a gentleman's competition or a nasty slugfest, depending on whether the contestants follow the rules, union-management relationships can be marked by constructive tension or self-defeating and destructive conflict.

Research and theory suggests a variety of factors that may be conducive or harmful to the development of union-management relations.[96] One prediction is that workers who form an occupationally homogeneous category and who are relatively isolated from the rest of society are more strike-prone than more heterogeneous workers who are integrated into society. For instance, longshoremen, lumberjacks, and miners have traditionally been somewhat more strike-prone than many other groups. Another prediction is that workers who have power (in the sense that they are located in the production process where they can halt production) will be more likely to strike than those located in a less critical spot. The type of organization, the dominant technology, and organizational size also seem to make a difference. Large organizations with batch and mass technologies tend to have poorer labor relations than smaller organizations with other types of technologies. Another interesting proposition is that more democratic unions will be more strike-prone. The reasoning behind this proposition is that when the leadership of a union is accountable to the membership and can be easily replaced, they are more likely to press unrealistic demands and to use the strike to maintain their power. This particular proposition remains in the realm of speculation, however, and has yet to be tested empirically.

The Movement toward Collaborative Relationships

In the last decade or so, substantial progress appears to have been made in developing more collaboration between union and management. In large part, the stimulus for these collaborative efforts appears to have been the increasing competition from foreign firms that has presented both management and unions with a common purpose—to produce more goods, more efficiently, or face ruin. The movement toward more collaborative relationships has appeared in several forms. One is in the form of more innovative approaches to arbitration. More contract provisions have been included in which both management and union have agreed to submit to an outside, neutral arbitrator if they cannot agree to a contract. For instance, in the 1970s the United Steelworkers and 10 steel companies signed the Experimental Negotiation Agreement, in which they agreed to submit disputed points to arbitration to avoid strikes or lockouts. Another procedure increasingly being used is *final offer arbitration*, in which the two parties agree that they will submit the final package to an arbitrator who will then choose between these two final offers. Traditional arbitration often appears to have what is called a "chilling effect" on negotiations, in that each side may stick to extreme positions in anticipation of the arbitrator's splitting the difference. Both laboratory[97] and field[98] research have shown that parties bargaining under a final offer arbitration rule have more of an incentive to move close together in their final offers than do those bargaining under traditional arbitration rules.

Another sign of increased collaboration is the inclusion in contracts of provisions for union-management committees. In 1970, 31 percent of contracts had such provisions, whereas 39 percent had such provisions in 1975, and 43 percent had them in 1979.[99] There are several types of union-management committees. Some have been in the form of *quality circles*, in which small groups of employees, usually only 7 to 10, meet regularly and voluntarily to make suggestions about improving the quality and reducing the costs of the product or service. Other types of plans that have been included in contract provisions include the Scanlon Plan, the Rucker Share-of-Production Plan, the Kaiser Plan, and the Lincoln Incentive Compensation Plan. All involve committees of workers that meet regularly to suggest ways to reduce costs and some mechanism whereby workers share in the profits resulting from cost reductions. The term *quality of work life* (QWL) has been used to refer to a concept of union-management collaboration aimed at broad improvements in the work environment. For instance, QWL projects at General Motors have included quality circles, job rotation and skill development, and teams of workers that meet periodically to discuss a variety of issues including safety and customer relations. Nadler and Lawler note that two distinctive elements appear to be a part of most QWL projects: (1) a concern about the impact of work on people as well as on organizational effectiveness and (2) the idea of participation in organizational problem solving and decision making.[100]

Schuster found evidence in several firms that joint labor and management committees were associated with substantial improvements in productivity.[101] However, before we become overly enthusiastic about such findings, we must recognize that anything as broad and often ill-defined as this concept is very difficult to evaluate rigorously. Still, the experience so far with QWL projects and other forms of collaborative relationships appears promising. They provide a channel of communication on issues that are not traditionally covered in labor contracts. Moreover, given the considerable difficulties that lie ahead for the American economy, management and unions have nothing to lose and a considerable amount to gain from experimenting with new modes of relating to one another.

SUMMARY

The mainstream of science and practice in I/O psychology deals primarily with what goes on inside the organizational system: human resource management and organizational behavior functions. However, as we saw at the outset, modern theory recognizes that organizations are not self-contained units. They are *open* in the sense that they carry on a number of important activities across the system's boundaries. In this chapter, we discuss three such boundary-spanning relations—each representing an identifiable subspeciality. None of the three accounts for more than about 5 percent of the total domain of I/O psychology. The first two, *consumer* and *engineering psychology*, have developed into somewhat autonomous fields with their own professional organizations, journals, and bodies of knowledge. Both, however, have to offer psychological information of value to important organizational functions. The former contributes data, theory, and techniques that are useful in advertising and marketing functions. The latter involves data, theory, and techniques that are useful in product and environment design.

The third illustration, *union-management relations*, is more a topic than a field; one, in fact, that has received very little attention from psychologists—I/O or otherwise. It does, however, constitute an important organizational reality, and one to which psychology should have more of a contribution to make. Not only are labor unions *organizations* to which millions of employees have significant work-related affiliations, they constitute a critical element in management functions of all kinds in the *employing organization*. Therefore, it seems appropriate for the student of

I/O psychology to understand at least a few key features of labor organizations and how they relate to work organizations. It is to this end that the third portion of the chapter is devoted.

NOTES

1. Perloff, R. (1968). Consumer analysis. *Annual Review of Psychology, 19*, 437–466.

2. Katona, G.; Stumpel, B., & Zahn, E. (1971). *Aspirations and affluence.* New York: McGraw-Hill.

3. For a discussion of this and several other models, see Watters, C.G. (1978). *Consumer behavior* (3d ed.). Homewood, Ill.: Richard D. Irwin.

4. Allen, C. B. (1981). Over 55: Growth market of the '80s. *Nation's Business, April,* 25–32.

5. Gerhold, P. E. J. (1974). Sweeping changes seen in brand ad research. *Advertising Age, 23,* 60–61.

6. Maneloveg, H.D. (1974). Media research's future: Is there any? *Advertising Age, 23,* 28.

7. Robertson, T.S., & Wind, Y. (1980) Organizational psychographics and innovativeness. *Journal of Consumer Research, 7,* 24–31.

8. Blum, M. L. (1977). *Psychology and consumer affairs.* New York: Harper & Row.

9. See Lehmann, D. R., (1979). *Market research and analysis.* Homewood, Ill.: Richard D. Irwin. Also Backstrom, C. H., & Hursh, G. D. (1963). *Survey research.* Evanston, Ill.: Northwestern University Press.

10. McGuire, W. (1968). Personality and attitude change: An information-processing theory. In A. G. Greenwald, T. C. Brock, & T. M. Ostrom (Eds.). *Psychological foundations of attitudes.* New York: Academic Press.

11. Edwards, W. (1971). How to use multiattribute utility measurement in social decision making. *IEEE Trans. Syst. Man. Cybern. 17,* 326–340. Also, Edwards, W., & Newman, J. R. (1982). *Multiattribute Evaluation.* Beverly Hills, Calif.: Sage Publications.

12. Britt, S. H. (1966). Behavior traits. In S. H. Britt (Ed.). *Consumer behavior and the behavioral sciences* (pp. 136–137). New York: John Wiley & Sons.

13. Robertson, T. S. (1970). *Consumer behavior.* Glenview, Ill.: Scott, Foresman.

14. Fishbein, M., & Ajzen, I. (1975). *Belief, attitude, intention, and behavior: An introduction to theory and research.* Reading, Mass.: Addison-Wesley Publishing.

15. Minard, P. W., & Cohen, J. B. (1979). Isolating attitudinal and motive influences in behavioral intentions models. *Journal of Marketing Research, XVI,* 102–10; and Ryan, M.J., & Bonfield, E. H. (1980). Fishbein's intentions model: A test of external and pragmatic validity. *Journal of Marketing, 44,* 82–95.

16. Wells, W. D. (1980). Do trends in attitudes predict trends in behavior? In R. W. Olshavsky (Ed.). *Attitude research enters the 80s* (p. 127). Chicago: American Marketing Associates.

17. Achenbaum, A. A. (1966). Knowledge is a thing called measurement. In L. Adler & I. Crespi (Eds.), *Attitude research at sea* (pp. 111–126). Chicago: American Marketing Association.

18. Aaker, D. A., & Day, G. S. (1974). A dynamic model of relationships among advertising, consumer awareness, attitudes, and behavior. *Journal of Applied Psychology, 59,* 281–286.

19. Mueller, E. (1957). Effects of consumer attitudes on purchases. *American Economic Review, 47,* 946–965.

20. Biederman, I., Mezzanotte, R. J., & Robinowitz, J. C. (1982). Scene perception: Detecting and judging objects undergoing relational violations. *Cognitive Psychology, 14,* 143–177.

21. LoSiuto, L. A., & Perloff, R. (1967). Influence of product preference on dissonance reduction. *Journal of Marketing Research, 4,* 286–290.

22. Holloway, R. J. (1967). An experiment on consumer dissonance. *Journal of Marketing Research, 31,* 39–43.

23. Perloff. Consumer analysis, 437–466.

24. Cialdini, R. B., Petty, R. E., & Cacioppo, J. T. (1981). Attitude and attitude change. *Annual Review of Psychology, 32,* 357–404; Cooper, J., & Croyle, R. T. (1984). Attitudes and attitude change. *Annual Review of Psychology, 35,* 395–426.

25. Robertson. *Consumer behavior.*

26. Yankelovich, D. (1966). New criteria for market segmentation. In S. H. Britt (Ed.). *Consumer behavior and the behavioral sciences* (pp. 334–335). New York: John Wiley & Sons.

27. Greenwald, A. G., & Leavitt, C. (1984). Audience involvement in advertising: Four levels. *Journal of Consumer Research, 11,* 581–592; Mitchell, A. A. (1979). Involvement: A potentially important mediator of consumer behavior. In W. H. Wilkie (Ed.). *Advances in consumer research* (Vol. 8). Ann Arbor, Mich.: Association for Consumer Research.

28. See, for example, B. J. Wattenberg in collaboration with R. M. Scammon (1965). *This U.S.A.: An unexpected family portrait of 194,067,296 Americans drawn from the Census.* New York: Doubleday.

29. Britt, S. H. (1960). What is the nature of the drive-in theatre audience? *Media/scope, 4,* 100–104.

30. Perloff. Consumer analysis, 437–466.

31. Schultz, D. (1973). *Psychology and industry today.* New York: Macmillan.

32. Szybillo, G. J., & Jacoby, J. (1974). Effects of different levels of integration on advertising preference and intention to purchase. *Journal of Applied Psychology, 59,* 274–280.

33. Miles, V. (1974). Avoid these errors in new product research. *Advertising Age, July,* 26–57; and Rogers, E. M., & Stanfield, J. D. (1968). Adoption and diffusion of new products: Emerging generalizations and hypotheses. In F. M. Bass, C. W. King, and E. Pessemier (Eds.) *Applications of the sciences in marketing management.* New York: John Wiley & Sons.

34. Donnelly, J. H. Jr., Etzel, M. J., & Roth, S. (1973). Relationship between consumers' category width and trial of new products. *Journal of Applied Psychology, 57,* 335–338.

35. Jacoby, J. (1971). Multiple-indicant approach for studying new product adopters. *Journal of Applied Psychology, 55,* 384–388.

36. Kassarjian, H. H. (1971). Personality and consumer behavior: A review. *Journal of Marketing Research, 8,* 401–418.

37. Kaponen, A. (1960). Personality characteristics of purchasers. *Journal of Advertising Research, 1,* 6–12.

38. Tucker, W. T., & Painter, J. J. (1961). Personality and product use. *Journal of Applied Psychology, 45,* 325–339.

39. Evans, F. B. (1959). Psychological and objective factors in the prediction of brand choice: Ford versus Chevrolet, *Journal of Business, 32,* 340–369.

40. Westfall, R. (1962). Psychological factors in predicting product choice. *Journal of Marketing, 26,* 34–40.

41. Worthing, P. M., Venkatesan, M., & Smith, S. (1973). Personality and product use revisited: An exploration with the personality research form. *Journal of Applied Psychology, 57,* 179–183.

42. Cohen, J. B. (1967). An interpersonal orientation to the study of consumer behavior. *Journal of Marketing Research, 4,* 270–278.

43. Noerager, J. P. (1979). An assessment of CAD—A personality instrument developed specifically for marketing research. *Journal of Marketing Research, XVI,* 53–59.

44. Blum. *Psychology and consumer affairs.*

45. Chubb, G. P. (1963). *Drivers' ability to control the velocity of an automobile as a function of initial velocity and extent of change.* Unpublished master's thesis, Ohio State University.

46. Kemeny, J. G. (Chairman). (1979). *Report of the President's Commission on the Accident at Three Mile Island.* Washington, D.C.: U.S. Government Printing Office.

47. Hopkins, C. O. (1981). HFS developing long-range plan for Nuclear Regulatory Commission. *Human Factors Bulletin, 24,* 1–3.

48. Howell, W. C., Johnston, W. A., & Goldstein, I. L. (1966). Complex monitoring and its relation to the classical problem of vigilance. *Organizational Behavior and human performance, 1,* 129–150; also Sussman, E. D., & Morris, D. F. (1971). Investigation of factors affecting driving alertness. *JSAS Catalog of Selected Documents in Psychology, 1,* 30.

49. Allen, R. B. (Ed.). (1984). Computer text editing. *Human Factors, 26* (4), (special issue); Card, S. K., Moran, T. P., & Newell, A. (1983). *The psychology of human-computer interaction.* Hillsdale, N.J.: Erlbaum; and Turner, P. A. (Ed.). (1983). Human factors and behavioral science. *Bell System Technical Journal, 62*(6), Part 3.

50. Landau, T. K., Dumais, S. T., Gomez, L. M., & Furnas, G. W. (1982). Human factors in data access. *Bell System Technical Journal, 61,* 2487–2509.

51. Tullis, T. S. (1981). An evaluation of alphanumeric, graphic, and color information displays. *Human Factors, 23,* 541–550; also Tullis, T. S. (1984). *Presenting the usability of alphanumeric displays.* Doctoral dissertation, Rice University.

52. McCarthy, R. L., Finnegan, J. P., Krumm-Scott, S., & McGarthy, G. E. (1984). Product information presentation, user behavior, and safety. *Proceedings of the Human Factors Society—28th Annual Meeting, 1,* 81–85.

53. Kantowitz, B. H., & Sorkin, R. D. (1983). *Human factors.* New York: John Wiley & Sons. Also Woodson, W. E. (1981). *Human factors design handbook.* New York: McGraw-Hill.

54. Hitt, W. D. (1961). An evaluation of five different abstract coding methods. *Human Factors, 3,* 120–130.

55. Wickins, C. D., Vidulich, M., & Sandry-Garza, D. (1984). Principles of S-C-R compatibility with spatial and verbal tasks: The role of display-control location and voice-interactive display-control interfacing. *Human Factors, 26,* 533–543.

56. Buckner, D. N., & McGrath, J. J. (Eds.). (1963). *Vigilance: A symposium.* New York: McGraw-Hill.

57. Broadbent, D. E., & Gregory, M. (1965). Effects of noise and signal rate upon vigilance analyzed by means of decision theory. *Human Factors, 7,* 155–162.

58. Fisk, A. D., & Schneider, W. (1981). Control and automatic processing during tasks which require sustained attention: A new approach to vigilance. *Human Factors, 23,* 737–750.

59. Posner, M. I., & McLeod, P. (1982). Information-processing models—In search of elementary operations. *Annual Review of Psychology, 33,* 477–514.

60. Ibid.

61. Smith, E. E. (1968). Choice reaction time: An analysis of the major theoretical positions. *Psychological Bulletin, 69,* 77–110; Taylor, D. A. (1976). Stage analysis of reaction time. *Psychology Bulletin, 83,* 169–191.

62. Kantowitz, B. H. (1982). Interfacing human information-processing and engineering psychology. In W. C. Howell & E. A. Fleishman (Eds.). *Human performance and productivity* (Vol. 2). Hillsdale, N.J.: Erlbaum; Lane, D. M. Limited capacity, attention allocation, and productivity. In Howell & Fleishman, ibid.

63. Shiffrin, R. M., & Schneider, W. (1977). Controlled and automatic human information processing: II. Perceptual learning, automatic attending, and a general theory. *Psychological Review, 84,* 127–190; Wickins, C. D. (1984). *Engineering psychology and human performance.* Columbus, Ohio: Merrill.

64. Beatty, J. (1982). Task-evoked pupillary responses, processing load, and the structure of processing resources. *Psychological Bulletin, 91,* 276–292; Moray, N. (1982). Subjective mental workload. *Human Factors, 24,* 25–40.

65. Wickins, C. D., Mountford, S. J., & Shreiner, W. (1981). Multiple resources, task-hemispheric integrity, and individual differences, in time-sharing. *Human Factors, 23,* 211–229.

66. Peterson, C. R., & Beach, L. R. (1967). Man as an intuitive statistician. *Psychological Bulletin, 68,* 29–46; Slovic, P., Fischoff, B., & Lichtenstein, S. (1977). Behavioral decision theory. *Annual Review of Psychology, 28,* 1–39.

67. Naylor, J. C., & Wherry, R. J., Sr. (1965). The use of simulated stimuli and the "JAN" technique to capture and cluster the policies of raters. *Educational and Psychological Measurement, 25,* 969–986; Hammond, K. R., & Summers, D. A. (1965). Cognitive dependence on linear and nonlinear cues. *Psychological Review, 72,* 215–224.

68. Slovic, P. (1982). Toward understanding and improving decisions. In W. C. Howell & E. A. Fleishman (Eds.). *Human performance and productivity* (Vol. 2). Hillsdale, N.J.: Erlbaum.

69. For a comprehensive review, see Kahneman, D., Slovic, P., & Tversky, A. (Eds.). (1982). *Judgment under uncertainty: Heuristics and biases.* New York: Cambridge.

70. Einhorn, H. J. (1980). Learning from experience and suboptimal rules in decision making. In T. S. Wallsten (Ed.). *Cognitive processes in choice and decision behavior.* Hillsdale, N.J.: Erlbaum.

71. Fishoff, B. (1982). Debiasing. In D. Kahneman, D. Slovic, & A. Tversky (Eds.). *Judgment under uncertainty: Heuristics and biases.* New York: Cambridge.

72. Einhorn, H. J., & Hogarth, R. M. (1981). Behavioral decision theory: Processes of judgment and choice. *Annual Review of Psychology, 32,* 53–88.

73. Schmidt, R. A. (1976). Control processes in motor skills. *Exercise and Sports Sciences Reviews, 4,* 229–261; also Schmidt, R. A., Zelaznik, H., Hawkins, B., Frank, J. S., & Quinn, J. T., Jr. (1979). Motor-output variability: A theory for the accuracy of rapid motor acts. *Psychology Review, 86,* 415–451.

74. Kelso, J. A. S. (1977). Motor control mechanisms underlying human movement reproduction. *Journal of Experimental Psychology: Human Perception and Performance, 3,* 529–543.

75. Alluisi, E. A., & Morgan, B. B., Jr. (1982). Temporal factors in human performance and productivity. In E. A. Alluisi and E. A. Fleishman (Eds.). *Human performance and productivity* (Vol. 3). Hillsdale, N.J.: Erlbaum.

76. Selye, H. (1976). *The stress of life.* New York: McGraw-Hill.

77. Hogan, R., & Hogan, J. C. Subjective correlates of stress and human performance. In E. A. Alluisi & E. A. Fleishman (Eds.). *Human performance and productivity* (Vol. 3). Hillsdale, N.J.: Erlbaum.

78. Poulton, E. C. (1966). Engineering psychology. *Annual Review of Psychology, 17,* 177–200.

79. Wing, J. F. (1965). Upper thermal tolerance limits for unimpaired mental performance. *Aerospace Medicine, 36,* 960–964.

80. Fanger, P. O. (1972). *Thermal comfort.* New York: McGraw-Hill.

81. Howell, W. C., & Kennedy, P. A. (1979). Field validation of the Fanger thermal comfort model. *Human Factors, 21,* 229–239; Howell, W. C., & Stramler, C. S. (1981). The contribution of psychological variables to the prediction of thermal comfort judgments in real work settings. *ASHRAE Transactions, 87,* Pt. 1; Rohles, F. H. Jr. (1971). Psychological aspects of thermal comfort. *ASHRAE Journal, 13,* 86–90.

82. Baritz, L. (1960). *The servants of power.* Middletown, Conn.: Wesleyan University Press.

83. Brett, J. M. (1984). Why employees want unions. In R. S. Schuler & S. A. Youngblood (Eds.). *Readings in personnel and human resource management* (2d ed.) (pp. 453–465). St. Paul, Minn.: West Publishing.

84. Youngblood, S. A., DeNisi, A. S., Molleston, J. L., & Mobley, W. H. (1984). The impact of work environment, instrumentality beliefs, perceived labor union image, and subjective norms on union voting intentions. *Academy of Management Journal, 27,* 576–590.

85. Peterson, F. (1963). *American labor unions: What they are and how they work.* New York: Harper & Row.
86. Rambo, W. W. (1982). *Work and organizational behavior.* New York: Holt, Rinehart & Winston.
87. Justice, B. W. The nature of collective bargaining. In R. S. Schuler & S. A. Youngblood (Eds.). *Readings in personnel and human resource management* (2d ed.) (pp. 466–478). St. Paul, Minn.: West Publishing.
88. French, W. L. (1982). *The personnel management process* (5th ed). Boston: Houghton Mifflin.
89. Fleishman, E. A., & Harris, E. E. (1962). Patterns of leadership behavior related to employee grievances and turnover. *Personnel Psychology, 15,* 43–56.
90. Ash, P. (1979). The parties to the grievance. *Personnel Psychology, 23,* 13–37.
91. Dalton, D. R., & Todor, W. D. (1979). Manifest needs of stewards: propensity to file a grievance. *Journal of Applied Psychology, 64,* 654–659.
92. Dalton, D. R., & Todor, W. D. (1982). Antecedents of grievance filing behavior: Attitude/behavioral consistency and the union steward. *Academy of Management Journal, 25,* 158–169.
93. Derber, M., Chalmers, W. E., & Edelman, M. T. (1962–1963). Types and variants in local union-management relationships. *Human Organizations, 21,* 264–271.
94. Brett, J. M. (1980). Behavioral research on unions and union management systems. In B. M. Staw & L. L. Cummings (Eds.). *Research in organizational behavior* (Vol. 2) (pp. 177–214). Greenwich, Conn: JAI Press.
95. Ibid.
96. Ibid.
97. Grigsby, D. W., & Bigoness, W. J. (1982). Effects of mediation and alternative forms of arbitration on bargaining behavior: A laboratory study. *Journal of Applied Psychology, 67,* 549–554.
98. Staudohar, P. D. (1975). Results of a final-offer arbitration of bargaining disputes. *California Management Review, 18,* 57–61.
99. Nadler, D. A., & Lawler, E. E. III. (1984). Quality of work life: Perspectives and Directions. In R. S. Schuler & S. A. Youngblood (Eds.). *Readings in personnel and human resource management* (2d ed.) (pp. 349–358). St. Paul, Minn.: West Publishing.
100. Ibid.
101. Schuster, M. (1983). The impact of union-management cooperation on productivity and employment. *Industrial and Labor Relations Review, 36,* 415–430.

10

Concluding Comments

Unlike the novel or even the biography, the textbook has no logical ending. Authors are justified simply in stopping once they have covered the requisite topics. Most, however, feel a compulsion to bring some sort of closure to the array of material they have presented, and we are no exception. Our concluding thought has to do with I/O psychology's impact on organizational affairs—past, present, and future. Broadly speaking, how much has it contributed, and what are its prospects for the future?

Our position, in a nutshell, is that despite its relative youth, the field of I/O psychology has proven its worth. It has made demonstrable and lasting contributions to virtually every facet of organizing, managing, developing, and serving people. It has advanced our basic understanding of work motivation, attitudes, group processes, individual differences, and so forth; knowledge which has led to specific principles and techniques that, in turn, have produced tangible improvements in both productivity and quality of work life. In the preceeding chapters we have attempted to illustrate these contributions—the scientific as well as the practical ones. But we have also illustrated, often by implication, that there is much yet to be learned, and even our current knowledge is frequently ignored, misunderstood, or misused in the organizational decision-making process. Organizations today are realizing only a fraction of the benefits that I/O psychology has to offer. Given the kind and magnitude of problems they will be facing in the next few decades, they can ill afford to squander that potential. Therefore, we devote the rest of this very brief concluding chapter to a consideration of what those problems are likely to be, and the obstacles that will need to be overcome if I/O psychology is to play an important role in addressing them.

PROBLEMS ON THE HORIZON

By most accounts, the problems facing our industrial/organizational/ management community as we approach the 21st century will become increasingly *human*-oriented and increasingly urgent. What will happen to the work force, for example, as automation continues to expand? What changes will be required in organizational design, management philosophies, career planning, work roles and values, skill requirements, compensation systems, and leisure activities?

Much has been written recently about the trend in the U.S. economy from a production to a service orientation. Certainly, this has important ramifications for the entire profile of the work force and, indeed, the very definition of work. Our industrial growth was founded on a base of plentiful resources and mass production. Service, however, is inherently less structured, more idiosyncratic and dynamic, more *human*. How well are our organizations prepared to make the necessary adjustments?

Or consider another widely recognized trend: the shifting U.S. demography. Our population is becoming older, the number of two-career families is increasing, and people continue their migration to warmer climates. As unrest persists in Latin America, Southeast Asia, the Middle East, and Africa, we can expect immigration from these areas (legal and otherwise) to continue growing. Certainly such an influx will have an impact on the work force. How will our social and industrial organizations cope with these demographic shifts?

Still another example is the proliferation of takeovers and mergers that is occurring among today's corporations—even very large ones. Attempting to blend the most compatible of organizations is no simple matter; integrating former competitors or organizations with very different structures, climates, or cultures is a virtual nightmare. The atmosphere of uncertainty and confusion can have a profound effect on both productivity and morale. Full assimilation of the two work forces and management systems can take years. Is there not some way to affect a smoother transition?

And finally, of course, there is the growing importance of international politics and practices in all our organizational affairs. What happens in the Japanese auto or steel or electronics industries has a direct bearing on the policies and practices formulated in Detroit, Pittsburgh, "Silicon Valley," and Washington, D.C. Because of the Japanese success story, for example, a virtual revolution has taken place in all aspects of our automobile industry: production methods, management philosophies, decision-making procedures, even union-management relationships. Likewise, the spectre of international terrorism has placed serious constraints on the activities of our large, multinational corporations on foreign soil. Organizations must think twice before investing heavily in new operations in certain developing countries, or before assigning key personnel to existing foreign operations.

It is our contention that I/O psychology has contributions to make in all of these existing or emerging problem areas. How much it contributes, however, will depend upon several considerations to which we now turn our attention.

CONDITIONS FOR PRODUCTIVE APPLICATION

The fact that I/O psychology has been underutilized to this point is due to several inhibiting conditions. Unless these are corrected, its contribution to the solution of future problems will continue to be limited.

The first inhibiting condition is simply one of attitude. Despite all the evidence to the contrary, the prevailing view among line managers is that "human relations" is something one does when one has time or money to spare; it is not a fundamental aspect of the management process. Implementing an effective performance-appraisal system, training program, or QWL program does take time and cost money. But it also pays dividends. Unfortunately, managers all too often fail to see beyond the initial costs. If the full potential of I/O psychology is to be realized, management must stop viewing those functions to which the field contributes most directly as luxuries.

A second condition has to do with the prevailing management philosophy. Most of today's managers have been schooled in the virtues of "Theory Y" (or "System 4" or "considerate") management concepts. At an intellectual level, they are also aware of the pitfalls in the antithetical "classical" view. They understand all about how people are supposed to be motivated through the opportunity to participate in decisions that affect them. Still, in our experience, the manager who really *believes* such things and practices them is rare. Scratch the Theory Y veneer and you quickly discover a Theory X core that is as solid as ever.

We recognize, of course, that it takes time for new ideas to sink in. But these are hardly new ideas! Moreover, we find the intuitive belief in the classical view almost as prevalent among our MBA students (and even undergraduates) as it is among practicing managers. One can only conclude that the "macho management" concept has become a part of our culture. It is interesting to note, in this regard, the success of the recent bestseller *In Search of Excellence*. Using a questionable survey method and seriously flawed logic, the authors nonetheless appear to have convinced America that they have identified what sets our most successful organizations apart. And what are these great insights? These prescriptions for excellence in organization and management? By the authors' own admission,[1] little more than the practice of what human-oriented scientists and theorists have known and been preaching since the 1930s! These are the very same principles to which managers have been exposed with so little effect in business schools, short courses, and OB or I/O psychology texts such as the present one, for *generations*. Apparently an appealing presentation of spurious evidence is having more of an impact on the management community than nearly 50 years of solid research findings. Fortunately, in this case, both lead to the same conclusions. Perhaps at long last the veneer is beginning to crack!

Unfortunately, not all the popular advice on human-organization relations to which managers are so readily drawn is equally constructive. This leads to our third inhibiting condition: management's gullibility and short-term perspective. As we noted in the first chapter, it is common for managers to accept on faith schemes for improving employee morale, motivation, productivity, leadership effectiveness, and other people-oriented nostrums that are totally without scientific merit. The promise of a "quick fix," a few big numbers, a testimonial or two, and a flashy brochure are often all that it takes. And no provisions are made for rigorous evaluation. Until organizations begin to take decisions regarding the human side of management as seriously as the technological and financial ones; until they learn how to discriminate between the legitimate and the illegitimate application of social science in general and psychology in particular, the real potential of these fields will continue to be squandered.

Finally, there is the matter of expectations. The reader may have begun this text with hopes of finding definitive answers to many of the problems that organizations face in managing human resources. Yet, research and theory in I/O psychology seldom have led to universal prescriptions that can be applied across all situations. More often than not the conclusion is that "more research is needed." Psychology as a science is still in its adolescence; as an adjunct to organization and management, in its infancy. Organizations must resist the temptation to demand conclusive answers for all people-related problems. And I/O psychology must resist the equally strong temptation to provide them. Often, both must be satisfied with a set of options—each with its pros and cons. At times, the organization will have to invest in research before making the final decisions, just as it would with a new product. However, if this set of realistic expectations becomes more commonplace than it is today, our understanding will grow and the range of plausible options for each kind of problem will progressively narrow.

Obviously, decisions must be made: even a narrow range of options is too many where the organization or manager is called upon to *act*. Some judgment will always be necessary, regardless of how successful we are in generating basic knowledge. Our point is simply that the judgment can be enlightened or unenlightened, and it is to that end that I/O psychology has a great deal to offer. The enlightened organization of the future, like those in the past, will have reasonable expectations of our science. It will make informed use of what we can offer rather than impulsive use of what we can't.

NOTE

1. Peters, T. J., & Waterman, R. H. (1982). *In search of excellence.* New York: Warner Books.

Name Index

A

Aaker, D.A., 405
Abrahams, N.M., 298
Abramowitz, S.I., 354
Achenbaum, A.A., 367, 405
Adams, F.F., 191
Adams, J.S., 70–71, 90
Adler, L., 367, 405
Ajzen, I., 405
Albright, D.W., 89
Aldag, R.J., 88
Alderfer, C.P., 54, 85, 88, 138
Alexander, R.A., 171
Alf, E., Jr., 298
Allen, C.B., 405
Allen, M.P., 171, 193
Allen, R.B., 407
Allison, T.J., 123, 140
Alluisi, E.A., 408
Anastasi, A., 297
Andrews, F.M., 140
Antoinetti, J.H., 352
Argyris, C., 326, 353
Arvey, R.D., 298–99
Asch, S.E., 119
Ash, P., 409
Ash, R.A., 235
Ashby, W., 113, 122, 139
Ashour, A.S., 177
Atkinson, J.W., 58, 88
Atkinson, R.C., 352
Auclair, G., 263, 297

B

Backstrom, C.H., 405
Baetz, J.L., 192

Baker, F., 39
Bales, R.F., 101, 120, 138–39
Balma, M.J., 300
Bamforth, K.W., 39, 135, 141
Bandura, A., 327, 353
Baritz, L., 408
Barnard, C., 26–27, 39
Barrett, G.V., 13, 40, 192, 212, 221, 236, 282, 299
Barrow, J.C., 193
Bartlett, C.J., 268–70, 297–98
Bass, B.M., 13, 90, 139, 167, 192–93, 212, 221, 236, 282, 299, 352
Bass, F.M., 406
Bass, H.R., 298
Beach, L.R., 89, 408
Beatty, J., 407
Beatty, R.W., 235–37
Becker, G.B., 89
Beckhard, R., 118, 139
Beer, M., 237
Bell, C.H., 79, 91, 141, 342, 354
Bem, D.J., 90
Bennis, W.G., 23, 39
Berger, M.A., 353
Berkowitz, L., 138
Bernardin, H.J., 235–37, 354
Biederman, L., 405
Bigoness, W.J., 409
Binet, A., 287
Birdwell, L.G., 87–88
Bishop, R.C., 910
Blackwell, R.D., 359
Blake, R.R., 139, 160, 192
Blanchard, K.M., 187–88, 195
Blau, P.M., 111, 139

Blencoe, A.G., 141, 236
Blood, M., 90
Blum, M., 405–6
Blumrosen, A.W., 298
Bochner, S., 193
Boehm, V.R., 298
Bolda, R.A., 297
Bonfield, E.H., 405
Borman, W.C., 299
Bouchard, T.J., 141
Bowers, D.G., 193
Boyatizis, R., 149, 192
Brayfield, A.H., 87
Bray, D.W., 299–300
Brenner, M.H., 354
Brett, J., 402, 408–9
Brief, A.P., 88
Britt, S.H., 405–6
Broadbent, D.E., 407
Brock, T.C., 405
Brousseau, K.R., 132, 141
Brown, C.W., 87, 288, 300
Brune, R.L., 297
Buchanan, P.C., 354
Buckley, M.R., 354
Buchner, D.N., 384, 407
Bugelski, B.R., 318, 325, 352
Burns, T., 34, 39, 122, 140
Buros, O.K., 286, 299
Byham, W.C., 192

C
Cacippo, J.T., 406
Calder, B.J., 90
Callendar, J.C., 298
Campbell, D.T., 14
Campbell, J.P., 53, 87–88, 141, 191, 232, 236–37, 297, 313, 338, 351, 354
Campbell, K.M., 90
Campbell, R.J., 300
Campion, J.E., 299
Campion, M.A., 299
Card, S.K., 407
Carledge, N., 76, 87, 89
Carlson, R.E., 299
Carroll, S.J., 192, 352
Carson, K.P., 171, 194
Cascio, W.F., 236, 265, 297
Cavander, J.W., 87
Chadwick-Jones, J.K., 87
Chalmers, W.E., 401
Chandler, A.D., 139
Chapanis, A., 376
Chemers, M.J., 138, 353
Cherrington, D.J., 47, 87, 89
Christal, R.E., 236
Chronbach, L.J., 297, 299
Chubb, G.P., 407
Cialdini, R.B., 406
Clark, R.A., 88, 193

Cleary, T.A., 271–72, 298
Cohen, J.B., 405–6
Cohen, S.L., 140, 192
Collins, B., 109, 140
Cook, M.S., 139
Cooper, J., 406
Cooper, W.H., 225–26, 236
Coors, A.E., 192
Cornelius, E.T., 236
Cosentino, J., 352
Cotton, J.L., 139
Coyle, B.W., 297
Craig, J.R., 193
Crespi, I., 367, 405
Crockett, W.H., 87
Crowe, B.H., 193
Croyle, R.T., 406
Cummings, L.L., 409
Cyart, R., 30, 39

D
Dachler, H.P., 13, 53, 88
Dale, E., 27
Dalton, D.R., 401, 409
Dansereau, F., 193
Davis, K., 39
Davis, L.E., 347, 354
Dawes, R.D., 87
Day, G.S., 405
Deci, E.L., 72–73, 82, 90
Decker, P.J., 353
Delberg, A.L., 141
DeLeo, P.J., 86, 89
DeNisi, A.S., 141, 195, 236, 408
Derber, M., 401
Dermer, J., 194
Dessler, G., 27, 39
Detterman, D.K., 300
Deutsch, M., 111, 139
Dickson, W.J., 39, 93, 137
Dieterly, D.L., 193
Dipboye, R.L., 90, 191, 280, 299
Dittrich, J.E., 141, 326, 353
Donnelly, J.H., Jr., 164, 193, 406
Dossett, D.L., 331, 353
Downey, R.G., 236
Dreher, G.F., 192, 300
Dumais, S.T., 407
Dunham, R.B., 88
Dunnette, M.D., 13, 57, 87–88, 91, 191, 236, 270, 297, 299, 338, 354, 376
Durand, D.E., 353
Dyer, F.J., 298
Dyer, L., 89

E
Easterbrook, J.A., 138
Edelman, M.T., 409
Eden, D., 353

Edwards, D.D., 323, 352
Edwards, W., 89, 405
Einhorn, H.J., 298, 408
Emery, F.E., 34, 39
Engel, J.F., 359
England, G.W., 87, 299
England, J.L., 62, 89
Entvisle, D.R., 88
Etzel, M.J., 406
Evans, F.B., 406
Evans, M.G., 194
Ezell, H.F., 191

F
Fairhurst, G.T., 140
Fanger, P.D., 408
Farr, J.L., 297
Farris, G.F., 193
Fay, C.H., 236
Fayol, H., 24, 39
Feather, N.T., 88
Feldman, D.C., 139
Festinger, L., 138, 140
Fiedler, F.E., 138, 175–78, 195, 336–37,
    353–54
Field, R.H.G., 195
Fine, S.A., 205–6, 235
Finnegan, J.P., 407
Fischoff, B., 408
Fishbein, M., 365–66, 405
Fisher, C., 87, 140
Fisk, A.D., 384, 407
Fleishman, E.A., 161, 192–93, 210–11,
    236, 323, 336, 352–53, 401, 407–9
Follett, M.P., 26–27, 39
Folley, J.D., Jr., 351–52
Fombrun, C., 139
Frank, J.S., 408
Freedman, R.D., 353
French, J.R.P., 161, 193, 342, 354
French, W.L., 141, 409
Friedman, A., 72, 90
Fromkin, H.L., 191
Fruchter, B., 297
Fryer, D.H., 237
Fulk, J., 195
Furnas, G.W., 407

G
Gagné, R.M., 302, 312–13, 352
Galbraith, J.D., 30, 34–35, 38–39, 138
Gerard, H., 140
Gerhold, P.E.J., 405
Ghiselli, E.E., 147, 191, 288, 297–98, 300
Gibb, J.R., 104, 138
Gitelson, R.A., 140
Gleser, G., 297
Gobdel, B.C., 165
Goldstein, A.P., 327

Goldstein, I.L., 13, 303–5, 307, 351–54,
    407
Gomez, L.M., 407
Goodman, P., 72, 90
Gordon, L.K., 191
Gough, H.G., 149, 191
Graen, G., 164, 177, 193, 335, 353
Grant, D.L., 299
Graves, J., 140
Gray, M.J., 139
Green, S.G., 170, 173, 193
Greenbaum, C.W., 138, 140
Greene, C.N., 47, 87, 166, 193, 195
Greenwald, A.G., 405–6
Gregory, M., 407
Griffin, R.W., 95, 138
Grigsby, D.W., 409
Guest, R.H., 137
Guetzkow, H., 109, 129, 140
Guilford, J.B., 297
Guion, R.M., 285–86, 289, 291, 297–300,
    346, 348, 354
Gulick, L., 24
Gullahorn, J.T., 116–17, 137
Gustafson, D.H., 141
Guzzo, R.A., 133, 141
Gyr, J., 129, 140

H
Hackman, J.R., 38, 60–61, 79, 81, 85, 88,
    90, 105, 132, 134, 138, 141, 296
Haga, W.J., 193
Hahn, C.P., 323, 352
Haire, M., 39, 297
Hakel, M.D., 57, 88, 299
Halderman, J., 141
Hall, D.T., 53, 88
Hall, H.L., 235
Hall, J., 141
Hammond, K.R., 408
Hamner, E.P., 87, 91
Hamner, W.C., 87, 91
Hamstra, B.W., 299
Haney, W.V., 138
Hare, A.P., 138, 141
Harrell, A.M., 89
Harris, E.F., 161, 192, 401, 409
Hartley, D., 354
Harvey, R.J., 236
Hankins, H., 408
Hayes, T.L., 236
Heinzmann, A.T., 309, 352
Hemphill, J., 157
Henderson, R., 237
Heneman, H.G., III, 89, 237, 299
Henry, E.R., 299
Herold, D.M., 195
Hersey, P., 187, 195
Herzberg, F., 54–57, 59, 78–79, 82, 85–
    86, 88, 90

Hickson, D.J., 28, 39
Hieser, R.A., 139
Hill, J.W., 90
Hinrichs, J.R., 192, 302, 351
Hitt, W.D., 407
Hodgson, J.D., 354
Hogan, J.C., 236, 408
Hogan, R.T., 408
Hogarth, R.M., 408
Holland, W.E., 137
Hollenbeck, J., 86
Holloway, R.J., 406
Holt, H.O., 352
Hopkins, C.O., 407
House, R., 179–81, 192, 195
Howard, A., 300
Howell, W.C., 13, 407–8
Hulin, C.L., 53, 62, 88–89, 90
Hulvershorn, P., 331, 353
Hunt, D.M., 352
Hunt, J.G., 192–93
Hunt, R.G., 39
Hunter, J.E., 53, 88, 265, 272–73, 292, 297–300
Hunter, R., 272–73, 297–99
Hursh, G.D., 405
Hymovitch, B., 140

I

Iaffaldano, M.J., 87
Ikeda, H., 89
Ilgen, D.W., 209, 235–36, 290, 297, 300
Ingham, A.G., 129, 140
Isenburg, D.J., 139
Ivancevich, J.M., 164, 193, 352

J

Jackson, K.W., 119–20, 353
Jacobs, T.O., 164, 193
Jacobson, E., 139
Jacoby, J., 372, 406
James, L.R., 348, 354
Jago, A.G., 195
Janis, I.L., 115, 139
Jeanneret, P.R., 235–36
Jensen, A.R., 297
Jerdee, T.H., 192
Jermier, J.M., 173–75
Jewell, L.N., 138
Johnson, D.W., 139
Johnson, R., 139
Johnston, W.J., 407
Jones, A.P., 348, 354
Jones, M.B., 128, 140
Jorgenson, D.C., 89
Justice, B.W., 409

K

Kagawa, M., 89
Kahn, R.L., 29–30, 39, 121, 139, 164, 193, 346, 354

Kahneman, D., 391, 408
Kallat, D.T., 359
Kane, J.S., 141
Karurgo, R.N., 43, 87
Kantowitz, B.H., 14, 394, 407
Kaplan, R.E., 141
Kaponen, A., 372
Kassarjian, H.H., 406
Katona, G., 356, 405
Katz, D., 29–30, 39, 121, 138–39, 164, 193, 346, 354
Katzell, R.A., 87, 298
Keller, R.T., 137
Kelley, H.H., 140
Kelman, H.C., 139
Kelso, J.A.S., 408
Kemeny, J.G., 407
Kendall, L.M., 230, 237
Kennedy, P.A., 408
Kerr, S., 159, 173–75, 192
Kidron, A.G., 353
King, C.W., 406
Kipnis, D., 165, 193
Kirchner, W.K., 339, 354
Kirk, R.J., 86
Kirkpatrick, D.L., 353
Klinger, E., 88
Knerr, C.S., 87, 89
Kolb, D.A., 330, 353
Komaki, J., 309, 352
Korman, A.K., 13, 69, 90, 150, 192, 195
Kromm-Scott, S., 407

L

Lakey, M.A., 236
Landy, F.J., 236
Lane, D.M., 407
Landaver, T.K., 407
Lang, J.R., 141, 326, 353
Larson, L.L., 192–93
Latane, B., 140
Latham, G.P., 89, 236–37, 299, 328, 353
Lawler, E.E., 38, 74–76, 83–84, 87–91, 129, 140–41, 191, 232, 236, 269, 409
Lawrence, P.R., 34, 39, 43
Lawshe, C.H., 263, 297, 300
Lawson, L., 309, 352
Leavitt, C., 406
Lehmann, D.R., 405
Leon, F.R., 89
Leonard, D.W., 86
Levine, E.L., 235
Levinger, G., 129, 140
Lichtenstein, S., 408
Lieberson, S., 171, 193
Likert, R., 345, 354
Lim, F.G., 193
Lincoln, J.R., 138
Locke, E.A., 61–64, 74, 76, 79, 87–89, 91, 192
Lofquist, L.H., 87

London, M., 352
Lord, R.G., 193
Lorsch, J.W., 34, 39
LoSiuto, L.A., 406
Lott, A.J., 140
Lott, B.E., 140
Lotz, R.E., 171, 193
Lowell, E.L., 88
Lusterman, S., 351

M

Maher, L., 353–54
Mahoney, R.A., 154, 171, 192, 194
Maier, N.R.F., 132, 141
Maneloveg, H.D., 405
March, J.G., 30, 39
Maruyama, G., 139
Maslow, A.H., 51–54, 59, 85, 87, 95, 103
Matsui, T., 89
Mayfield, E.C., 299
Mayo, E., 18
McCarthy, G.E., 407
McCarthy, R.L., 407
McClelland, D.C., 85, 88, 149, 158–60, 192, 335, 353
McClintock, C.G., 89
McCormick, E.J., 208–9, 230, 235–36, 264, 290, 300, 383
McGehee, W., 87, 351–53
McGrath, J.J., 384, 407
McGregor, D., 52, 87
McGuire, W., 362, 405
McIntyre, J.M., 353
McKeachie, W.I., 322, 352
McKenzie, R.C., 297
McKinney, A.C., 353
McLeod, P., 386, 407
Mecham, R.C., 235–36
Menlo, A.J., 76
Merrihue, H.F., 87
Mezzanotte, R.J., 405
Michael, C., 352
Miles, M.B., 88, 343–44, 354
Miles, V., 406
Miller, J., 138
Miller, R.S., 140
Minard, P.W., 405
Miner, J.B., 13, 39, 148–49, 191, 352
Mintzberg, H., 145, 154, 192
Mischel, W., 192
Mitchell, A.A., 406
Mitchell, J.L., 210, 236
Mitchell, T.R., 79, 89, 91, 95, 138, 170, 173, 179, 193, 195
Mobley, W.H., 408
Molleston, J.L., 408
Mooney, J., 24
Moore, D.L., 139
Moran, T.P., 407
Moray, N., 407
Morgan, B.B., Jr., 408

Morris, D.F., 407
Morris, C.G., 105, 134, 138
Morsh, J.E., 207, 235
Moses, J.L., 192
Mountford, S.J., 408
Mouton, J., 139, 160, 192
Mowday, R.T., 45, 87, 90
Muchinsky, P.M., 87
Muczyk, J.P., 352
Mueller, E., 405
Muldrow, T., 297
Munsterburg, H., 4, 89
Murray, H., 50–51, 58, 87

N

Nadla, D.A., 409
Nash, A.N., 148, 191, 352
Naylor, J.C., 408
Nebeker, D.M., 179, 195
Nelson, D., 139
Nemeroff, W.F., 352
Neuhauser, J.J., 352
Newell, A., 407
Newman, J.R., 405
Nida, S., 140
Noerager, J.P., 406
Nord, W.R., 87
Nougaim, K.E., 53, 88
Nunnally, J.C., 237
Nystrom, P., 89, 192

O

O'Connor, J.F., 171, 193
Odewahn, C.A., 191
O'Gara, P.W., 90
Ohnesorge, J.P., 299
Ohtsuka, Y., 89
Oldham, G., 60–61, 79, 81, 85
O'Leary, V.S., 268–70, 297–98
Olsharsky, R.W., 405
Opsahl, R.L., 91
O'Reilly, C.H., 139
Organ, D.W., 47, 80, 91
Orife, J.N., 79, 91
Osborn, R.N., 192
Osburn, H.G., 298
Ostrom, T.M., 405
Owens, W.A., 299

P

Paine, F.T., 352
Painter, J.J., 372, 406
Panian, S.K., 171, 193
Parker, D.F., 89
Parsons, H.M., 39, 139
Pasmore, W., 141
Patchen, M., 88
Payne, R., 88
Pearlman, K., 298–99
Peckham, V., 140
Pelz, D.C., 140

Peres, H., 236
Perloff, R., 405–6
Perrow, C., 39
Pessemier, E., 406
Peters, T.J., 414
Peterson, C.R., 89, 408
Peterson, D.A., 299
Peterson, F., 409
Petrullo, L., 139
Petty, M., 87
Pfeffer, J., 95, 138
Pheysey, D.C., 28, 39
Pimoff, E.S., 300
Podsakoff, P.M., 166, 193
Porter, L.W., 38–39, 45, 86–87, 90, 129, 140, 296
Posner, B.Z., 314, 319, 326, 328–29, 352–53
Posner, M.I., 386, 407
Poulton, E.C., 408
Pritchard, R.D., 86, 89, 90
Pugh, D.S., 28, 38–39
Purcell, L.M., 299

Q–R

Quaintance, M.K., 210, 236
Quinn, J.T., Jr., 408
Quinn, R.P., 191, 193
Rambo, W.W., 409
Randolph, W.A., 141, 314, 319, 326, 328–29, 352–53
Rapaport, A., 89
Rauschenberbger, J., 53, 88, 297
Raven, B., 140, 161, 193
Ravid, G., 353
Reddin, W.J., 187, 195
Reilly, R.R., 236, 297
Reitz, H.J., 87, 138
Ritchie, J.B., 354
Roback, H.B., 354
Roberts, K.H., 88, 139
Robertson, T.S., 405
Robinowtz, J.C., 405
Roche, G.R., 352
Roethlisberger, F., 39, 93, 137
Rogers, E.M., 406
Rohles, F.H., Jr., 408
Roscoe, S.N., 352
Rosen, N.A., 171, 194
Rosenbaum, M.E., 139
Rosenthal, R.A., 193
Roth, S., 406
Rousseau, D.M., 236
Rubin, I., 118, 139, 353
Rush, M., 193
Russell, J.T., 262
Ryan, M.J., 405

S

Saad, F.E., 236
Saari, L.M., 89, 299, 328, 354
Sackett, P.R., 192, 300

Salancik, G., 90, 95, 138
Sales, S.M., 91
Sanders, M.S., 383
Sandry-Garza, D., 407
Sands, L., 192
Sands, W.A., 297
Scammon, R.M., 406
Scandura, T.A., 353
Schein, E.H., 103, 105, 138, 140
Scherf, G.W.H., 54, 88
Schlenker, B.R., 140
Schmidt, F.L., 193, 265, 272–73, 292, 297–300
Schmidt, R.A., 408
Schmidt, W.H., 155–56, 192
Schmitt, N., 53, 88, 297–99
Schmuck, R.A., 343–44, 354
Schneider, B., 88, 193, 296–97
Schneider, W., 384, 407–8
Schoenfeldt, L.F., 299
Schriesheim, C.A., 159, 192, 195
Schuler, R.S., 40, 91, 195, 298, 408–9
Schultz, D., 406
Schuster, M., 404, 409
Schwab, D.P., 89, 299
Schwartz, D.F., 139
Schweiger, D.M., 192
Scott, W.D., 4
Seashore, S.E., 140, 193
Seely, W., 297
Seligman, D., 298
Selye, H., 408
Shani, A., 141
Shaw, K.N., 89
Shaw, M.E., 93, 137, 139–40
Shea, D.J., 353
Sheldon, A.S., 24
Sherman, J.D., 191
Sherwood, J.J., 339, 354
Shiffrin, R.M., 407
Shovar, M.N., 139
Simon, H.A., 27, 30, 39, 390
Simonds, R.H., 79, 91
Sirota, D., 79, 91
Sistrunk, F., 235
Skinner, B.F., 41, 317, 352
Skon, L., 139
Slovic, P., 408
Smart, G., 139
Smith, E.E., 407
Smith, J.E., 171, 194
Smith, P.C., 230, 237
Smith, S., 373, 406
Snarely, B.K., 140
Snoek, J.D., 193
Sommer, R., 94, 138
Sorcher, M., 327, 353
Sorkin, R.D., 14, 394, 407
Sparks, C.P., 152, 298, 300
Sparks, D.L., 192
Sperling, S.M., 297

Spielberger, C.D., 300
Stahl, M.J., 89, 149, 192
Stalker, G.M., 34, 39, 122, 140
Stanfield, J.D., 406
Stanley, J.C., 14
Starbuck, W.H., 89
Staudohar, P.D., 409
Staw, B.M., 67, 89, 90, 192, 409
Steele, T.P., 89
Steers, R.M., 45, 86–87, 90, 296
Steiner, I.D., 107–8, 127, 138
Sternberg, R.J., 300
Stogdill, R.M., 124, 140, 157, 167, 191–92
Stramler, C.S., 408
Stumpel, B., 405
Stumpf, S.A., 352–53
Summers, D.A., 408
Sussman, E.D., 407
Suttle, J.L., 74–76, 87, 89–90
Szybillo, G.J., 406

T

Tabor, J.M., 191
Tannenbaum, R., 155–56, 181, 192
Taylor, D.A., 407
Taylor, F.W., 17–18, 24, 39, 92–93, 137
Taylor, H.C., 262
Taylor, J.C., 167
Tenopyr, M.L., 236, 297
Thayer, P.W., 299, 351–52
Thomas, J.C., 193
Thompson, J.D., 138, 354
Tichy, N., 139
Tiffin, J., 230, 264
Timmons, J.A., 353
Todor, W.D., 401, 409
Torrance, E.P., 139
Triandis, H., 62, 89
Trist, E.L., 34, 39, 135, 141
Trumbo, D., 299
Tsui, A.S., 144, 191
Tucker, W.T., 372, 406
Tuckman, B.W., 96, 138
Tullar, W.I., 353
Tullis, T.S., 379–80, 407
Turner, P.A., 407
Tversky, A., 391, 408

U

Ulmstot, D.D., 79, 91
Ulrich, L., 299
Underwood, W.J., 339, 354
Urwick, L., 24

V

Valenzi, E.R., 167, 193
Van DeVan, A.H., 141
Van Zelst, R.H., 133, 141
Vaughn, J.A., 307, 352
Vecchio, R.P., 72, 90, 165, 193
Venkatesan, M., 373, 406
Vertinsky, I., 139
Vidulich, 407

Vittori, F.L., 352
Von Bergen, C.W., 86
Vroom, V.H., 64–67, 81, 91, 156, 181–87, 195

W

Wahba, M.A., 87–88
Walker, C.J., 137
Wallace, M.J., Jr., 236
Walsten, T.S., 89, 408
Walton, R.E., 134, 141
Walter, G.A., 88
Wanous, J.P., 43, 87, 239, 296–97
Waterman, R.H., 414
Waters, J.A., 141
Watson, W.H., 141
Wattenberg, B.J., 406
Watters, C.G., 405
Weber, M., 18–19, 23, 39
Weick, K.E., Jr., 90, 191, 232, 236
Weiner, N., 171, 194
Weiss, D.J., 87, 141
Weiss, J.A., 132
Wells, W.D., 405
Welsh, P., 352
Wendler, E.R., 195
Westfall, R., 406
Wexley, K.N., 88, 195, 236–37, 298, 351
Wherry, R.J., 237, 408
White, J.K., 88
White, S.E., 95, 138, 141, 326, 353
Wiback, K., 191
Wickens, C.D., 388–89, 407–8
Wiley, W.W., 205–6, 235
Wilkie, W.H., 406
Wilkinson, I., 193
Williams, B.H., 352
Williams, M.S., 141
Williges, R.C., 352
Wilson, H.A., 352
Wind, Y., 405
Wing, J.F., 408
Winter, D.G., 88
Wolfe, D., 193
Wolfson, A.D., 79, 91
Woodman, R.W., 339, 354
Woodward, J., 27–29, 39
Worthing, P.M., 373, 406
Wright, D.R., Jr., 299

Y

Yankelovich, D., 8, 370, 406
Yetton, P.W., 91, 156, 195
Youngblood, S.A., 298, 399, 408–9
Yukl, G.A., 88–89, 167, 298, 193, 195

Z

Zahn, E., 405
Zawack, R.A., 141, 342, 354
Zedeck, S., 236
Zelaznik, H., 408
Ziller, R.C., 139

Subject Index

A

Absolute judgment procedures, 227, 229–31
Achievement motivation, 58–60
Achievement-training, 59, 335
Adverse impact (in selection), 266, 268–78
  defined, 277
Advertising, 356, 360–61
  effectiveness measures, 358–59
  Journal of Advertising Research, 374
  subliminal, 366–68
Affirmative action (in selection), 276
Air Force Task Inventory method, 205–8
Albemarle v. *Moody* case, 275
American Psychological Association (APA), 8
  I/O Division, 278
American Psychologist, 215
American Telephone and Telegraph Co. (AT&T), 9, 293
Application in psychology, 3, 7–9
Assessment centers, 293
Attitudes
  and consumer behavior, 357–58, 363–69
  changes in, 366
  defined, 363
  measurement, 365–66
  work related, 43–48
Attraction-selection process, 239–41
Attribution Theory (of leadership), 170
ARRO, 8
Autonomous work group, 135
Authority, 164

B

β (in TSD), 385–86
Bakke v. *University of California* case, 276

Behavior modification programs, 42, 80–82
Behavioral description procedures
  job analysis, 203–9
  performance appraisal, 219, 227, 231–33
Behavioral intentions, 365
Behavioral modeling, 327–28
Behavioral observation scales (BOS), 231
Behaviorally anchored rating scales (BARS), 230–31
Behaviorism, 42, 80–82
Biases in subjective ratings, 224–27, 280
Biographical data (BIB), 281–82
Bootstrapping, 390
Brainstorming, 132
Bureaucratic model, 23
Buros yearbook, 284, 286
Business games, 322–24

C

CAD scales, 373
California Personality Inventory, 149, 291
Case method of training, 325–26
Central tendency bias, 225, 228
Checklist, weighted, 220, 231–33
Classical theory of organization, 22–26
Classification method in job evaluation, 213
Cleary model; *see* Fairness in selection
Climate; *see* Organizational, climate
Closed-loop processes, 392
Coefficient (reliability), 249–50
  of equivalence, 250
  of internal consistency, 249–50
  of stability, 249
Cognitive consistency and dissonance
  in consumer behavior, 368
  in word motivation, 67–69

Cognitive process in consumer behavior, 369
Cognitive structures, states, strategies, traits, 386
Cohesiveness of groups, 122–24
College Entrance Board Test, 285
Communication
  breakdowns, 99–101
  capacity, 34–5, 387
  functions, 101–3
  information overload, 34
  model of, 99
  theory, 34–36
Comparable, 212, 214–15
Comparative judgment procedures, 227–29
Compensation systems, 211–16
Competitive reward systems, 110–12
Compliance, 119, 373
Composition of groups, effects of
  homogeneity-heterogeneity, 128–29
  size, 129–30
  task ability, 127–28
Computer assisted instruction, 320–22
Computer software design, 378–80
Concern for people; *see* Consideration in leadership
Conference method of training, 324–25
Conformity, 119
Connecticut v. *Teal* case, 276
Consensus decision making, 131
Consideration in leadership, 157–61
Consumer
  behavior, 356
  Journal of Consumer Research, 374
  marketing variables in, 356, 358
  measurement of, 358–60
  person variables in, 360–73
  psychology, 6
    defined, 355–56
    variables and models, 357–60
Context effects, 225–26
Contingency theories of leadership
  Fiedler's theory, 175–78
  Hersey and Blanchard, 187–88
  Path-goal theory, 178–81
  Reddin's 3-D model, 187
  Vroom and Yetton's model, 181–86
Control (experimental), 10–11, 333
Cooperative reward systems, 110–12
Core job characteristics, 60–61
Correlation
  coefficient, 249, 254–9
  eta, 257
  phi, 257
  point-biserial, 257
  r, 254
  R, 258
  tetrachoric, 257

Criterion
  composite, 217
  contamination and deficiency, 224
  measures (performance evaluation), 217–18
  multiple, 217
  problem (leadership effectiveness), 143–44
  in selection, 245–46, 253–54
  ultimate, 217
Critical incident technique
  in job analysis, 201–2
  in performance evaluations, 219, 230–31, 233
  in testing two-factor theory, 55
Cross-validation, 253–54
CRT, 387, 391–92

D

d' (in TSD), 386
Decision theory
  behavioral, 32–34, 64
  and detection of signals, 384–86
  economic, 19, 33–34
  heuristics, 390–91
Demographics, 358, 360, 370–72
Dependent variables, 10
Depth interviews, 362
Design of training evaluations, 331–34
Dictionary of Occupational Titles (DOT), 199
Differentiation, 31, 34–36
Discriminability of items, 232
Disseminator, 145
Distributed practice, 310
Disturbance handler (role of manager), 145

E

Economic psychology, 356, 366
Educational Testing Service, 8
Ego needs, 52
Emergent leadership, 143
Encounter group training, 337–40
Engineering psychology, 5–6, 374–95
Entrepreneur (role of manager), 145
Entropy, 31, 34–35
Equal Employment Opportunity
  Acts of 1964, 1972, 274
  Commission (EEOC), 274
Equipotentiality, 376
Equity
  external, 212, 215–16
  individual, 212, 216
  internal, 212–215
  theory, 70–72
ERG theory, 54
Essex Corporation, 8
Evaluation of training, 331–34

Existence needs, 54
Expectancy
  chart, tables, 261–63
  concept, 64, 239
  cutoff level, 261
  theory; see Valence-instrumentality-ex-
    pectancy (VIE) theory
Expected utility (EU), 263
Experimental design, 11, 33–34
Experimentation, 11–12
Exxon Corporation, 9, 292

F

Factor comparison method, 212–13
Fail-safe design, 378
Fairness in selection, 243, 265–78
  definition problem, 265–67
  legal considerations, 274–78
  models, 271–74
  philosophical considerations, 266–67
  technical considerations, 267–74
Faking in testing, 290–91
Favorability of items, 231–33
Fear of failure, 58
Feedback
  as core job characteristic, 60–61
  as moderator of goalsetting effects, 63
  in training, 308–9
Fidelity in simulation, 323
Fiedler's contingency theory; see Contin-
  gency theories of leadership, 175–78
Figurehead (role of manager), 145
Fixed interval schedule of reinforcement,
  307
Fixed ratio schedule of reinforcement, 308
Focused-group interview, 362
Forced choice method in performance eval-
  uation, 231–32
Forced distribution procedures, 228–29
Four Factor Theory Questionnaire
  (FFTQ), 167
Friendship group, 96
Functional Job Analysis (FJA), 204–5

G

General characteristics philosophy, 4
General Clerical Test, 286
General Electric Corporation, 9
General systems theory, 19–20, 30–32
g-factor, 286–87
Goal setting theory, 61–64
Gray market, 357–58
Griggs v. *Duke Power* case, 275
Group behavior
  composition, 127–30
  conflict, 114–15
  development, 96
  effectiveness, 97–98
  external environment, 106–15

Group behavior (*continued*)
  formation, 96–97
  interventions, 130–36
  process, 98–106
  structure, 115–127
  types, 96–97
Group problem solving, 131–33
Group (social) theories of organization, 15
Group structure
  cohesiveness, 122–24
  interaction patterns, 116–17
  norms, 118–20
  roles, 120–22
  status, 125–27
Groupthink, 114–15
Growth needs, 54
Guiding of behavior, 309–10

H

Halo effect, 225–26
Hard-core unemployed, training of, 340–
  42
Hawthorne effect, 332
Hay and Associates, 8
Herzberg's two-factor theory; see Two-
  factor theory, 54–57
Homogeneity-heterogeneity of group,
  128–29
Human analysis (in assessing training
  needs), 305
Human factors engineering, 6, 377
Human information processing, 386–91
Human relations movement, 18–19
Human relations training, 336
Hygiene factors, 56

I

Imitation, 309–10
In-basket technique, 293
Incentive systems, 216
Independent variables, 10
Individual differences
  approach, 4
  in consumer psychology, 360, 369–73
  and personnel decisions, 241–43
Individualistic reward system, 110–12
Industrial and organizational psychology
  content, 5–7
  defined, 1
  history, 4–7
  methodological orientation, 4–5
  objectives, 2–4
  research techniques, 9–12
Influence tactics, 163
Information processing theory, 34–36
Innovation (basis for market segmentation), 371–72
Instrumental conditioning, 307

Instrumentality
  defined, 64–67
  of pay, 83
  theory; see Valence-instrumentality-ex-
    pectancy (VIE) theory
Intelligence
  concepts, 286
  quotient (IQ), 287
  tests, 287
  validity, 287–8
Interaction process analysis, 101–3
Interface (person-machine), 377, 381
Internalization, 119
Interview techniques
  in job analysis, 201–3
  in selection, 278–81
Involvement (market segmentation), 371

J

Jackson's personality research form, 373
Job analysis, 201–11
Job-centered philosophy (selection), 244
Job characteristics model, 60–61
Job description
  approaches to, 198–201
  concept, 197–98
  methods, 201–11
Job involvement, 43, 45
Job requirements
  defined, 198
  in job analysis, 210–11
Job specification, 198
Johari window, 103, 338

K–L

Kaiser Aluminum v. Weber case, 276
Knowledge of results, 60–61
Landscaped offices, 94
Law of requisite variety, 122
Lawshe expectancy tables, 261–63
Leader Match, 336–37
Leadership
  appointed versus emergent, 143
  Behavior Description Questionnaire,
    157–60
  effectiveness, 143–44
  nominal, 143
  Opinion Questionnaire, 158–59
  role, 120–22, 145
  theories
    behavioral, 153–68
    contingency, 175–88
    situational, 168–75
    versus supervision, 143
    training, 335–37
    trait, 146–53
Learning to learn, 311
Least Preferred Coworker (LPC) scale,
  176–78
Lecture, 317–19

Leniency bias, 225, 228
Liaison (role of manager), 145
Linking pins, 121

M

Macro organization theories, 22–36
Maintenance needs, 56
Management by objectives, 77–78
Management theories (classical), 22–26
Managerial grid program, 160–61
Market segmentation, 360, 369–73
Marketing Research, Journal of, 374
Massed practice, 310
Matrix organizational design, 35–36
Mechanistic organizational structure, 34
Mental
  age, 287
  workload, 387–88
  processing capacity, 387–88
Minnesota Multiphasic Personality Inven-
  tory (MMPI), 291
Modeling (behavioral), 309–11
Moderator variables in validation, 268–72
Monitor (role of manager), 145
Monitoring (task), 382–83
Motivation
  achievement theory, 58–60
  cognitive consistency theory, 67–69,
    368
  cognitive evaluation theory, 72–73
  concept, 41–42
  and consumer behavior, 361–63
  need theory, 50–61
  radical behaviorism, 41–42
  valence-instrumentality-expectancy
    theory, 64–67
Multiple constituencies (of a leader), 144
Myart v. Motorola case, 275

N

Naturalistic observation, 11–12
Need
  hierarchy theory, 51–54
  theories, 50–61
Needs assessment (training), 304–5
Negative reinforcement, 307
Negotiator (role of manager), 145
Neoclassical theory of organizations, 26–
  27
Network analysis, 116
Neutralizers of leadership, 173–74
Nominal
  group technique, 132
  leader, 143
Normal distribution, 242–43
Norms
  concept, 118–20
  return potential model, 119–20
  types of conformity, 119

O

Off-the-job training, 317–28
On-the-job training, 314–17
Open systems theory, 19–20, 30–32
Open-loop processing, 392
Operations research, 30
Organization
  analysis, 304
  theory (OT)
    background, 16–22
    defined, 16
    human-oriented (micro), 16, 36–37
    macro, 16, 22–36
Organizational
  behavior (OB), 15–16
  climate, 344–48
  development (OD), 342–48
  maintenance, 37
  psychology, 1–2, 16
Organizations analysis, 304
Otis (selection test), 286
Overload, information; see Communication
Overprediction, 271

P

Paired-comparison method, 228
Partial reinforcement schedules, 307–8
Participative management, 155–56
Path-goal theory of leadership, 178–81
Pay, 82–84
Peer ratings, 226–27
Performance
  evaluation, 197, 216–33
    objective measures, 221–24
    subjective measures, 224–33
  relation to satisfaction, 37
Person-centered philosophy (selection), 244
Personality
  concepts, 289–90
  and consumer behavior, 372–73
  tests, 290–92, 373
    projective, 290–91
    self-report, 291–92
  traits, 289–90, 372–73
Personalized system of instruction, 320–22
Personnel psychology, 5, 15
Personnel and human resource management (PHRM), 15
Personnel Development Services (PDS), 292
Physical abilities (in job analysis), 210–11
Physiological needs, 51–52
Placement, 243–44
Planned change, 301–2, 343
POC functions, 388
Point system (job evaluation), 212–15

Position Analysis Questionnaire (PAQ), 208–10
Positive reinforcement, 307–8
Posttest only design, 332
Potential productivity (group), 127
Power position (contingency theory), 175–78
Practitioners, 7–10, 12–13
Prediction
  individual, 261–63
  institutional, 261–63
  under and over, 271
  use of regression in, 255–57, 271
Predictors
  concept, 244–47, 267–71
  description and classification, 278–93
Pretest sensitization, 333
Primary
  market, 369
  Mental Abilities Test (PMA), 287
Principles of training, 312–13
Principles for the Validation and Use of Personnel Selection Procedures, 278
Procedural justice, 12
Process
  consultation, 130–31
  group, 98–106
  loss, 127
  theories of motivation, 61–73
Product
  liability litigation, 380
  variables, 358
Professional and Management Position Questionnaire (PMPQ), 209–10
Profile of organizational characteristics, 345
Programmed instruction, 320–22
Project (or product) organizational design, 35
Projective techniques, 51, 290–91
Psychological Corporation, 8

Q–R

Quality (performance), 221
Quantity (performance), 221
Race
  and leadership success, 147
  in selection, 263–78
Random assignment, 333–34
Ranking method
  in job evaluation, 212–13
  in performance evaluation, 228
Rater training, 340
Rating
  biases, 224–27
  graphic scales, 229–31
Rationality in decision making, 33, 263–64, 363, 390–91
Ravens Progressive Matrices test, 287
Realistic job preview, 239–41

Recruiting, 238–41
Regression, 256–57
Reinforcement, 307–8
Relevance (in selection), 278
Reliability
  defined, 248–49
  measures, 249–50
Research
  applied (mission-oriented), 9
  basic (fundamental), 9–10
Resource allocator (role of manager), 145
Return potential model, 119–20
Reward systems
  diagnosing effectiveness of, 82–84
  effects of group, 110–12
Role
  concepts, 120–21
  playing, 326–27
  set, 121
  stress, 121–22
  types, 120–21
Rorschach test, 290–91

S

Safety needs, 52
Satisfaction (work)
  changes in, 78, 80
  measurement, 43–44
  relations to behavior, 36–37, 45–48
"Satisficing" (versus maximizing), 33
Schedules of reinforcement, 307–8
Science, 2–3
Science Research Associates, 8
Scientific management, 17–18
Scientific method, 2–3, 10–11
Selection (personnel)
  actuarial versus diagnostic, 245–47
  as a decision function, 263–65
  efficiency, 259
  evaluation of, 247–65
  expectancy in, 259–65
  fairness in, 265–78
  guidelines, 276–78
  models and logic, 241–47
  moderator variables in, 268–71
  ration and success rate, 259
  as a system function, 294
Self-actualization needs, 51–52
Self-consistency, 67–69
Self-esteem, 67–69
Self-interest group, 96–97
Self-report techniques, 290–91
Sensitivity training, 337–40
Sentence Completion Test, 148
Sex as a predictor of leadership success, 147
Shaping of behavior, 309–10
Shrinkage formulae (in validation), 254
Signal detection (TSD), 381, 384–86

Simulation techniques of training, 322–24
Situational approaches to leadership, 168–75
Social
  attribution theory, 170
  desirability errors, 365–66
  information processing, 95
  loafing, 129
  needs, 51–52, 94–95
Socioemotional group process, 101–2
Sociotechnical approach, 134
Spokesperson, 145
S-R compatibility, 382
Stanford-Binet test, 287
States (cognitive), 386
Status in groups, 127
Stress, stressors, 393
Stringency bias, 225
Strategies (cognitive), 386
Strong Vocational Interest Blank, 148
Structure
  group, 115–127
  initiating, in leadership, 157–61
  of Intellect Model, 266
  organic versus mechanistic, 34
  macro theories, 22–36
Structures (cognitive), 386
Styles of leaderships
  autocratic versus democratic, 155–56
  consideration, 157–61
  initiation of structure, 157–61
Subordinate ratings, 227
Subsample methods; see Reliability, measures
Substitutes for leadership, 173–74
Supervisory
  Behavior Description Questionnaire, 159–61
  support (leadership), 167
Survey
  research, 362
  Research Center, University of Michigan, 356
Systems view in
  design (person-machine system), 374–77
  organizations, 20–21, 30–32
  selection and placement, 294

T

Target population, 369
Task
  additive, 108
  conjunctive, 108
  discretionary, 108
  disjunctive, 108
  divisible, 108–9
  feedback, 60–61
  identity, 60–61

Task (*continued*)
  inventory method (job analysis), 205–7
  tracking, 391–92
  unitary, 108
Task-oriented group processes, 101–3
Taylor-Russell tables, 261–62
Team building, 338–39
Team management, 134
Technology theory, 27–29
Tests
  achievement, 285
  aptitude, 285–86
  defined, 382–85
  general intelligence, 286–89
  objective versus subjective, 284
  paper-and-pencil, 284
  performance, 284
  personality, 289–92
  power, 284
  speeded or timed, 284
  standardized, 283–84
Test-retest methods; *see* Reliability, measure
T-groups training, 337–40
Thematic Apperception Test (TAT), 58–60, 290
Theories X and Y, 52–53
Three Mile Island accident, 377–78
Throughput, 31
Training
  assessments phase, 304–5
  defined, 302
  evaluation of, 331–32
  methods
    audiovisual techniques, 319–20
    behavioral modeling, 327–28
    case method, 325–26
    conference, 324–25
    laboratory, 337–40
    lecture, 317–19
    on-the-job, 314–17
    programmed instruction, 320–22
    role playing, 326–27
    simulation, 322–24
  principles, 312–13
Traits
  cognitive, 386
  defined, 241–42, 244, 386

Traits (*continued*)
  illustrated, 245–46
  in leadership, 147–53
Tracking tasks, 391–92
Transfer of training, 310–12
Transparency in testing, 290
"Truth-in-testing" legislation, 283
Two-factor theory, 54–57

U
Uncertainty (task), 34–35, 109–10
Underprediction, 271
Uniform guidelines, in selection, 276–78
U.S. Training and Employment Service (USTES)
  identified, 199
  system for job analysis, 201–5
  system for job description, 199–201
Utility
  in consumer behavior, 365
  in decision theory, 33–34, 390
  in selection, 263–65

V
Valence-instrumentality-expectancy (VIE) theory, 64–67, 239
Validity
  concepts, 250–52
  defined, 250
  differential, 268–71
  generalization, 272–74
  measurement, 252–54
  moderated, 268
  single-group, 268–71
Vertical dyad linkage (VDL) theory, 164–65
VIE theory, 64–67
Vigilance, 382–86
Vroom-Yetton model, 181–86

W
Warnings, 378
Washington v. *Davis* case, 275–76
Wonderlic (personnel test), 287
Worker function scales, 204–5
Work-oriented methods (job analysis), 201, 206
Worker-oriented methods (job analysis), 201, 203

ABOUT THE AUTHORS

William C. Howell is the Herbert S. Autrey Professor of Psychology and Administrative Science at Rice University. He graduated Phi Beta Kappa from the University of Virginia in 1954, and earned his Ph.D. in Psychology from the same institution in 1958. Previous positions include the Directorship of the Human Performance Center at the Ohio State University and a professorship in the Ohio State psychology department. He has chaired the psychology department at Rice since 1970 and served as consultant to numerous corporations and government agencies. His research, which has led to a number of papers and books, was recognized in 1979 by Division 21 of the American Psychological Association through the Franklin V. Taylor award. Dr. Howell is a Fellow of the American Psychological Association, and has held a variety of offices in this and other professional and scientific organizations. He is a consulting editor on several journals, including the *Journal of Applied Psychology* and *Organizational Behavior and Human Decision Processes.*

Robert L. Dipboye received his B.A. from Baylor University and his M.S. and Ph.D. in Psychology from Purdue University–West Lafayette. He has taught in the Stokely School of Management at the University of Tennessee–Knoxville and the Krannert Graduate School of Industrial Administration at Purdue. Currently, he is professor of Psychology and Adminstrative Science at Rice University, where he serves as director of the graduate program in Industrial and Organizational Psychology and the Center for Applied Psychological Systems. Professor Dipboye has published numerous articles on topics related to industrial and organizational psychology. He is also a licensed psychologist in the state of Texas and consults with several major corporations.

A NOTE ON THE TYPE

The text of this book was set via computer-driven cathode-ray tube in 10/12 Century Schoolbook, a typeface based on a design drawn in 1894 by L. B. Benton and T. L. DeVinne for the *Century* magazine. Century Schoolbook is an excellent example of a refined Egyptian typeface. The Egyptian family of faces is characterized by thick slab serifs and little contrast between thick and thin strokes. The large x-height and simple letter forms of Century Schoolbook make it very legible.

Composed by Eastern Graphics, Binghamton, New York.

Printed and bound by Malloy Lithographing, Inc., Ann Arbor, Michigan.

11-1201-03   ISBN 0-256-03396